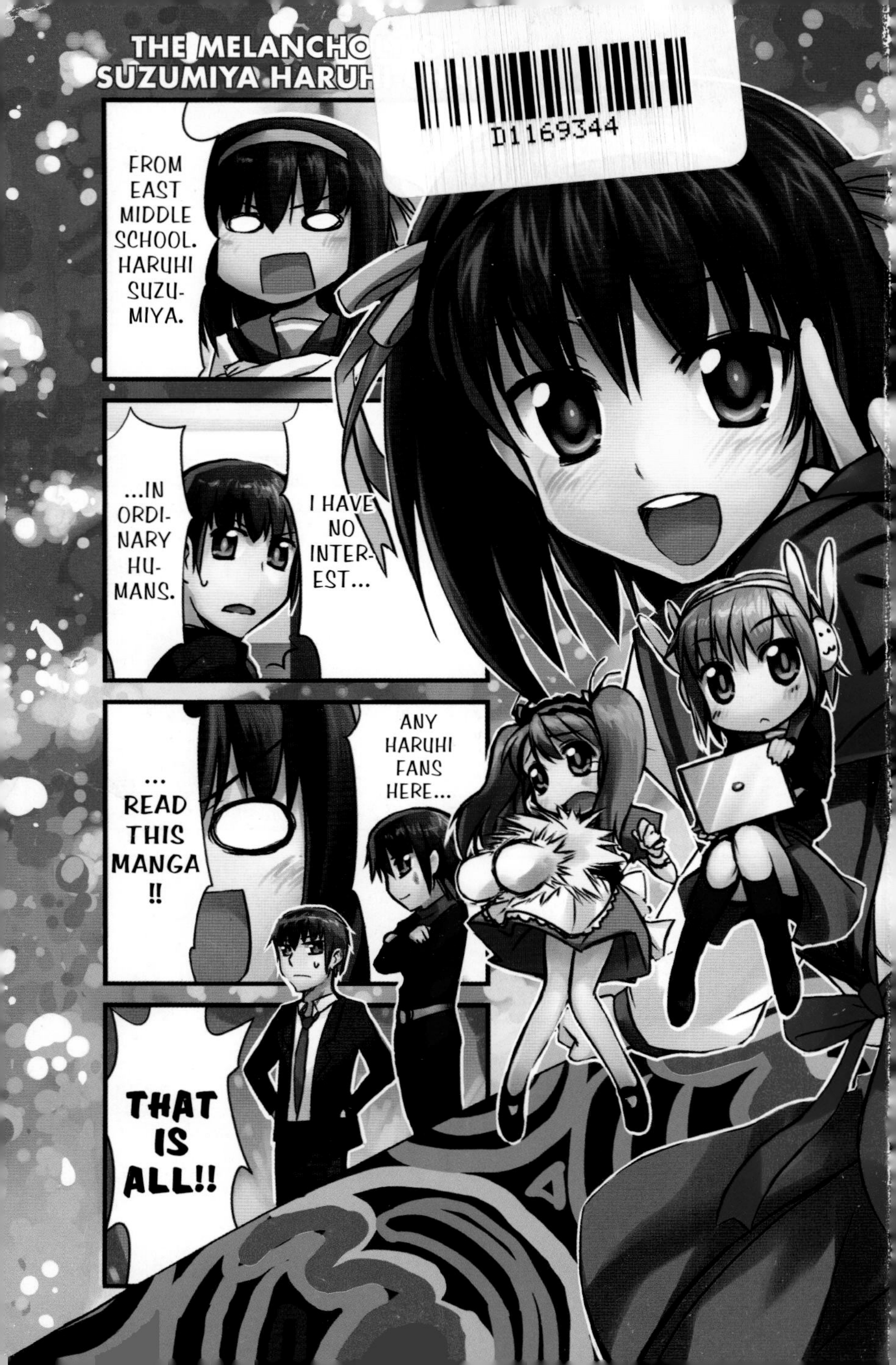
THE MELANCHO[...] SUZUMIYA HARUH[...]
FROM EAST MIDDLE SCHOOL. HARUHI SUZUMIYA.
I HAVE NO INTEREST...
...IN ORDINARY HUMANS.
ANY HARUHI FANS HERE...
... READ THIS MANGA!!
THAT IS ALL!!

SHOUT

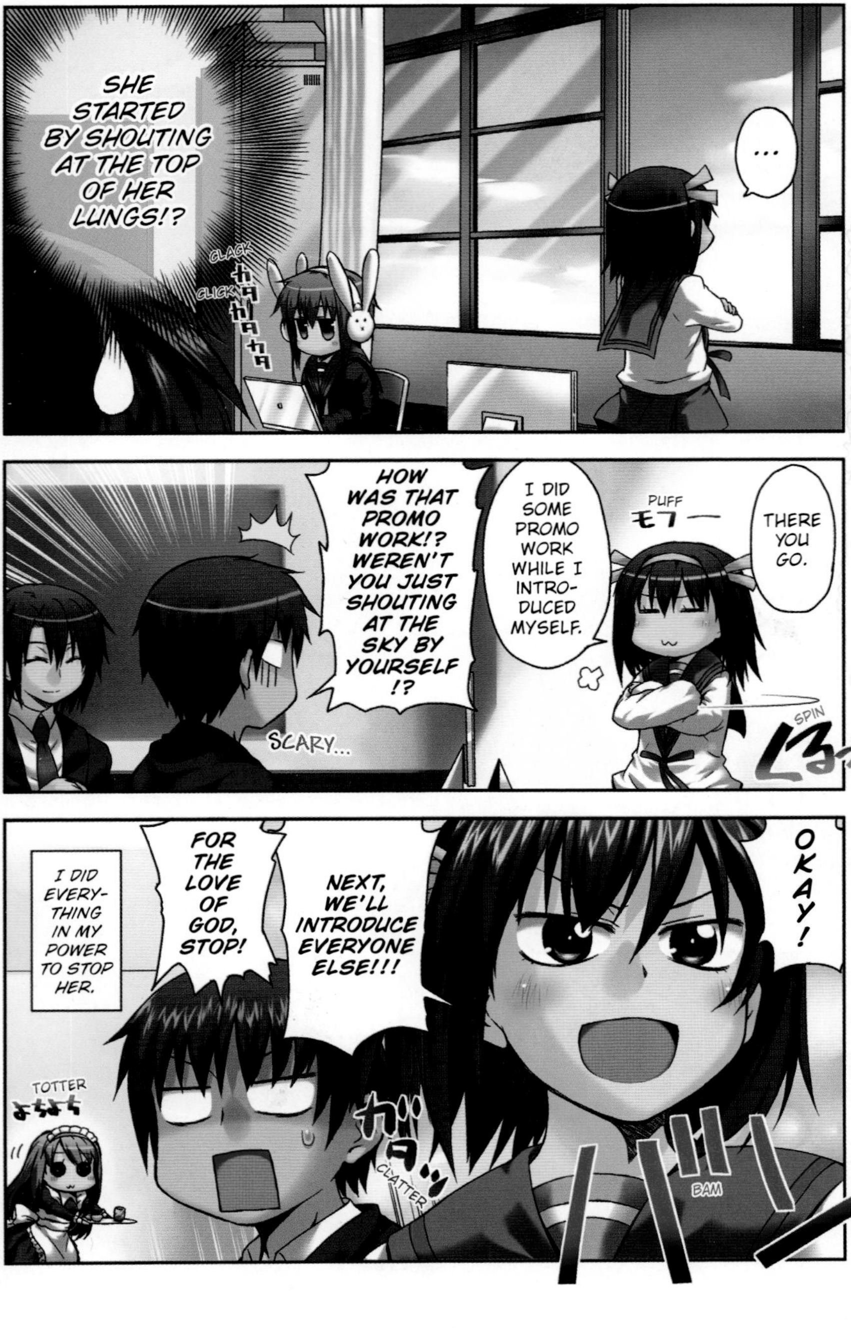

...
CLACK
CLICK
SHE STARTED BY SHOUTING AT THE TOP OF HER LUNGS!?
THERE YOU GO.
PUFF
I DID SOME PROMO WORK WHILE I INTRODUCED MYSELF.
SPIN
HOW WAS THAT PROMO WORK!? WEREN'T YOU JUST SHOUTING AT THE SKY BY YOURSELF!?
SCARY...
OKAY!
NEXT, WE'LL INTRODUCE EVERYONE ELSE!!!
BAM
FOR THE LOVE OF GOD, STOP!
CLATTER
I DID EVERYTHING IN MY POWER TO STOP HER.
TOTTER

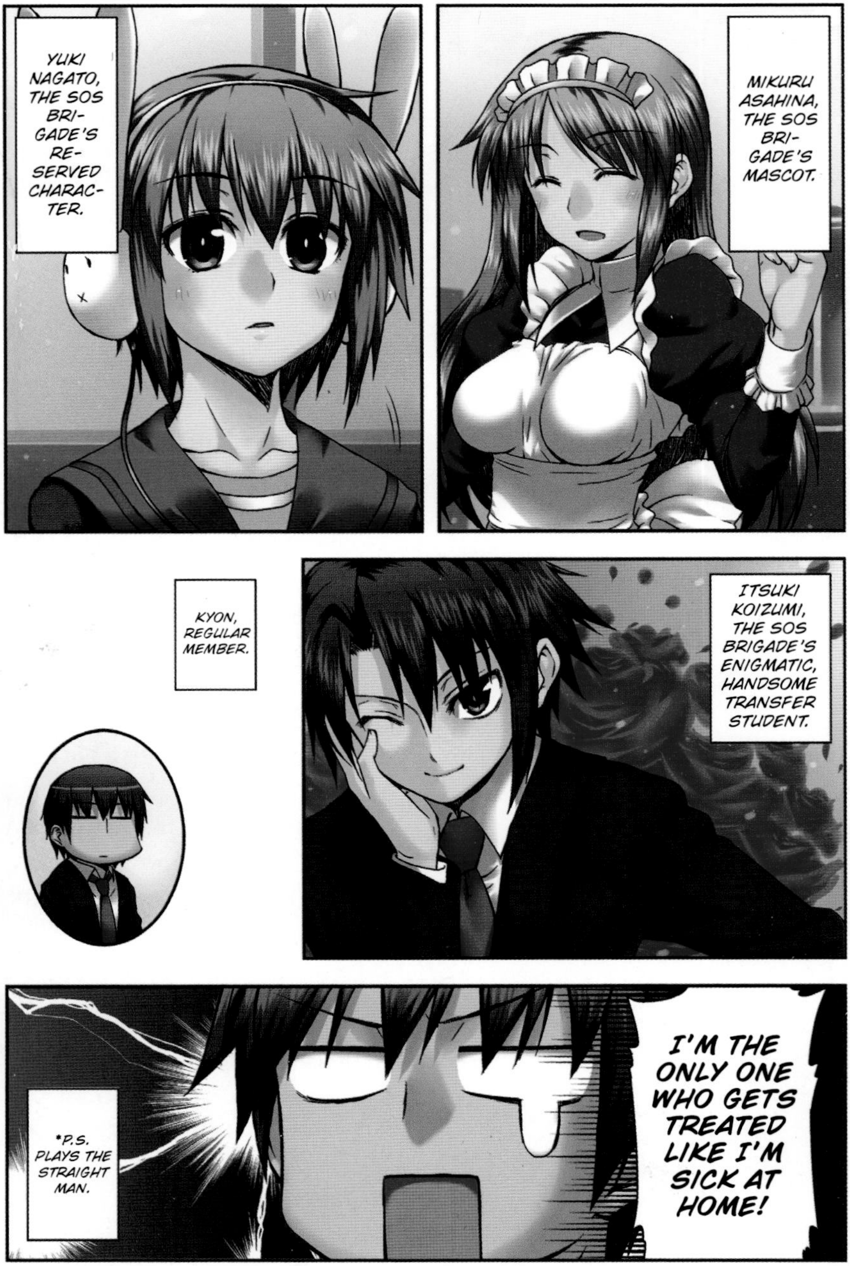
MIKURU ASAHINA, THE SOS BRI-GADE'S MASCOT.
YUKI NAGATO, THE SOS BRI-GADE'S RE-SERVED CHARAC-TER.
ITSUKI KOIZUMI, THE SOS BRIGADE'S ENIGMATIC, HANDSOME TRANSFER STUDENT.
KYON, REGULAR MEMBER.
I'M THE ONLY ONE WHO GETS TREATED LIKE I'M SICK AT HOME!
*P.S. PLAYS THE STRAIGHT MAN.

The Melancholy of Suzumiya Haruhi-chan 01

INDEX

THE MELANCHOLY of SUZUMIYA
HARUHI·CHAN

The Untold Adventures of the SOS Brigade

YUKI.N> **This story is a work of fiction and bears no relation to any real people, organizations, or events.**

STORY: **NAGARU TANIGAWA** ART: **PUYO** CHARACTERS: NOIZI ITO

BELIEVE

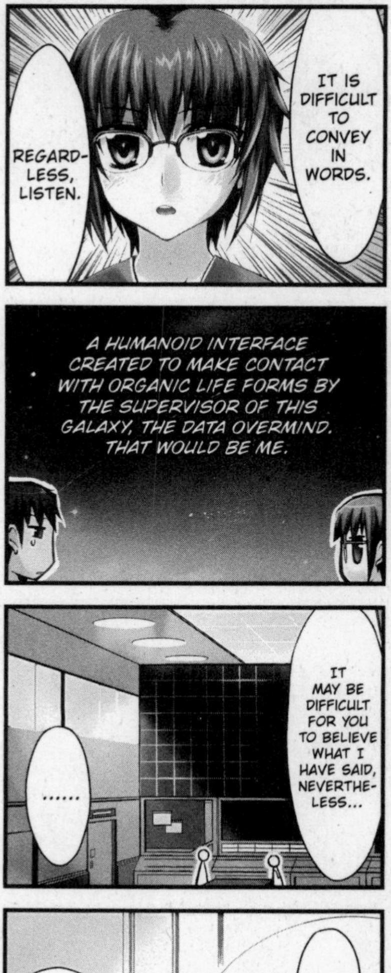
IT IS DIFFICULT TO CONVEY IN WORDS.
REGARDLESS, LISTEN.
A HUMANOID INTERFACE CREATED TO MAKE CONTACT WITH ORGANIC LIFE FORMS BY THE SUPERVISOR OF THIS GALAXY, THE DATA OVERMIND. THAT WOULD BE ME.
IT MAY BE DIFFICULT FOR YOU TO BELIEVE WHAT I HAVE SAID, NEVERTHELESS...
......
BELIEVE ME.
I'D HAVE A HARDER TIME IF YOU TOLD ME NOT TO BELIEVE YOU...

FLIP BOOK

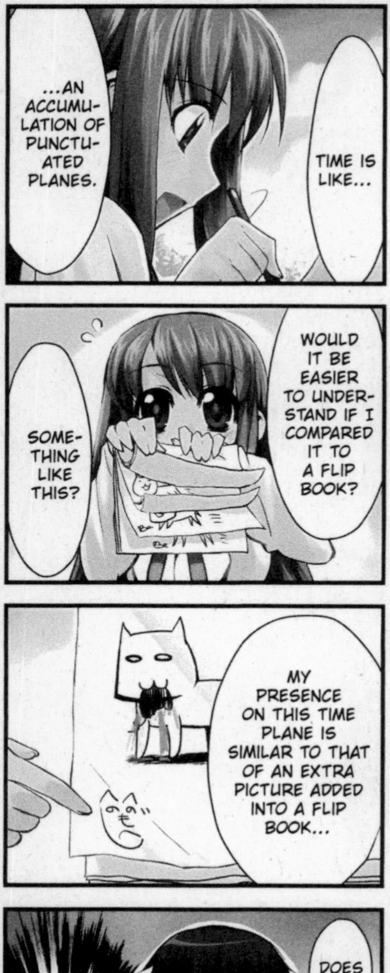
TIME IS LIKE...
...AN ACCUMULATION OF PUNCTUATED PLANES.
WOULD IT BE EASIER TO UNDERSTAND IF I COMPARED IT TO A FLIP BOOK?
SOMETHING LIKE THIS?
MY PRESENCE ON THIS TIME PLANE IS SIMILAR TO THAT OF AN EXTRA PICTURE ADDED INTO A FLIP BOOK...
DOES THAT HELP?
THAT'S ONE SCARY CAT!

ASSIST

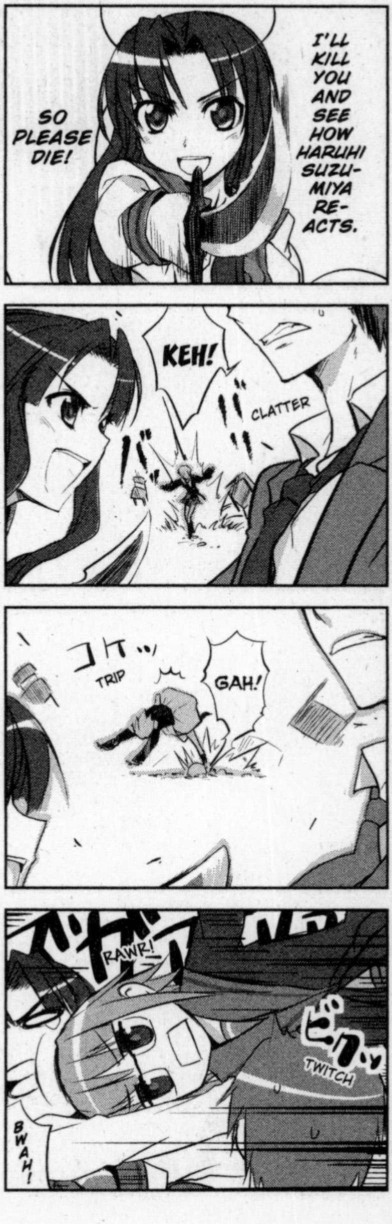
I'LL KILL YOU AND SEE HOW HARUHI SUZUMIYA RE-ACTS.
SO PLEASE DIE!
KEH!
CLATTER
GAH!
TRIP
RAWR!
TWITCH
BWAH!

TWIST

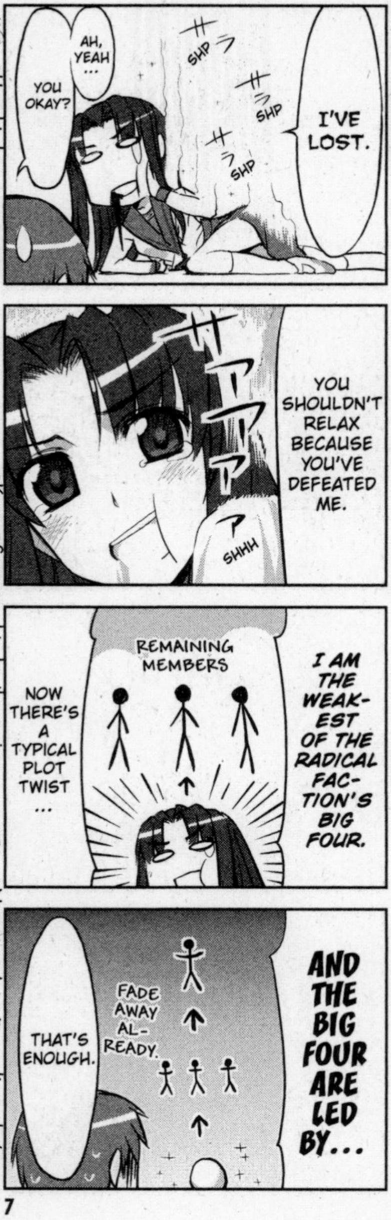
I'VE LOST.
SHP
SHP
SHP
AH, YEAH ...
YOU OKAY?
YOU SHOULDN'T RELAX BECAUSE YOU'VE DEFEATED ME.
SHHH
I AM THE WEAK-EST OF THE RADICAL FAC-TION'S BIG FOUR.
REMAINING MEMBERS
NOW THERE'S A TYPICAL PLOT TWIST ...
AND THE BIG FOUR ARE LED BY...
FADE AWAY AL-READY.
THAT'S ENOUGH.

•Haruhi-chan •SOS Brigade brigade chief. Selfish, pushy, eccentric, and cute.

•Kyon •Supposed to be the main character in this story. Still stuck as the straight man in this work.

•Nagato •A taciturn alien who's always reding. Defeated Asakura-san by head-butting her.

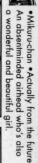

•Mikuru-chan •Actually from the future. An absentminded airhead who's also a wonderful and beautiful girl.

•Koizumi •An enigmatic transfer student who happens to be an esper. A smug and detestable stud who's always smiling.

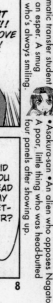

•Asakura-san •An alien who opposes Nagato. A poor, little thing who was head-butted four panels after showing up.

LOVE LETTER

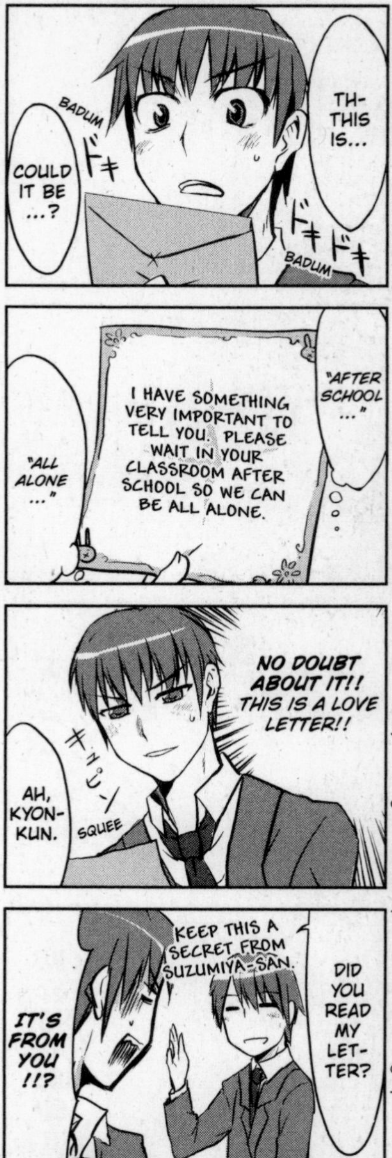
TH- THIS IS...
BADUM ドキ
COULD IT BE ...?
ドキドキ BADUM
"AFTER SCHOOL ..."
I HAVE SOMETHING VERY IMPORTANT TO TELL YOU. PLEASE WAIT IN YOUR CLASSROOM AFTER SCHOOL SO WE CAN BE ALL ALONE.
"ALL ALONE ..."
NO DOUBT ABOUT IT!! THIS IS A LOVE LETTER!!
キュピーン SQUEE
AH, KYON-KUN.
DID YOU READ MY LETTER?
KEEP THIS A SECRET FROM SUZUMIYA-SAN.
IT'S FROM YOU!!?

THOROUGH INVESTIGATION

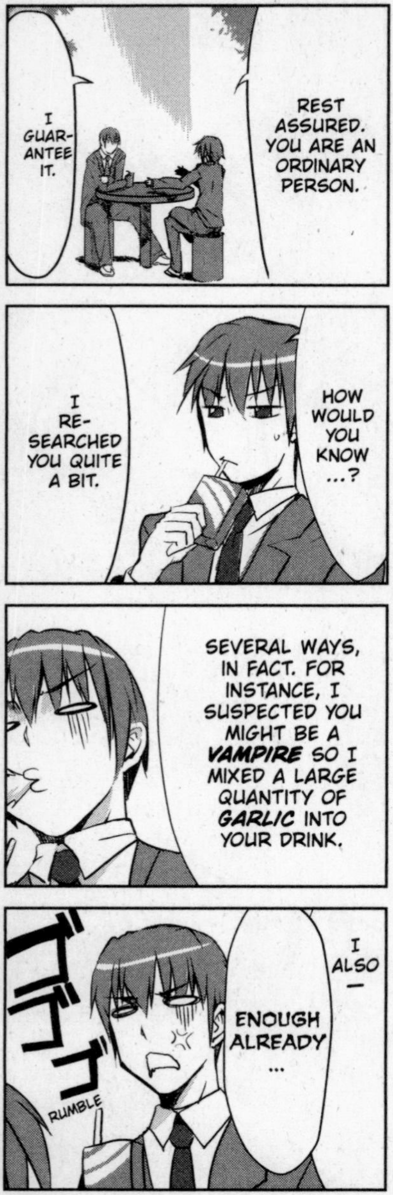
REST ASSURED. YOU ARE AN ORDINARY PERSON.
I GUARANTEE IT.
HOW WOULD YOU KNOW ...?
I RESEARCHED YOU QUITE A BIT.
SEVERAL WAYS, IN FACT. FOR INSTANCE, I SUSPECTED YOU MIGHT BE A VAMPIRE SO I MIXED A LARGE QUANTITY OF GARLIC INTO YOUR DRINK.
I ALSO —
ENOUGH ALREADY ...
ゴゴゴ RUMBLE

HARUHI-CHAN'S COLLECTION OF SPECIAL ATTACKS

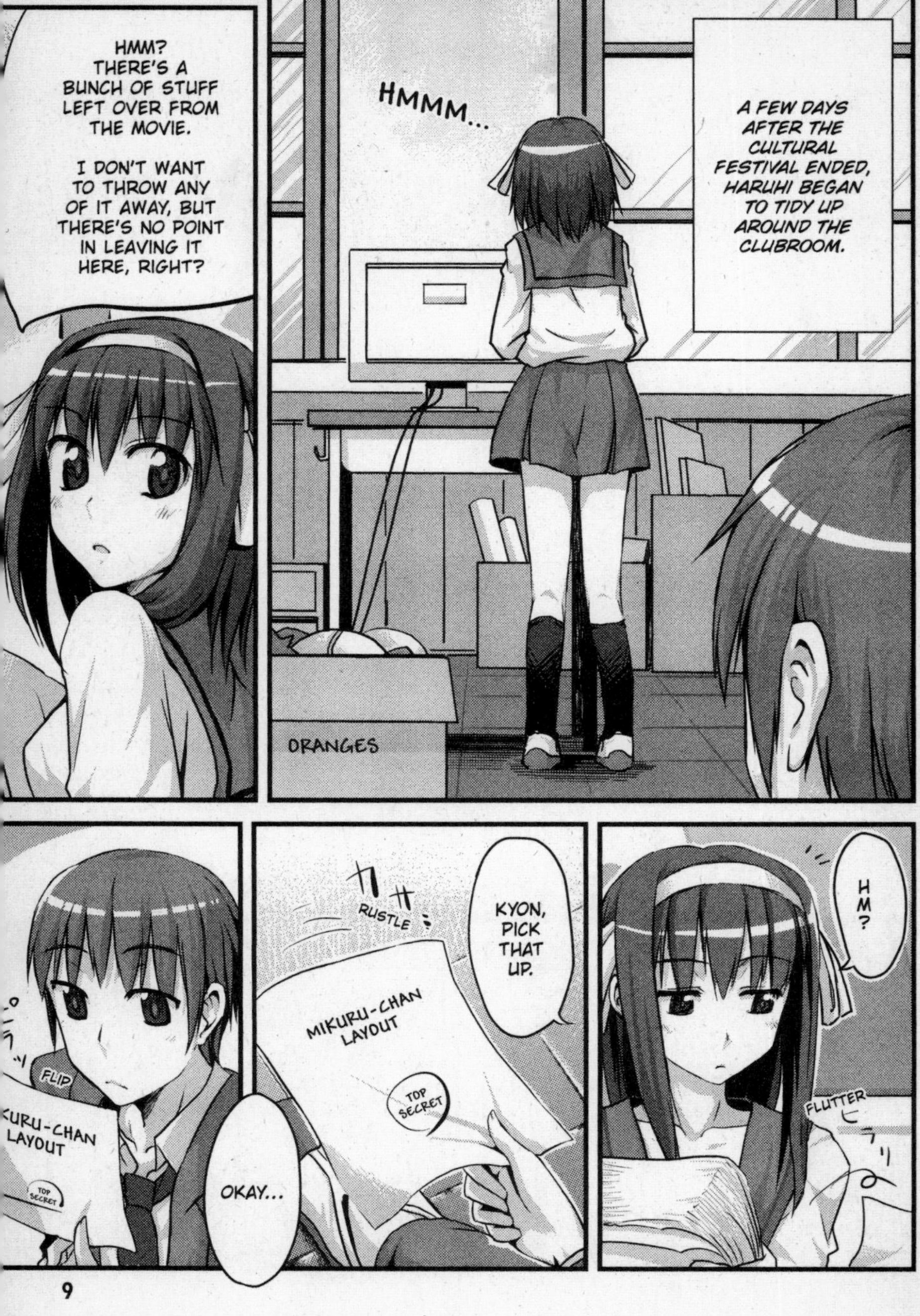
A FEW DAYS AFTER THE CULTURAL FESTIVAL ENDED, HARUHI BEGAN TO TIDY UP AROUND THE CLUBROOM.
HMMM...
ORANGES
HMM? THERE'S A BUNCH OF STUFF LEFT OVER FROM THE MOVIE.
I DON'T WANT TO THROW ANY OF IT AWAY, BUT THERE'S NO POINT IN LEAVING IT HERE, RIGHT?
HM?
FLUTTER
KYON, PICK THAT UP.
RUSTLE
MIKURU-CHAN LAYOUT
TOP SECRET
OKAY...
FLIP
KURU-CHAN LAYOUT
TOP SECRET

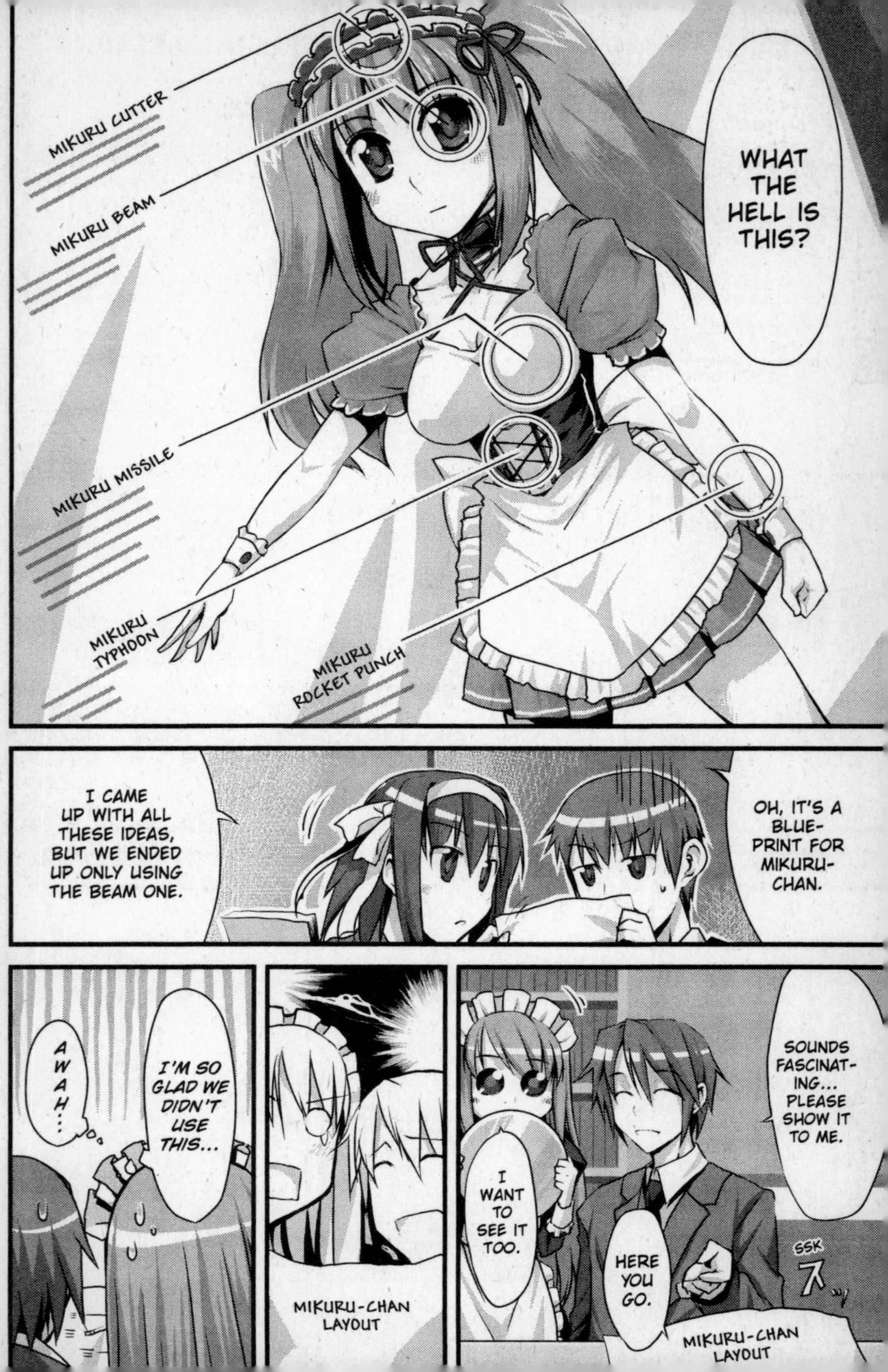
WHAT THE HELL IS THIS?
MIKURU CUTTER
MIKURU BEAM
MIKURU MISSILE
MIKURU ROCKET PUNCH
MIKURU TYPHOON
OH, IT'S A BLUE-PRINT FOR MIKURU-CHAN.
I CAME UP WITH ALL THESE IDEAS, BUT WE ENDED UP ONLY USING THE BEAM ONE.
SOUNDS FASCINATING... PLEASE SHOW IT TO ME.
SSK
I WANT TO SEE IT TOO.
HERE YOU GO.
MIKURU-CHAN LAYOUT
MIKURU-CHAN LAYOUT
I'M SO GLAD WE DIDN'T USE THIS...
AWAH...

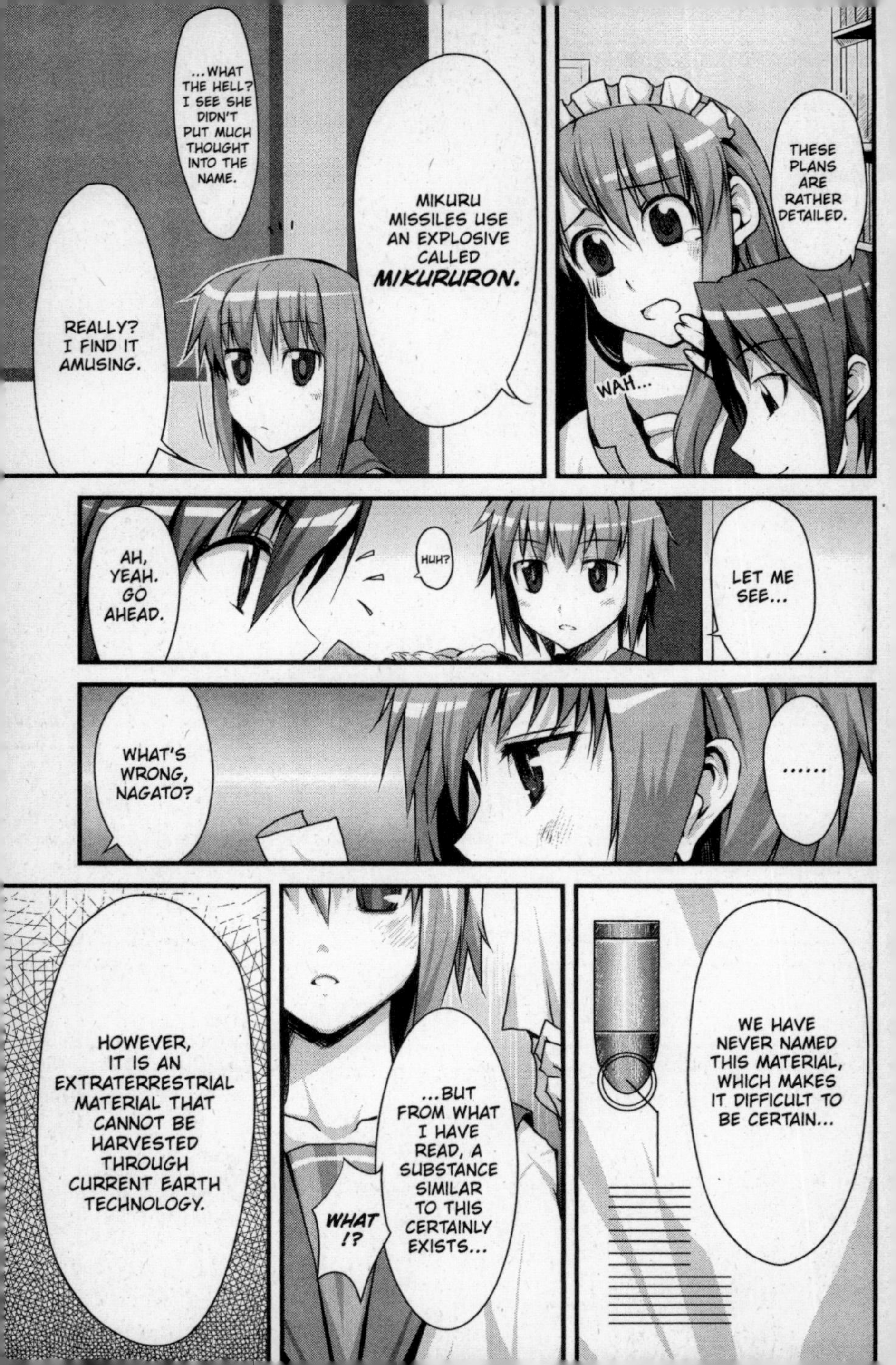
THESE PLANS ARE RATHER DETAILED.
WAH...
MIKURU MISSILES USE AN EXPLOSIVE CALLED MIKURURON.
...WHAT THE HELL? I SEE SHE DIDN'T PUT MUCH THOUGHT INTO THE NAME.
REALLY? I FIND IT AMUSING.
LET ME SEE...
HUH?
AH, YEAH. GO AHEAD.
......
WHAT'S WRONG, NAGATO?
WE HAVE NEVER NAMED THIS MATERIAL, WHICH MAKES IT DIFFICULT TO BE CERTAIN...
...BUT FROM WHAT I HAVE READ, A SUBSTANCE SIMILAR TO THIS CERTAINLY EXISTS...
WHAT!?
HOWEVER, IT IS AN EXTRATERRESTRIAL MATERIAL THAT CANNOT BE HARVESTED THROUGH CURRENT EARTH TECHNOLOGY.

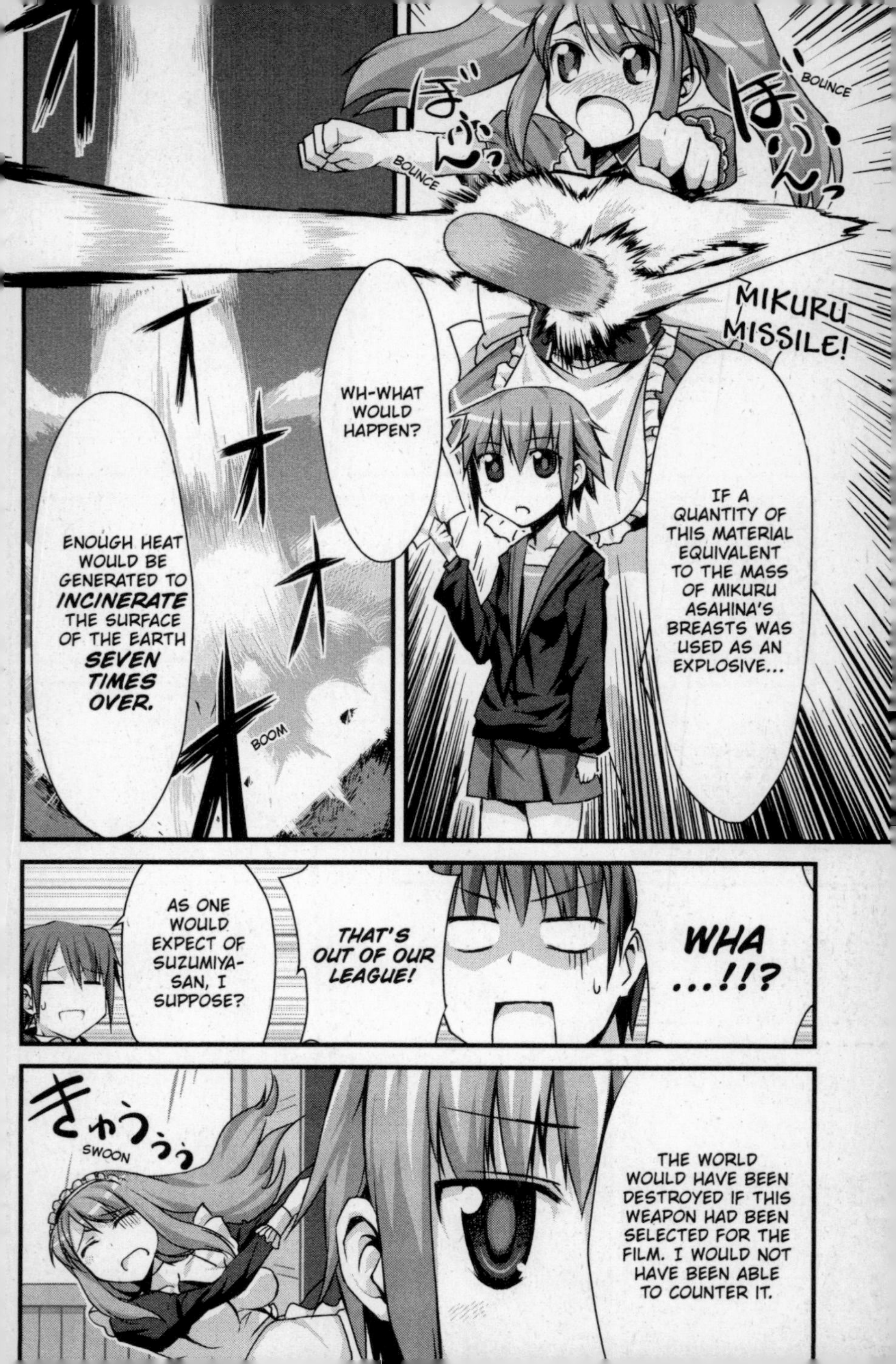

ぼいんっ
BOUNCE
ぼいんっ
BOUNCE
MIKURU MISSILE!
IF A QUANTITY OF THIS MATERIAL EQUIVALENT TO THE MASS OF MIKURU ASAHINA'S BREASTS WAS USED AS AN EXPLOSIVE...
WH-WHAT WOULD HAPPEN?
オオオオ
ENOUGH HEAT WOULD BE GENERATED TO INCINERATE THE SURFACE OF THE EARTH SEVEN TIMES OVER.
BOOM
WHA ...!!?
THAT'S OUT OF OUR LEAGUE!
AS ONE WOULD EXPECT OF SUZUMIYA-SAN, I SUPPOSE?
THE WORLD WOULD HAVE BEEN DESTROYED IF THIS WEAPON HAD BEEN SELECTED FOR THE FILM. I WOULD NOT HAVE BEEN ABLE TO COUNTER IT.
きゅううう
SWOON

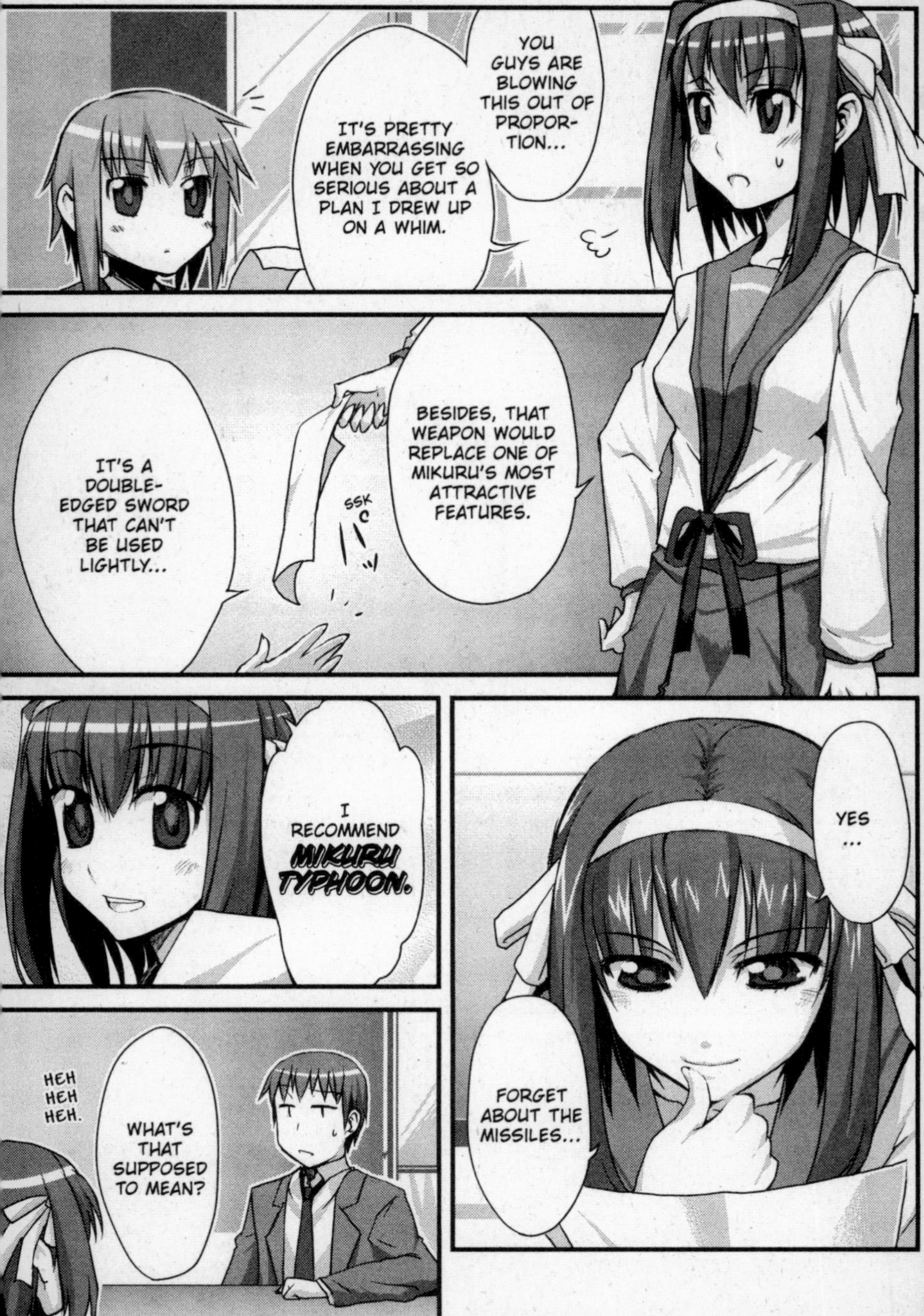
YOU GUYS ARE BLOWING THIS OUT OF PROPOR-TION...
IT'S PRETTY EMBARRASSING WHEN YOU GET SO SERIOUS ABOUT A PLAN I DREW UP ON A WHIM.
BESIDES, THAT WEAPON WOULD REPLACE ONE OF MIKURU'S MOST ATTRACTIVE FEATURES.
SSK
IT'S A DOUBLE-EDGED SWORD THAT CAN'T BE USED LIGHTLY...
YES ...
FORGET ABOUT THE MISSILES...
I RECOMMEND MIKURU TYPHOON.
HEH HEH HEH.
WHAT'S THAT SUPPOSED TO MEAN?

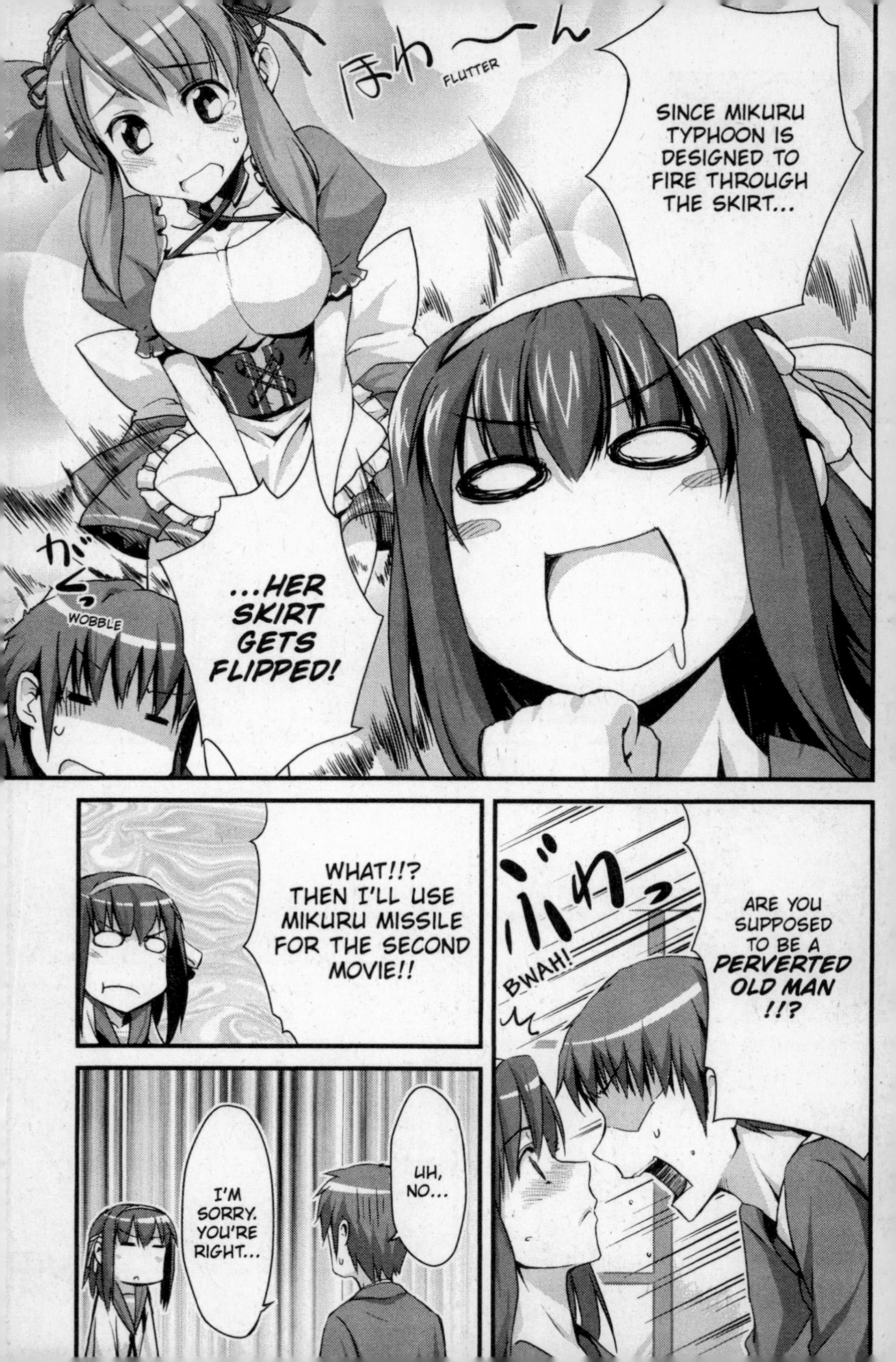
SINCE MIKURU TYPHOON IS DESIGNED TO FIRE THROUGH THE SKIRT...
ほわ～ん
FLUTTER
...HER SKIRT GETS FLIPPED!
がくっ
WOBBLE
ARE YOU SUPPOSED TO BE A PERVERTED OLD MAN !!?
ぶわっ
BWAH!
WHAT!!? THEN I'LL USE MIKURU MISSILE FOR THE SECOND MOVIE!!
UH, NO...
I'M SORRY. YOU'RE RIGHT...

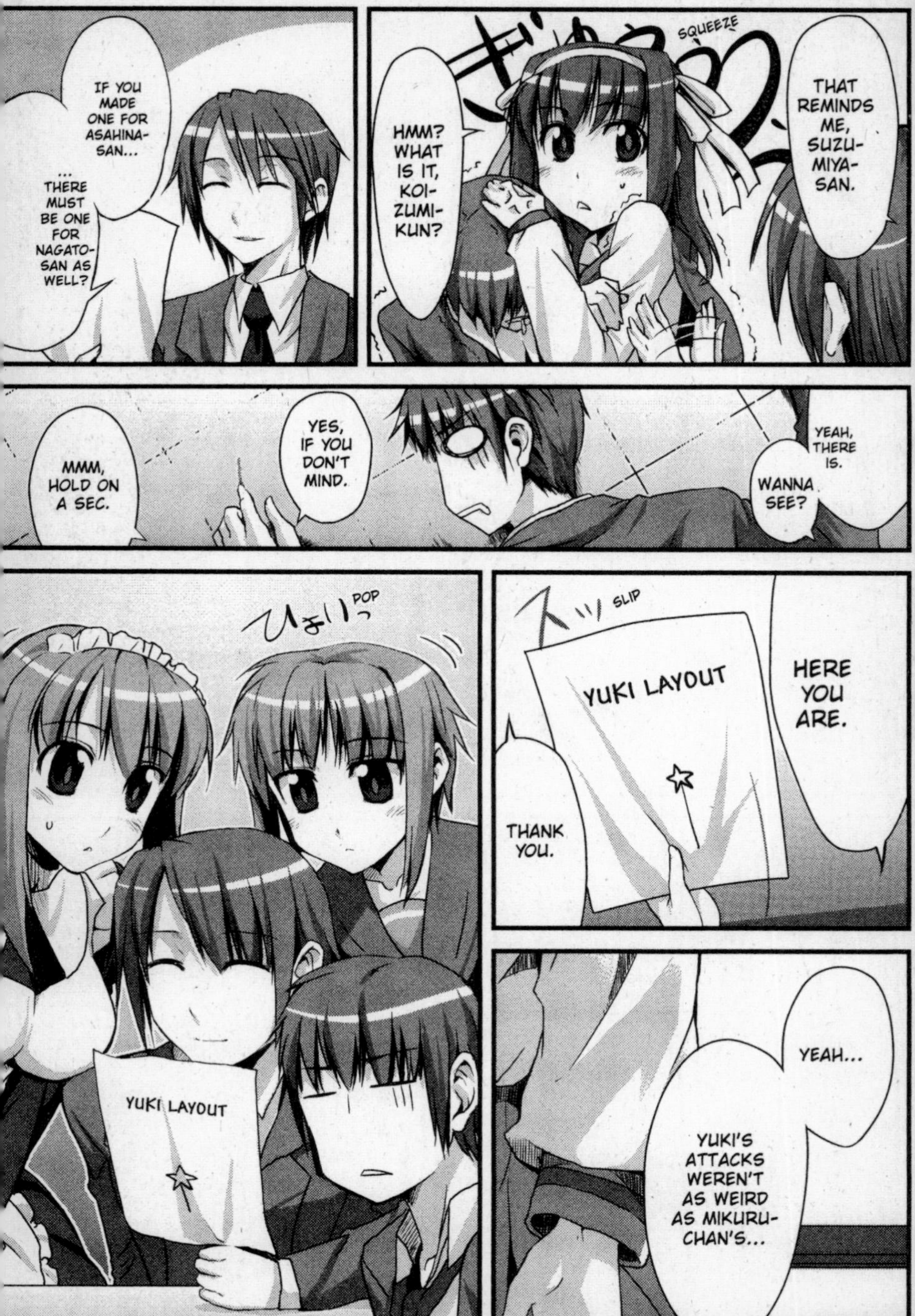
THAT REMINDS ME, SUZUMIYA-SAN.
SQUEEZE
HMM? WHAT IS IT, KOIZUMI-KUN?
IF YOU MADE ONE FOR ASAHINA-SAN...
...THERE MUST BE ONE FOR NAGATO-SAN AS WELL?
YEAH, THERE IS.
WANNA SEE?
YES, IF YOU DON'T MIND.
MMM, HOLD ON A SEC.
HERE YOU ARE.
SLIP
YUKI LAYOUT
THANK YOU.
YEAH...
YUKI'S ATTACKS WEREN'T AS WEIRD AS MIKURU-CHAN'S...
POP
YUKI LAYOUT

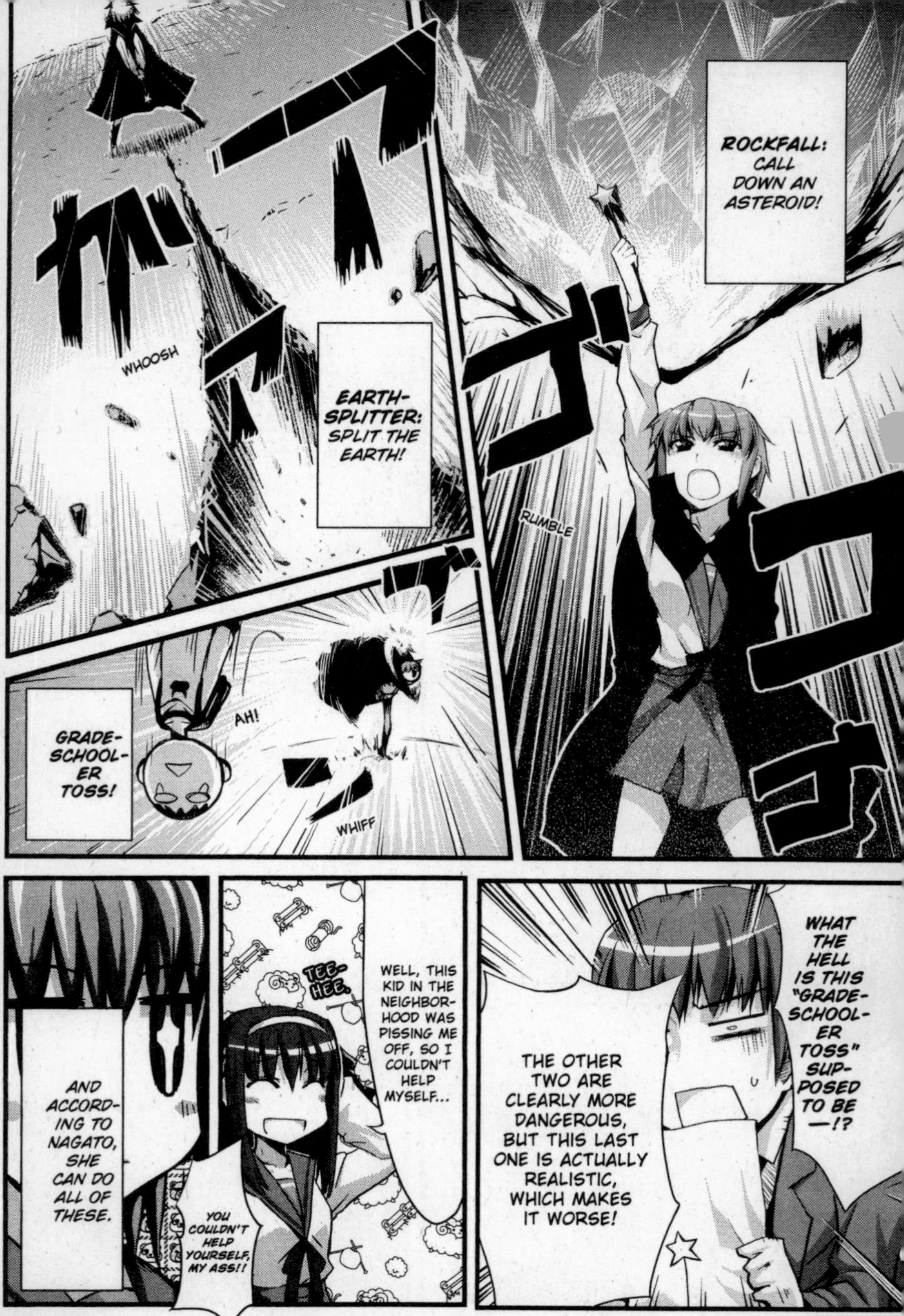
ROCKFALL: CALL DOWN AN ASTEROID!
RUMBLE
WHOOSH
EARTH-SPLITTER: SPLIT THE EARTH!
GRADE-SCHOOLER TOSS!
AH!
WHIFF
WHAT THE HELL IS THIS "GRADE-SCHOOLER TOSS" SUPPOSED TO BE—!?
THE OTHER TWO ARE CLEARLY MORE DANGEROUS, BUT THIS LAST ONE IS ACTUALLY REALISTIC, WHICH MAKES IT WORSE!
WELL, THIS KID IN THE NEIGHBORHOOD WAS PISSING ME OFF, SO I COULDN'T HELP MYSELF...
TEE-HEE.
YOU COULDN'T HELP YOURSELF, MY ASS!!
AND ACCORDING TO NAGATO, SHE CAN DO ALL OF THESE.

VOICE

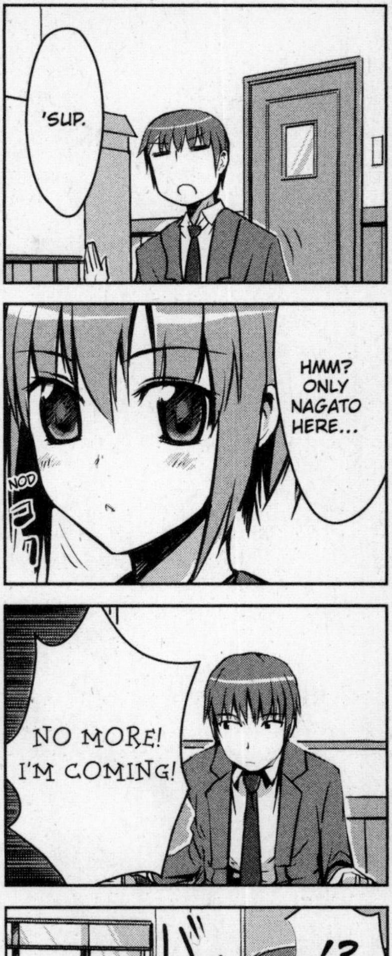
'SUP.
HMM? ONLY NAGATO HERE...
NOD
NO MORE! I'M COMING!
!?
TURN
...
...!?

NAGATO'S HOBBY

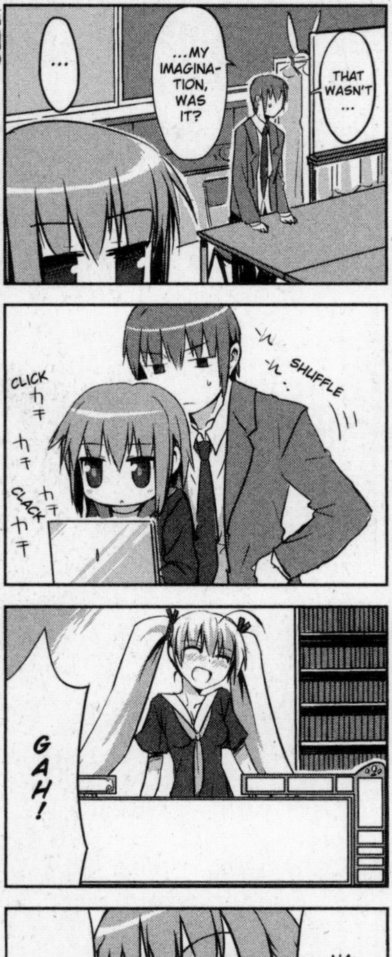
THAT WASN'T ...
...MY IMAGINATION, WAS IT?
...
SHUFFLE
CLICK
カチ
カチ
CLACK
カチ
カチ
GAH!
NA-GATO... IS THAT INTERESTING?
FASCINATING.
R-REALLY...

•Little-sister heroine
•Heroine in the game Nagato is playing. Wonder what the game's about?

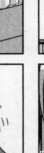

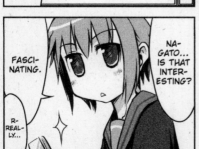

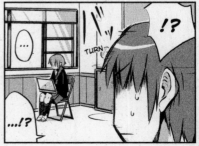

BEWARE OF SOUND LEAKAGE

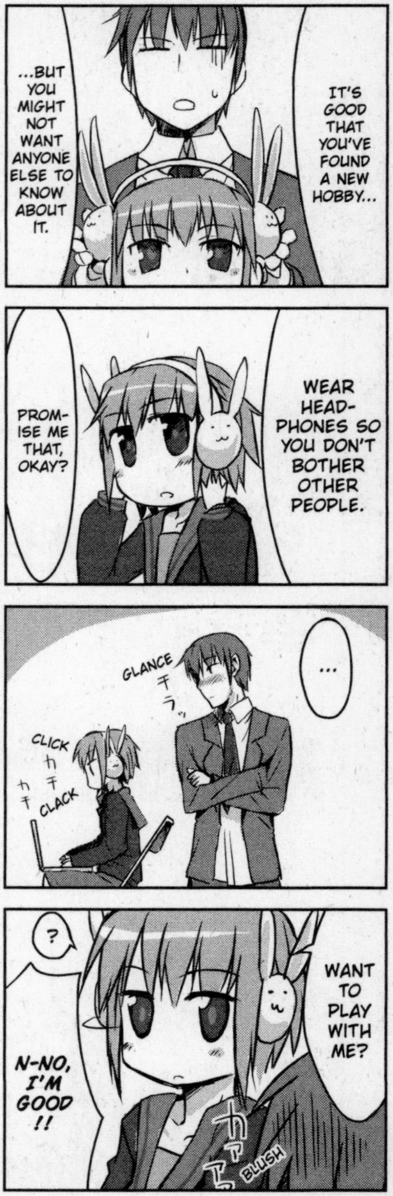
IT'S GOOD THAT YOU'VE FOUND A NEW HOBBY...
...BUT YOU MIGHT NOT WANT ANYONE ELSE TO KNOW ABOUT IT.
WEAR HEAD-PHONES SO YOU DON'T BOTHER OTHER PEOPLE.
PROM-ISE ME THAT, OKAY?
...
GLANCE
チラッ
CLICK
カチ
カチ
CLACK
WANT TO PLAY WITH ME?
?
N-NO, I'M GOOD!!
カァァ
BLUSH

TRUE TALES OF CLOSED SPACE

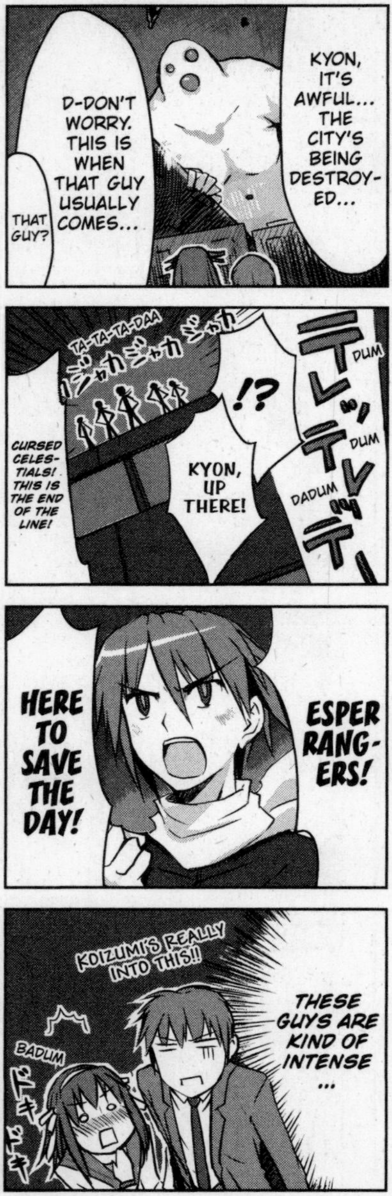
KYON, IT'S AWFUL... THE CITY'S BEING DESTROY-ED...
D-DON'T WORRY. THIS IS WHEN THAT GUY USUALLY COMES...
THAT GUY?
テレッ
DUM
テレッ
DUM
テー
DADUM
!?
KYON, UP THERE!
TA-TA-TA-DAA
ジャカジャカジャカ
CURSED CELES-TIALS! THIS IS THE END OF THE LINE!
ESPER RANG-ERS!
HERE TO SAVE THE DAY!
THESE GUYS ARE KIND OF INTENSE...
KOIZUMI'S REALLY INTO THIS!!
BADUM
ドキドキ

POINTLESS COLOR CODING

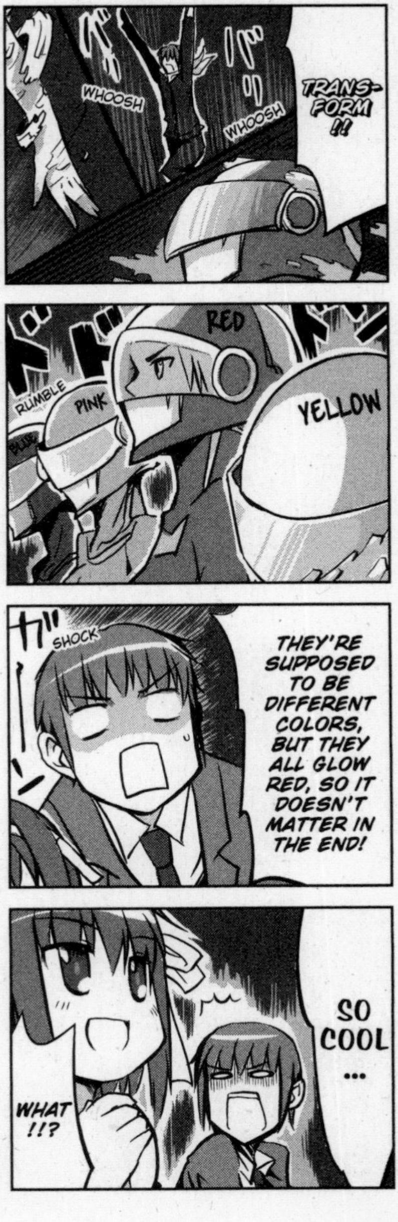
TRANSFORM!!
WHOOSH
WHOOSH
RED
YELLOW
PINK
RUMBLE
BLUE
THEY'RE SUPPOSED TO BE DIFFERENT COLORS, BUT THEY ALL GLOW RED, SO IT DOESN'T MATTER IN THE END!
SHOCK
SO COOL...
WHAT!!?

KYON PLAYS STRAIGHT MAN

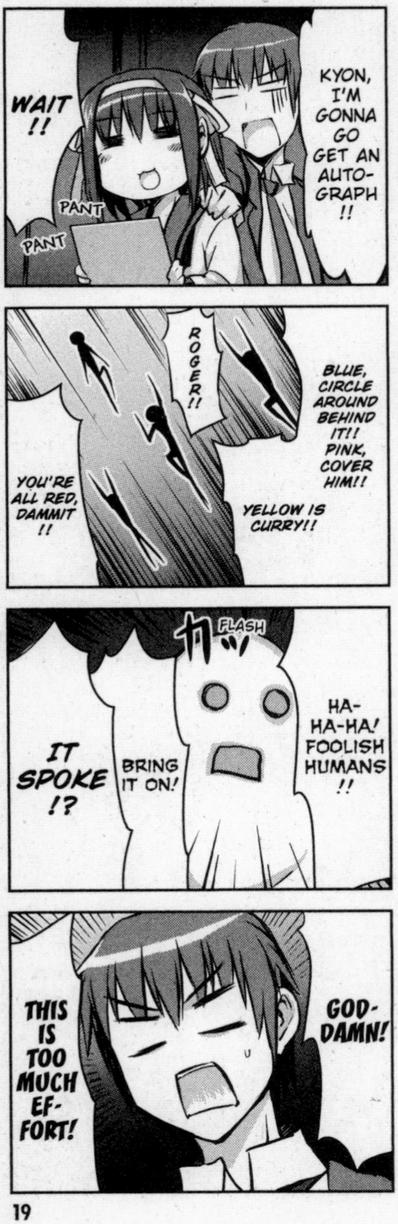
KYON, I'M GONNA GO GET AN AUTOGRAPH!!
WAIT!!
PANT
PANT
BLUE, CIRCLE AROUND BEHIND IT!! PINK, COVER HIM!!
ROGER!!
YELLOW IS CURRY!!
YOU'RE ALL RED, DAMMIT!!
FLASH
HA-HA-HA! FOOLISH HUMANS!!
BRING IT ON!
IT SPOKE!?
GODDAMN!
THIS IS TOO MUCH EFFORT!

INSPIRE

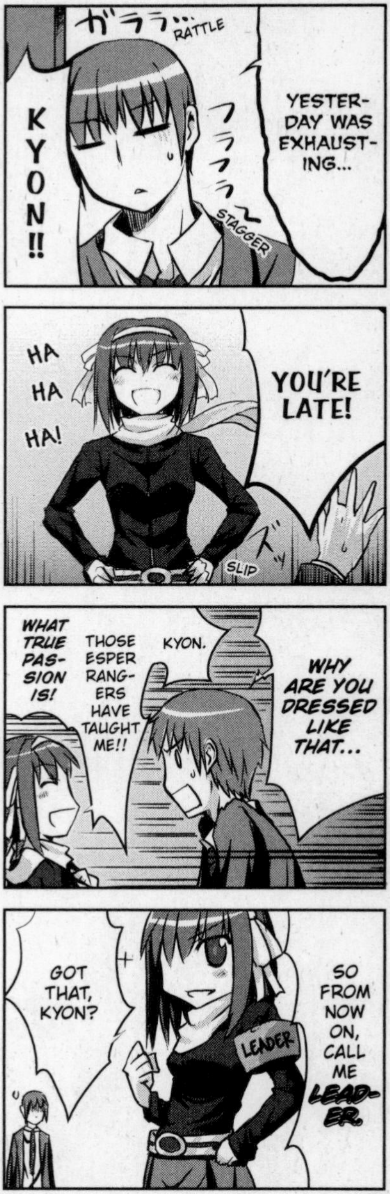
YESTER-DAY WAS EXHAUST-ING...
ガラララ… RATTLE
KYON!!
フラフラ～ STAGGER
YOU'RE LATE!
HA HA HA!
ズッ SLIP
WHY ARE YOU DRESSED LIKE THAT...
KYON.
THOSE ESPER RANG-ERS HAVE TAUGHT ME!!
WHAT TRUE PAS-SION IS!
SO FROM NOW ON, CALL ME LEAD-ER.
GOT THAT, KYON?
LEADER

COSPLAY

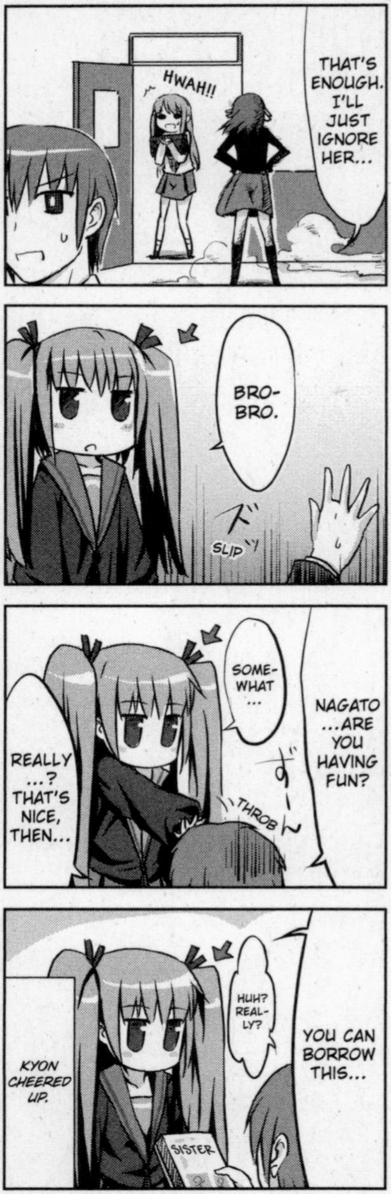
THAT'S ENOUGH. I'LL JUST IGNORE HER...
HWAH!!
BRO-BRO.
ズッ SLIP
NAGATO ...ARE YOU HAVING FUN?
SOME-WHAT ...
ずぅ～ん THROB
REALLY ...? THAT'S NICE, THEN...
YOU CAN BORROW THIS...
HUH? REAL-LY?
SISTER
KYON CHEERED UP.

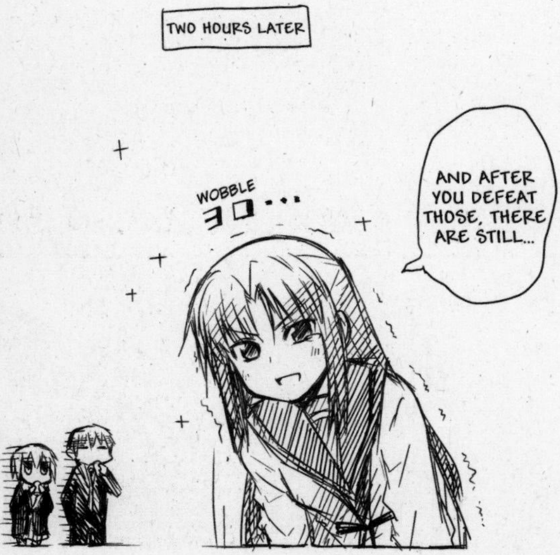
TWO HOURS LATER
AND AFTER YOU DEFEAT THOSE, THERE ARE STILL...
WOBBLE
ヨロ…

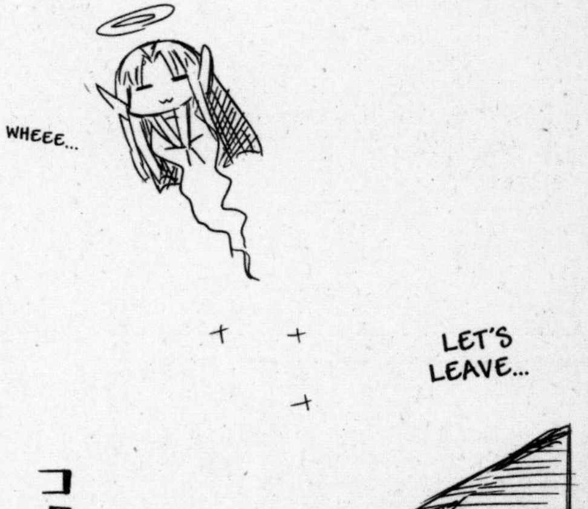
WHEEE...
LET'S LEAVE...
コクッ
NOD

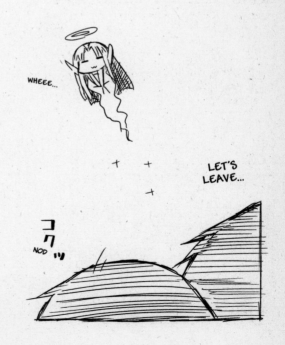

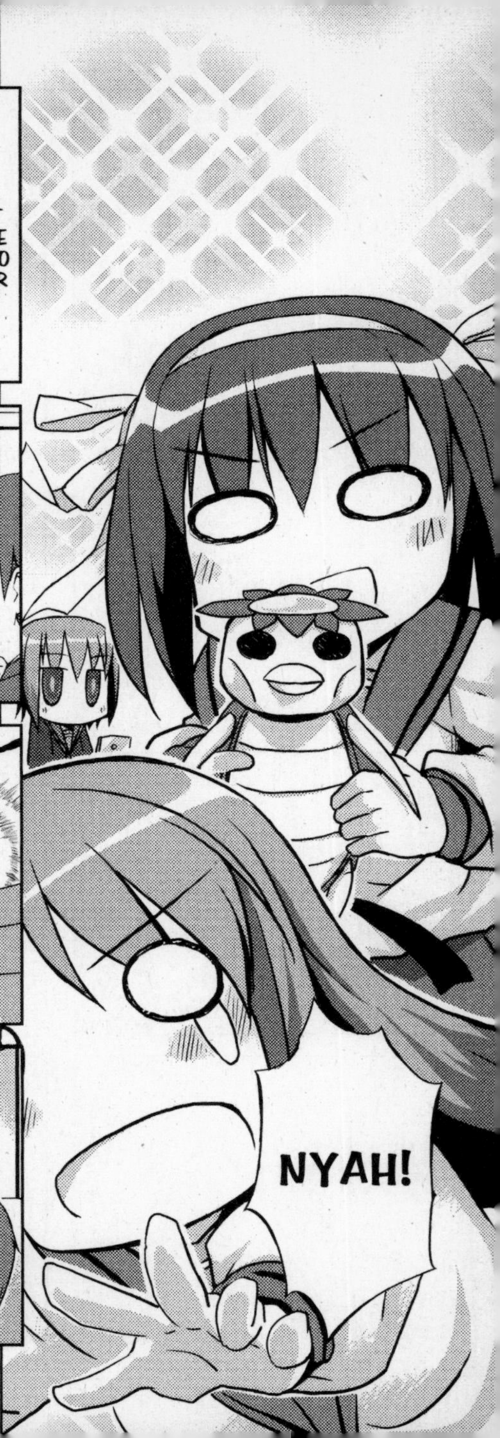
NYAH!

BORED

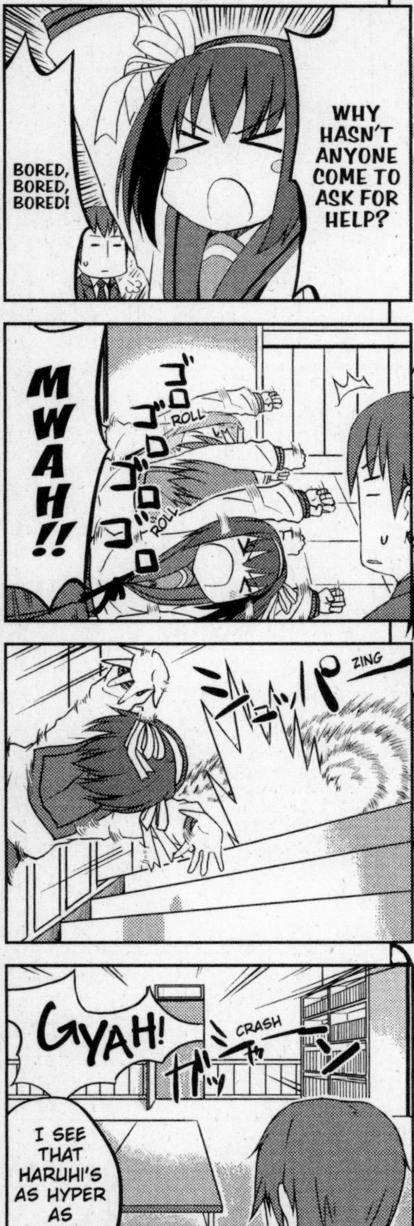
WHY HASN'T ANYONE COME TO ASK FOR HELP?
BORED, BORED, BORED!
ROLL
ROLL
MWAH!!
ZING
CRASH
GYAH!
I SEE THAT HARUHI'S AS HYPER AS ALWAYS.

•Haruhi-chan •SOS Brigade brigade chief. Seems to have trouble standing still.

•Kyon •Supposed to be the main character in this story. Busy delivering riposte after riposte in disgust.

•Nagato •A taciturn alien who's always reading. Recently became hooked on naughty games.

REQUEST

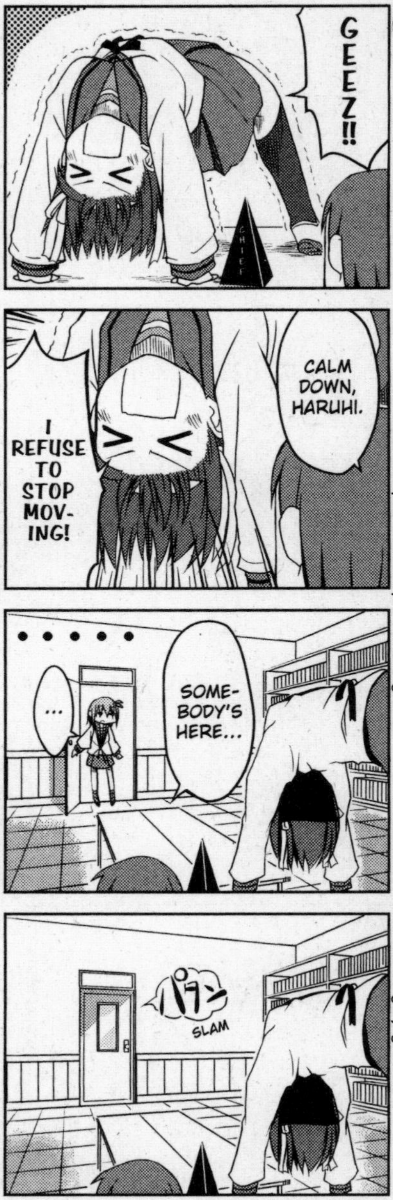
GEEZ!!
CALM DOWN, HARUHI.
I REFUSE TO STOP MOVING!
SOME-BODY'S HERE...
...
• • • • •
SLAM

FREEFALL

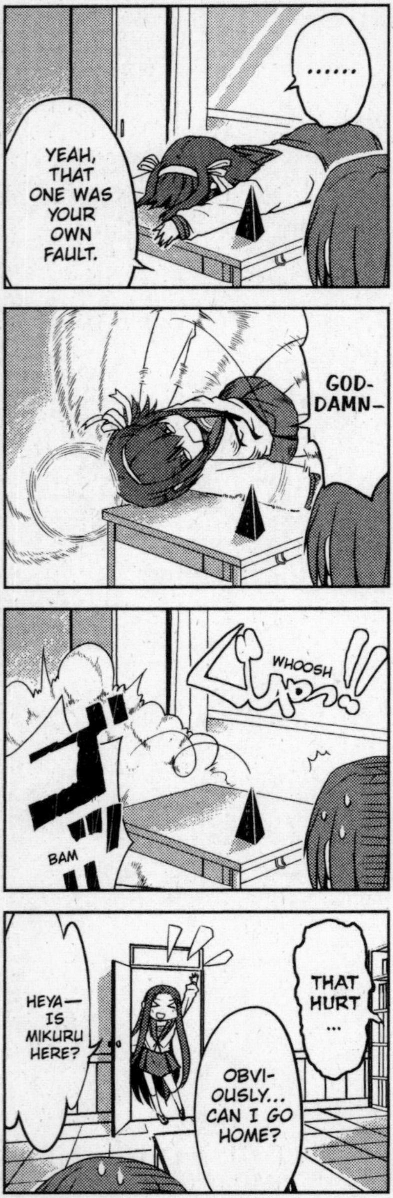
....
YEAH, THAT ONE WAS YOUR OWN FAULT.
GOD-DAMN—
WHOOSH
BAM
THAT HURT ...
OBVIOUSLY... CAN I GO HOME?
HEYA— IS MIKURU HERE?

LEGEND OF MIKURU

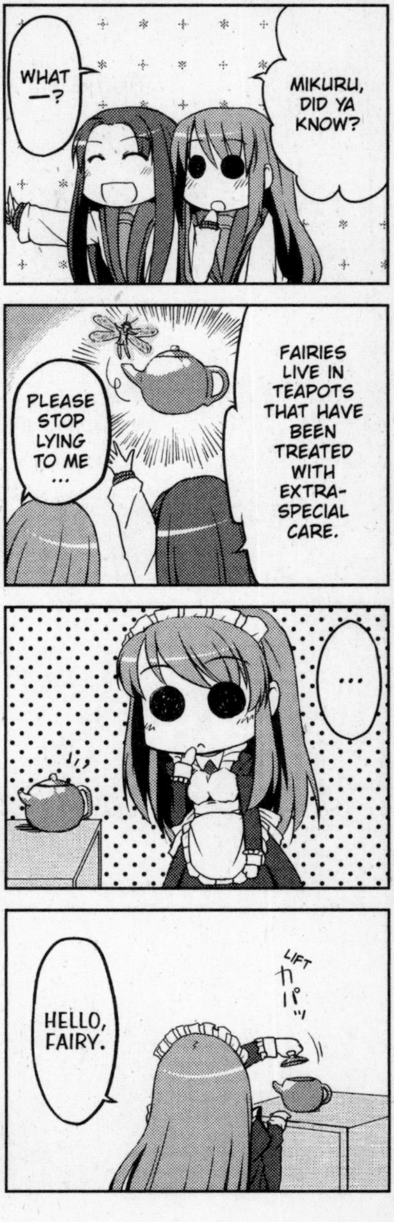
MIKURU, DID YA KNOW?
WHAT—?
FAIRIES LIVE IN TEAPOTS THAT HAVE BEEN TREATED WITH EXTRA-SPECIAL CARE.
PLEASE STOP LYING TO ME ...
...
カパッ
LIFT
HELLO, FAIRY.

FAIRY

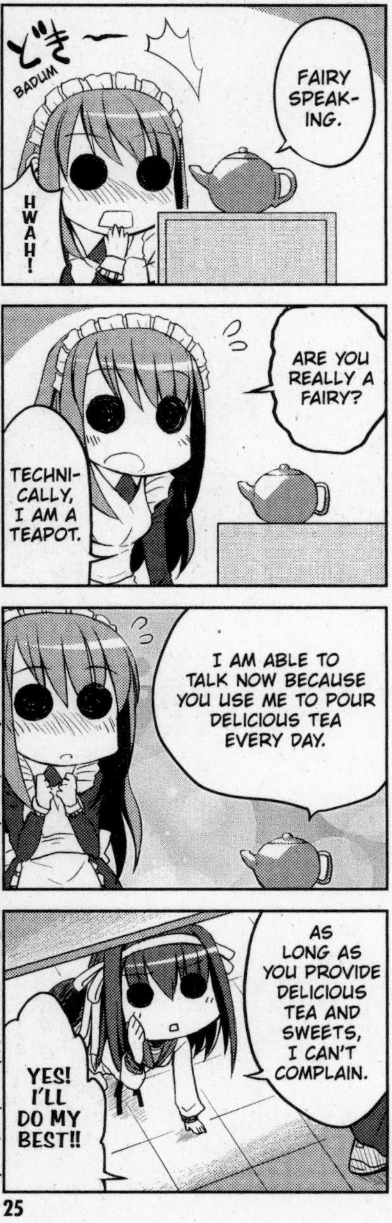
FAIRY SPEAKING.
どき〜
BADUM
HWAH!
ARE YOU REALLY A FAIRY?
TECHNICALLY, I AM A TEAPOT.
I AM ABLE TO TALK NOW BECAUSE YOU USE ME TO POUR DELICIOUS TEA EVERY DAY.
AS LONG AS YOU PROVIDE DELICIOUS TEA AND SWEETS, I CAN'T COMPLAIN.
YES! I'LL DO MY BEST!!

•Mikuru-chan •Actually from the future. Seems to be the type that's easily fooled.

•Koizumi •An enigmatic transfer student who happens to be an esper. He's always smiling, but he may actually be mean at heart.

•Tsuruya-san •Mikuru-chan's rich classmate. Sneaked in her first appearance this time.

THE SHOCK OF MIKURU ASAHINA

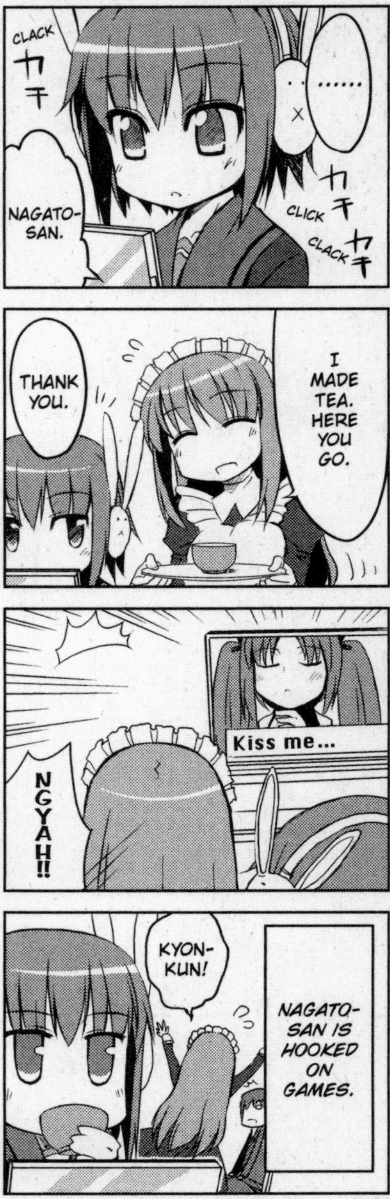
......
CLACK カチ
CLICK カチ
CLACK カチ
NAGATO-SAN.
I MADE TEA. HERE YOU GO.
THANK YOU.
Kiss me...
NGYAH!!
NAGATO-SAN IS HOOKED ON GAMES.
KYON-KUN!

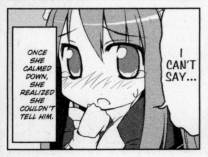

•Little sister heroine
•Heroine in the game Nagato is playing. Progress in her route has been made.

•Computer Society President
•Regular victim of Haruhi's capriciousness. First appearance on the next page.

•Asakura-san •An alien who opposes Nagato. A poor, little thing who was head-butted by Nagato and destroyed.

I CAN'T SAY...

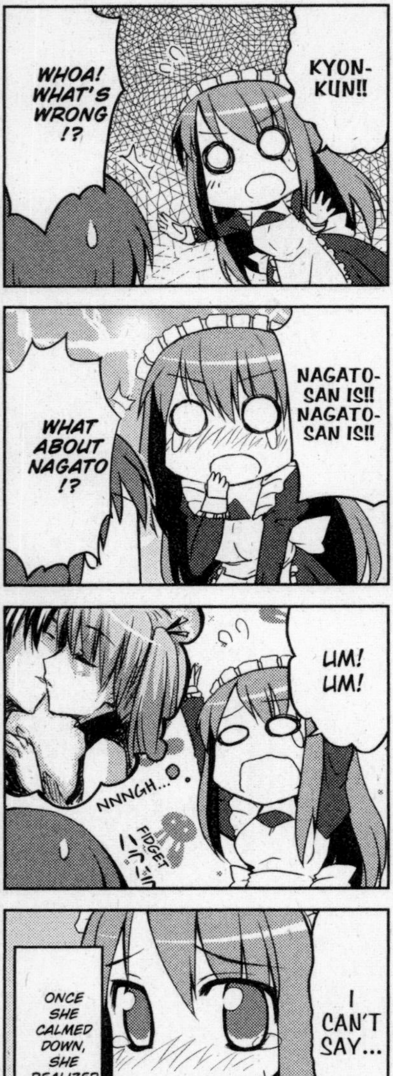
KYON-KUN!!
WHOA! WHAT'S WRONG!?
NAGATO-SAN IS!! NAGATO-SAN IS!!
WHAT ABOUT NAGATO!?
UM! UM!
NNNGH...
FIDGET
I CAN'T SAY...
ONCE SHE CALMED DOWN, SHE REALIZED SHE COULDN'T TELL HIM.

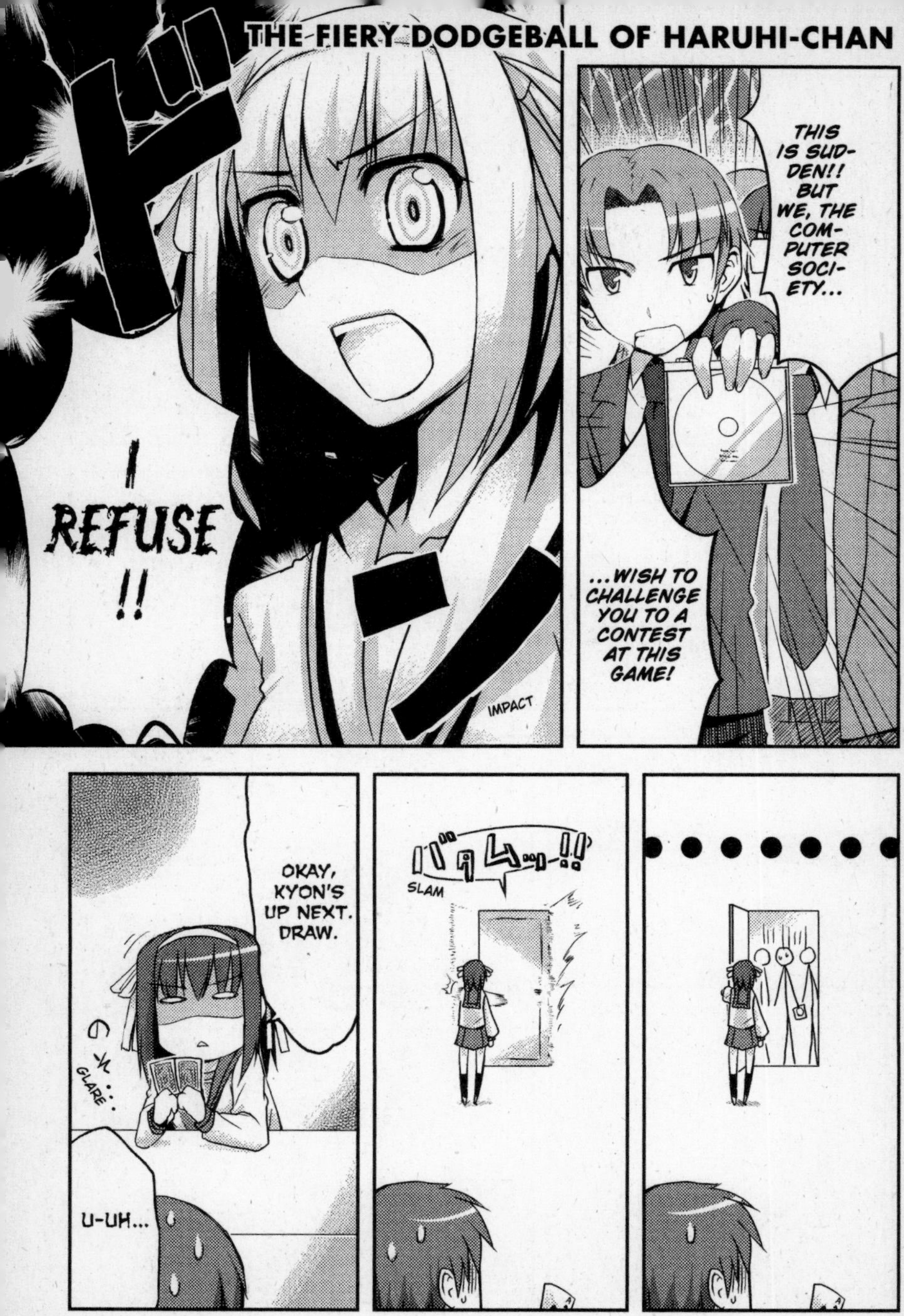
THIS IS SUDDEN!! BUT WE, THE COMPUTER SOCIETY...
...WISH TO CHALLENGE YOU TO A CONTEST AT THIS GAME!
I REFUSE !!
IMPACT
• • • • • • •
SLAM
OKAY, KYON'S UP NEXT. DRAW.
GLARE...
U-UH...

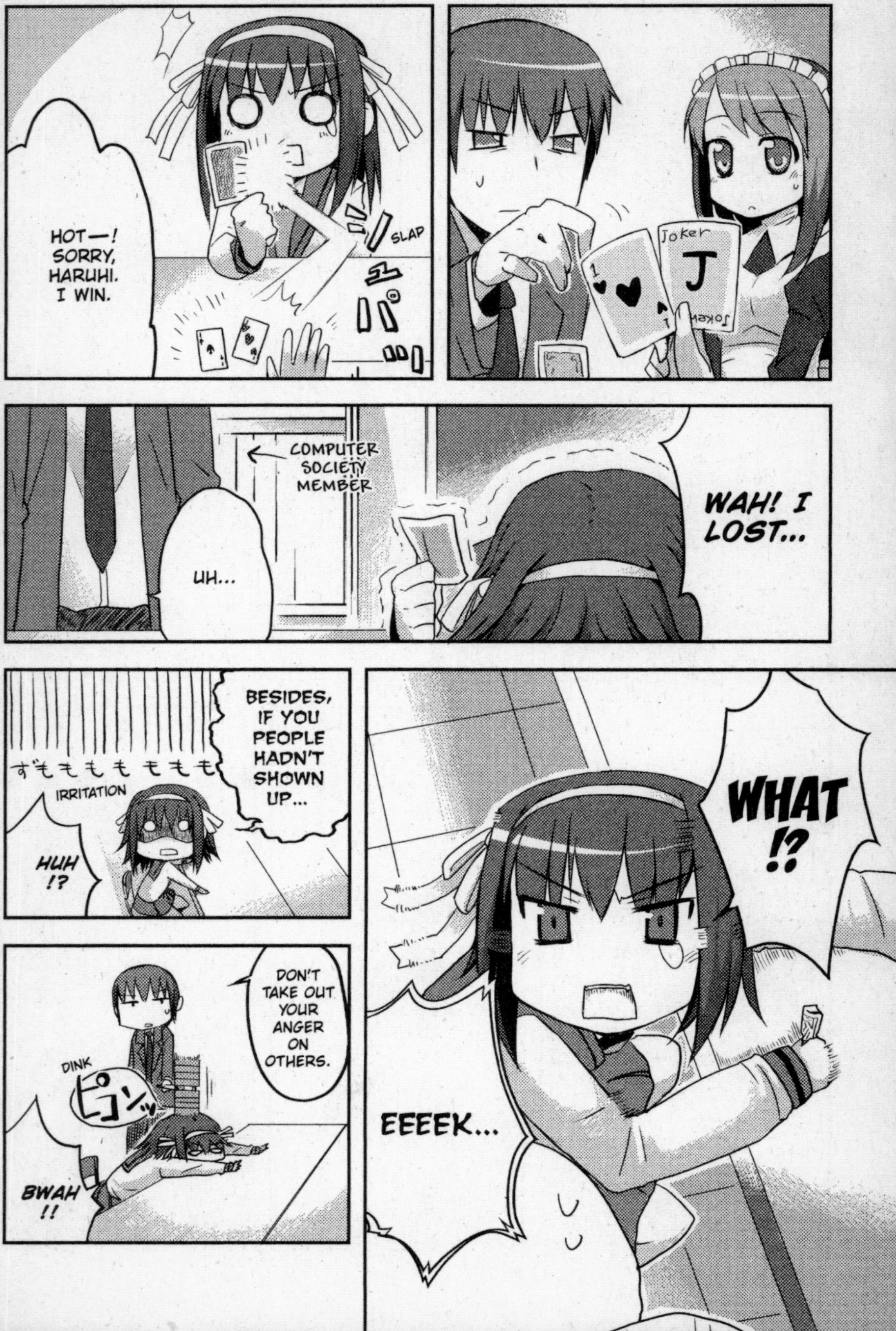
Joker
J
HOT—! SORRY, HARUHI. I WIN.
SLAP
WAH! I LOST...
COMPUTER SOCIETY MEMBER
UH...
WHAT !?
EEEEK...
BESIDES, IF YOU PEOPLE HADN'T SHOWN UP...
ずもももも ももも
IRRITATION
HUH !?
DON'T TAKE OUT YOUR ANGER ON OTHERS.
DINK
ピコンッ
BWAH !!

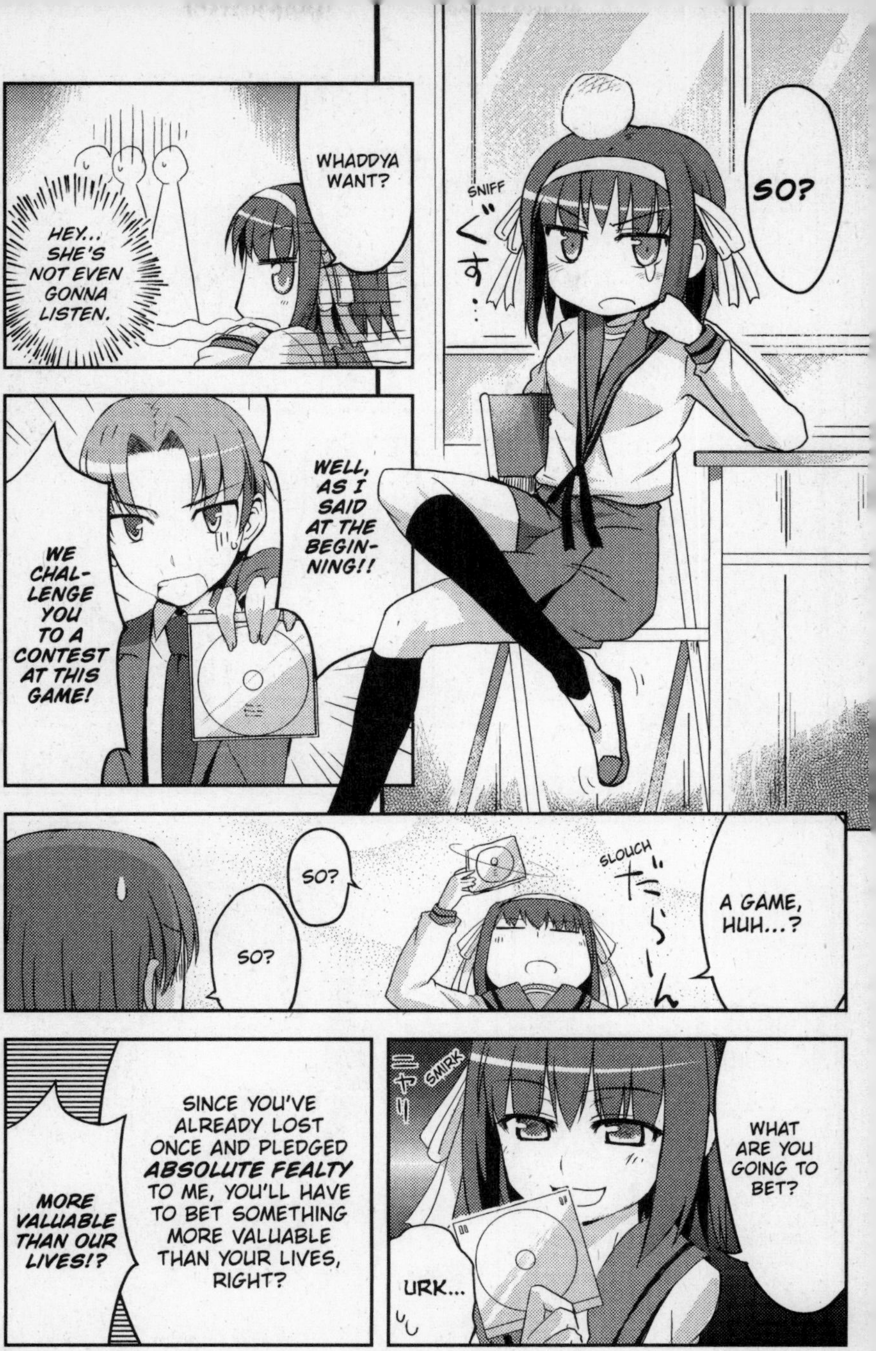
SO?
SNIFF
ぐす・・
WHADDYA WANT?
HEY... SHE'S NOT EVEN GONNA LISTEN.
WELL, AS I SAID AT THE BEGIN-NING!!
WE CHAL-LENGE YOU TO A CONTEST AT THIS GAME!
A GAME, HUH...?
SLOUCH
だらーん
SO?
SO?
WHAT ARE YOU GOING TO BET?
SMIRK
ニヤリ
URK...
SINCE YOU'VE ALREADY LOST ONCE AND PLEDGED **ABSOLUTE FEALTY** TO ME, YOU'LL HAVE TO BET SOMETHING MORE VALUABLE THAN YOUR LIVES, RIGHT?
MORE VALUABLE THAN OUR LIVES!?

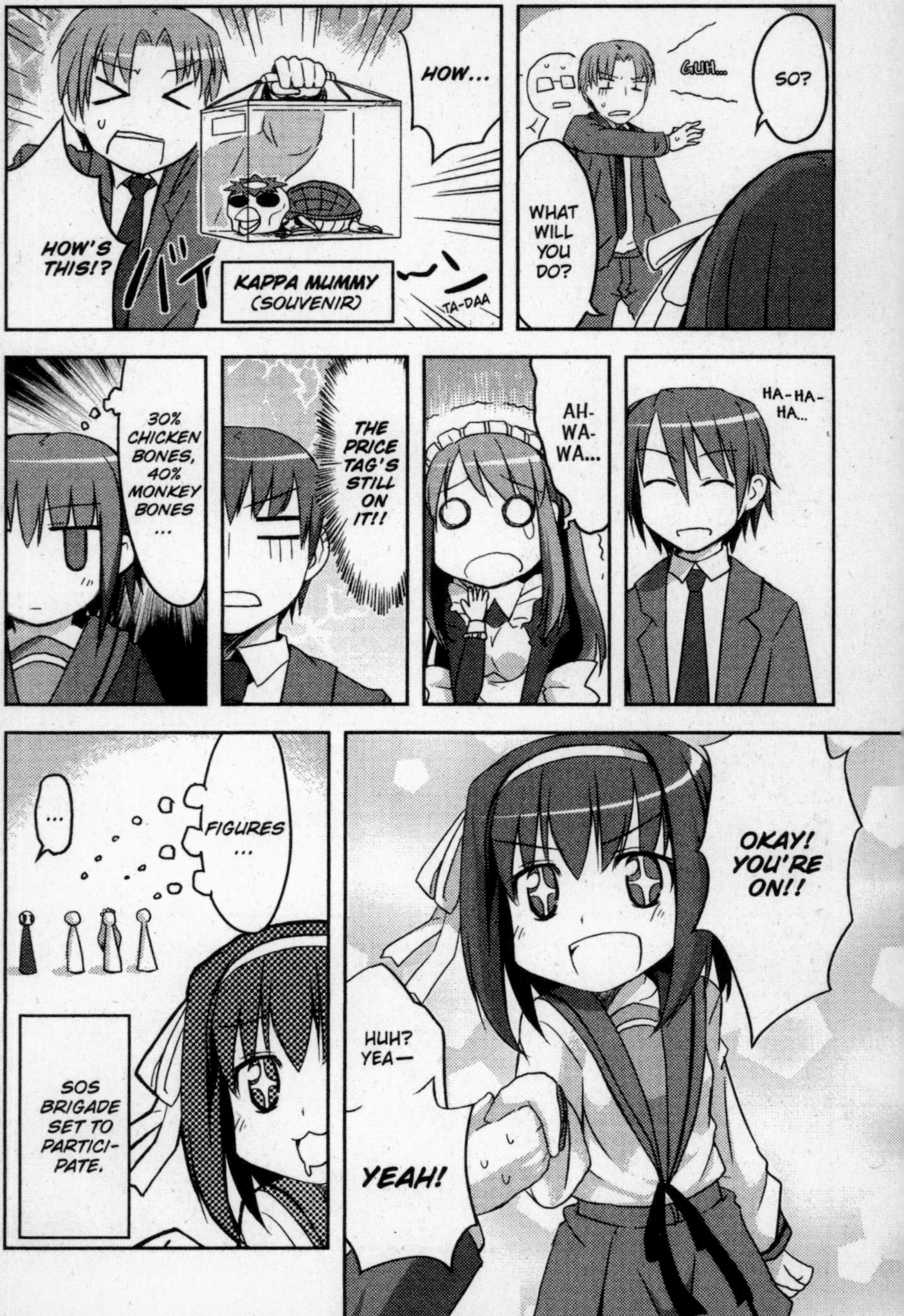
SO?
GUH...
WHAT WILL YOU DO?
HOW...
HOW'S THIS!?
KAPPA MUMMY (SOUVENIR)
TA-DAA
HA-HA-HA...
AH-WA-WA...
THE PRICE TAG'S STILL ON IT!!
30% CHICKEN BONES, 40% MONKEY BONES ...
OKAY! YOU'RE ON!!
HUH? YEA—
YEAH!
FIGURES ...
...
SOS BRIGADE SET TO PARTICI-PATE.

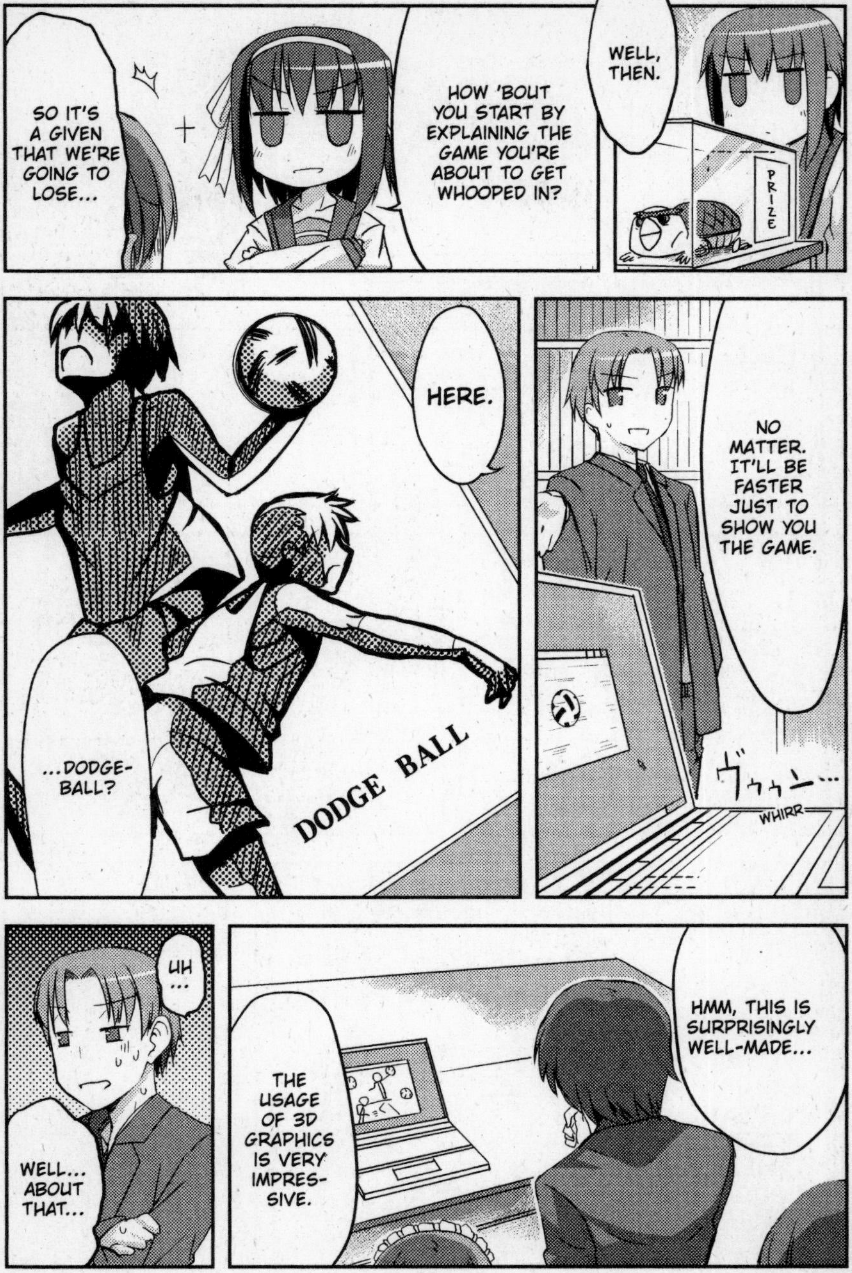
WELL, THEN.
PRIZE
HOW 'BOUT YOU START BY EXPLAINING THE GAME YOU'RE ABOUT TO GET WHOOPED IN?
SO IT'S A GIVEN THAT WE'RE GOING TO LOSE...
NO MATTER. IT'LL BE FASTER JUST TO SHOW YOU THE GAME.
WHIRR
HERE.
DODGE BALL
...DODGE-BALL?
HMM, THIS IS SURPRISINGLY WELL-MADE...
THE USAGE OF 3D GRAPHICS IS VERY IMPRESSIVE.
UH ...
WELL... ABOUT THAT...

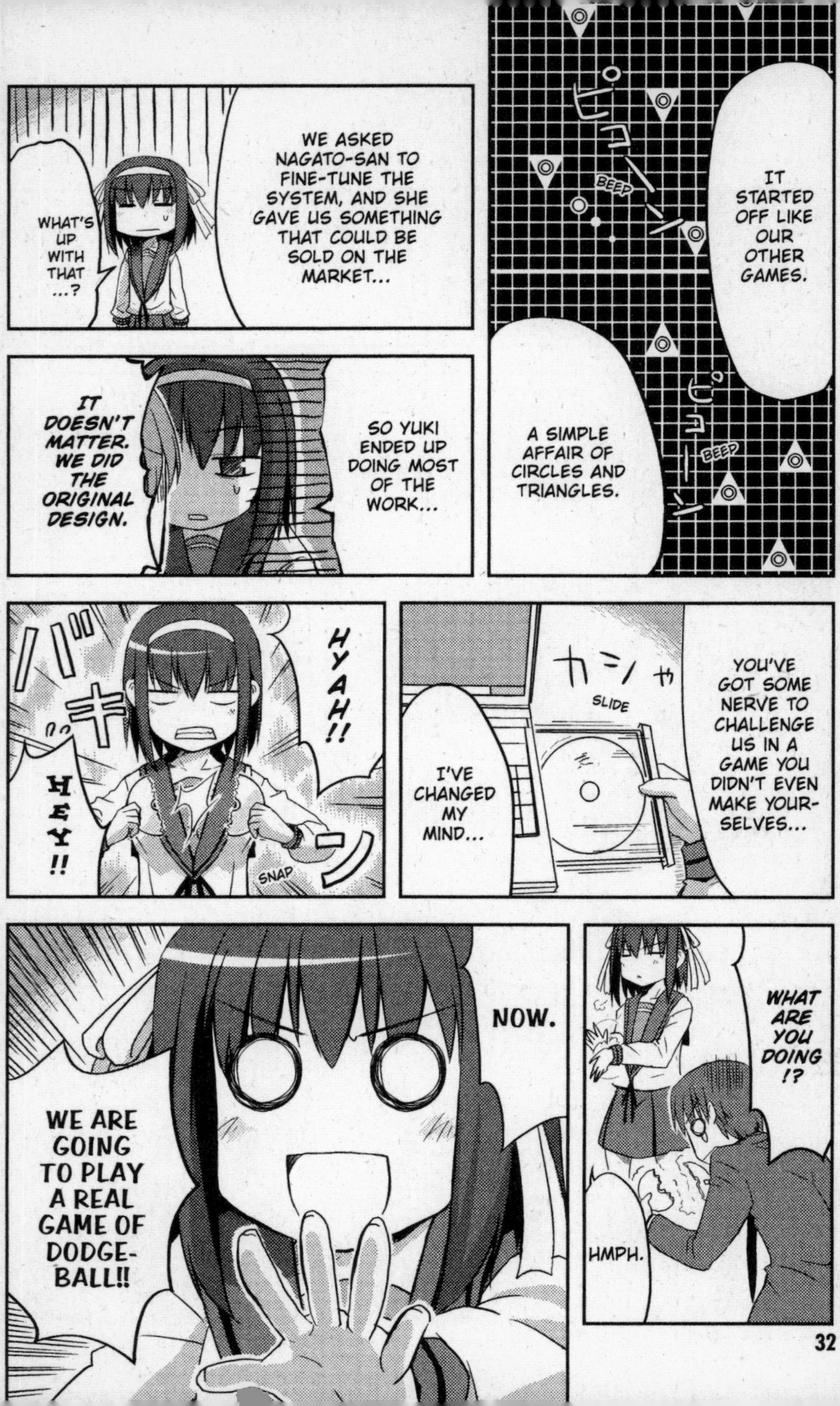
IT STARTED OFF LIKE OUR OTHER GAMES.
BEEP
A SIMPLE AFFAIR OF CIRCLES AND TRIANGLES.
BEEP
WE ASKED NAGATO-SAN TO FINE-TUNE THE SYSTEM, AND SHE GAVE US SOMETHING THAT COULD BE SOLD ON THE MARKET...
WHAT'S UP WITH THAT ...?
SO YUKI ENDED UP DOING MOST OF THE WORK...
IT DOESN'T MATTER. WE DID THE ORIGINAL DESIGN.
YOU'VE GOT SOME NERVE TO CHALLENGE US IN A GAME YOU DIDN'T EVEN MAKE YOUR-SELVES...
SLIDE
I'VE CHANGED MY MIND...
HYAH!!
HEY!!
SNAP
WHAT ARE YOU DOING!?
HMPH.
NOW.
WE ARE GOING TO PLAY A REAL GAME OF DODGE-BALL!!

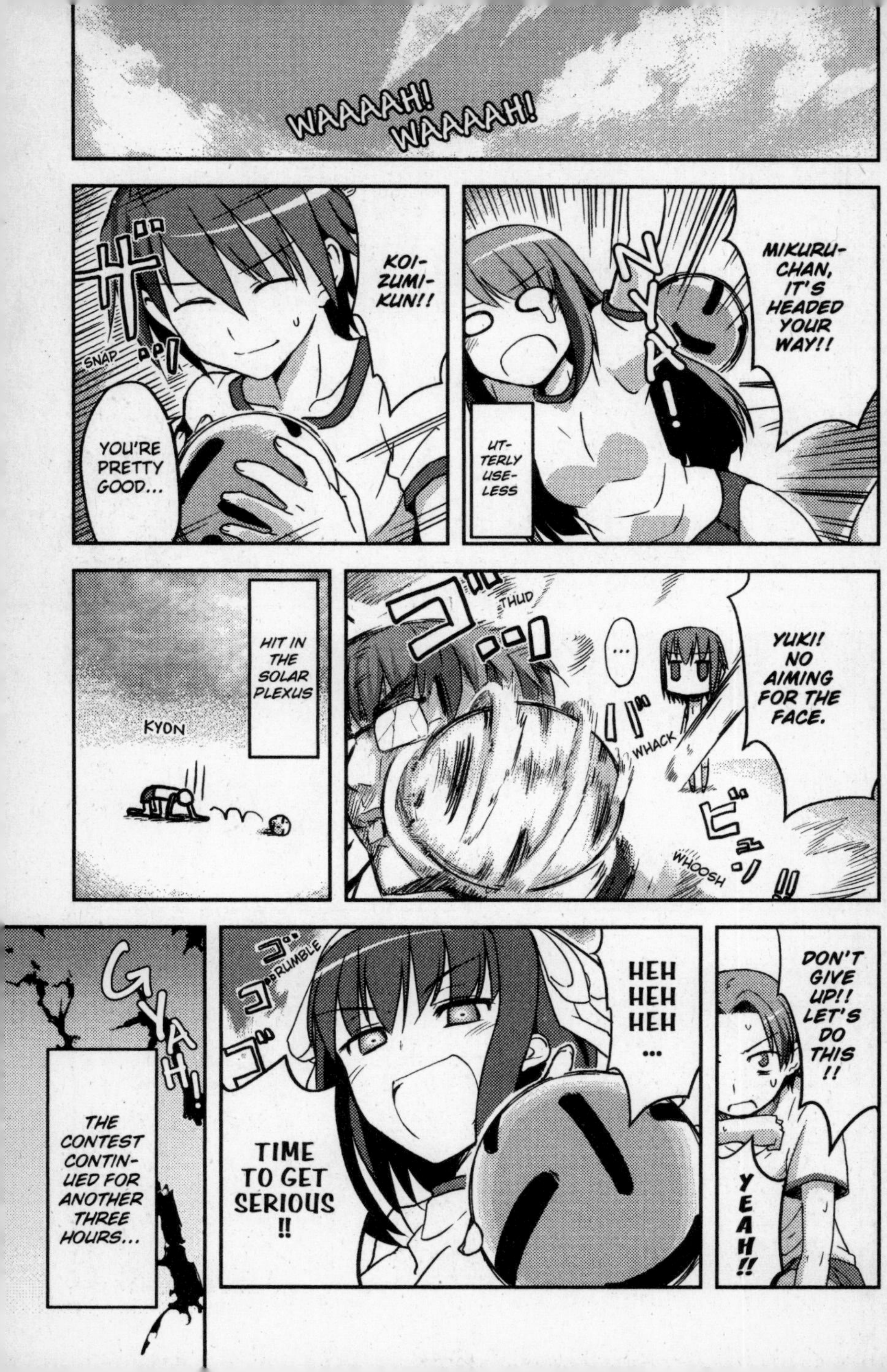
WAAAAH! WAAAAH!
MIKURU-CHAN, IT'S HEADED YOUR WAY!!
NYA-!
UT-TERLY USE-LESS
KOI-ZUMI-KUN!!
SNAP
YOU'RE PRETTY GOOD...
YUKI! NO AIMING FOR THE FACE.
...
THUD
WHACK
WHOOSH
HIT IN THE SOLAR PLEXUS
KYON
DON'T GIVE UP!! LET'S DO THIS!!
YEAH!!
HEH HEH HEH...
RUMBLE
TIME TO GET SERIOUS!!
GYAH!
THE CONTEST CONTIN-UED FOR ANOTHER THREE HOURS...

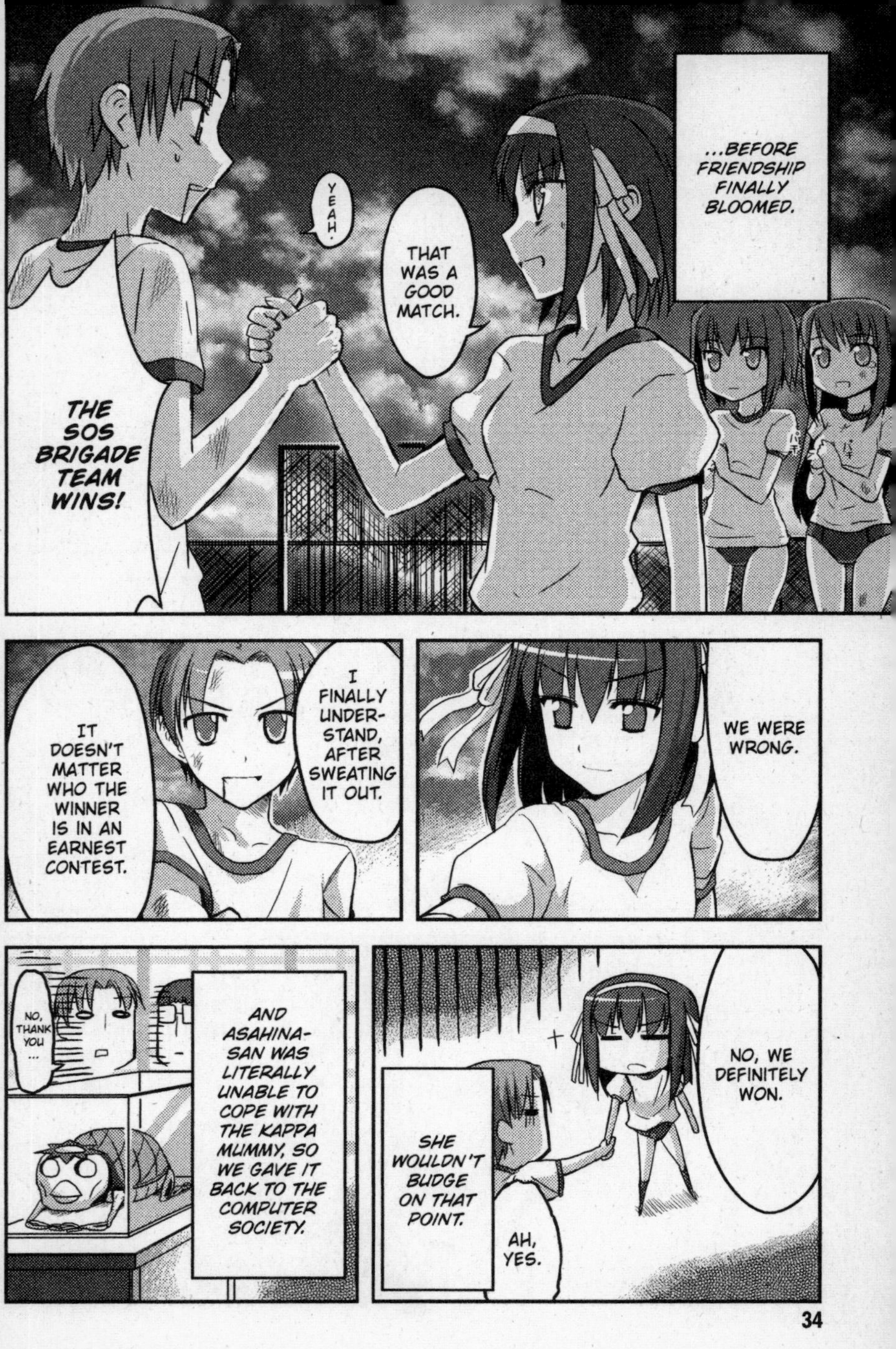
...BEFORE FRIENDSHIP FINALLY BLOOMED.
THAT WAS A GOOD MATCH.
YEAH.
THE SOS BRIGADE TEAM WINS!
WE WERE WRONG.
I FINALLY UNDER-STAND, AFTER SWEATING IT OUT.
IT DOESN'T MATTER WHO THE WINNER IS IN AN EARNEST CONTEST.
NO, WE DEFINITELY WON.
SHE WOULDN'T BUDGE ON THAT POINT.
AH, YES.
AND ASAHINA-SAN WAS LITERALLY UNABLE TO COPE WITH THE KAPPA MUMMY, SO WE GAVE IT BACK TO THE COMPUTER SOCIETY.
NO, THANK YOU...

BOOKS VS. GAMES

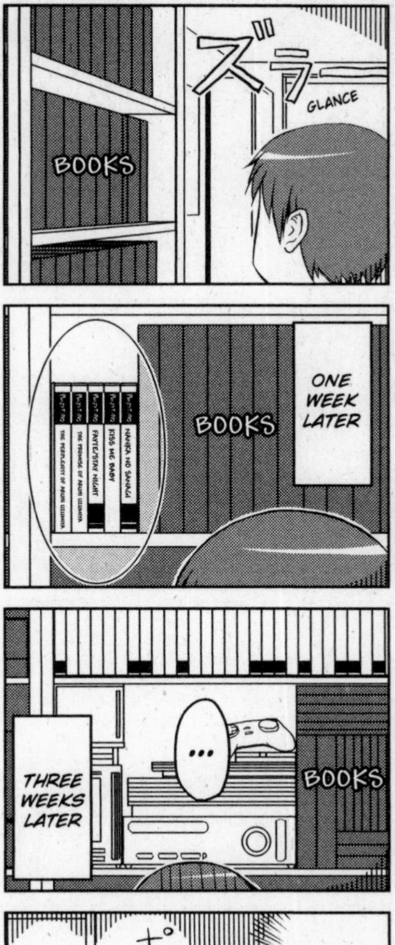
ズラー
GLANCE
BOOKS
ONE WEEK LATER
BOOKS
NANIKA NO SANAGI
KISS ME BABY
FAYTE/STAY NIGHT
THE PROMISE OF ARUHI UZUMIYA
THE PERPLEXITY OF ARUHI UZUMIYA
BOOKS
...
THREE WEEKS LATER
HANG IN THERE! HANG IN THERE!!
ポン...
POOF
BOOKS

SISTER

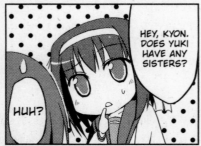

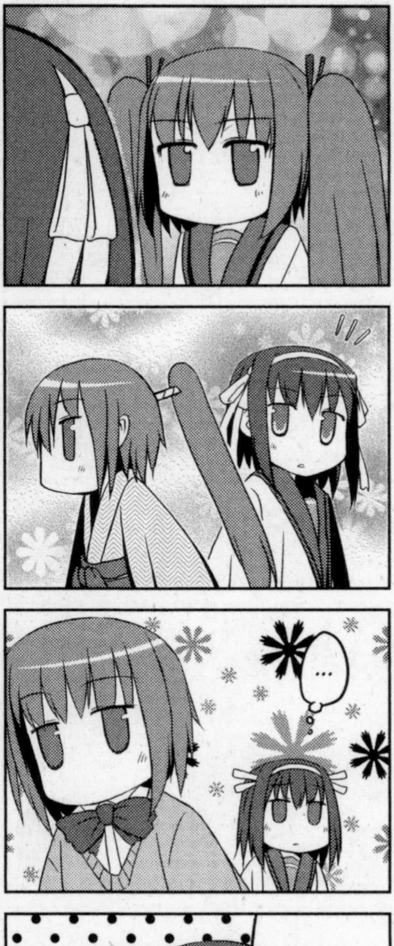
...
HEY, KYON. DOES YUKI HAVE ANY SISTERS?
HUH?

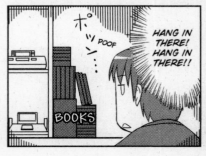

ONWARD, ESPER RANGERS

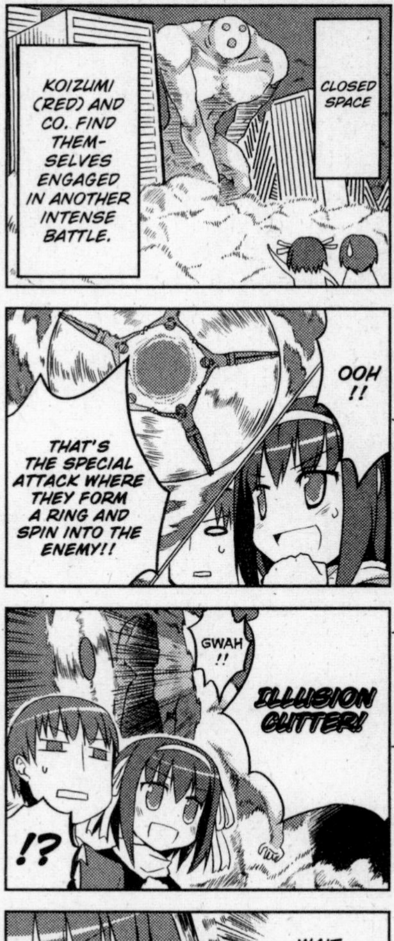
CLOSED SPACE
KOIZUMI (RED) AND CO. FIND THEM-SELVES ENGAGED IN ANOTHER INTENSE BATTLE.
OOH!!
THAT'S THE SPECIAL ATTACK WHERE THEY FORM A RING AND SPIN INTO THE ENEMY!!
GWAH!!
ILLUSION CUTTER!
!?
WAIT... HOW DOES SHE KNOW THE NAME OF THE ATTACK!?
RED, HANG IN THERE!

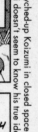

•Red
•A psyched-up Koizumi in closed space. Haruhi doesn't seem to know his true identity.

•Celestial
•Here, it can talk and multiply, to help create a superhero atmosphere.

NEVER GIVE UP, ESPER RANGERS

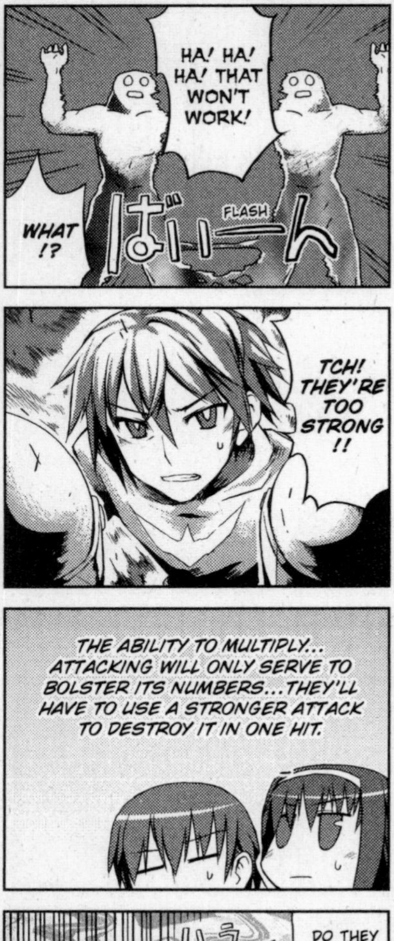
HA! HA! HA! THAT WON'T WORK!
FLASH
ばぃーん
WHAT!?
TCH! THEY'RE TOO STRONG!!
THE ABILITY TO MULTIPLY... ATTACKING WILL ONLY SERVE TO BOLSTER ITS NUMBERS...THEY'LL HAVE TO USE A STRONGER ATTACK TO DESTROY IT IN ONE HIT.
DO THEY HAVE A MOVE THAT'S POWER-FUL ENOUGH...?
ハラ
FIDGET
ハラ
A GUIDE-BOOK!?
TOP SECRET
GUIDE BOOK

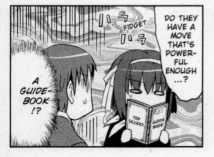

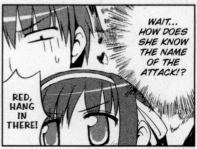

SHINE ON, ESPER RANGERS

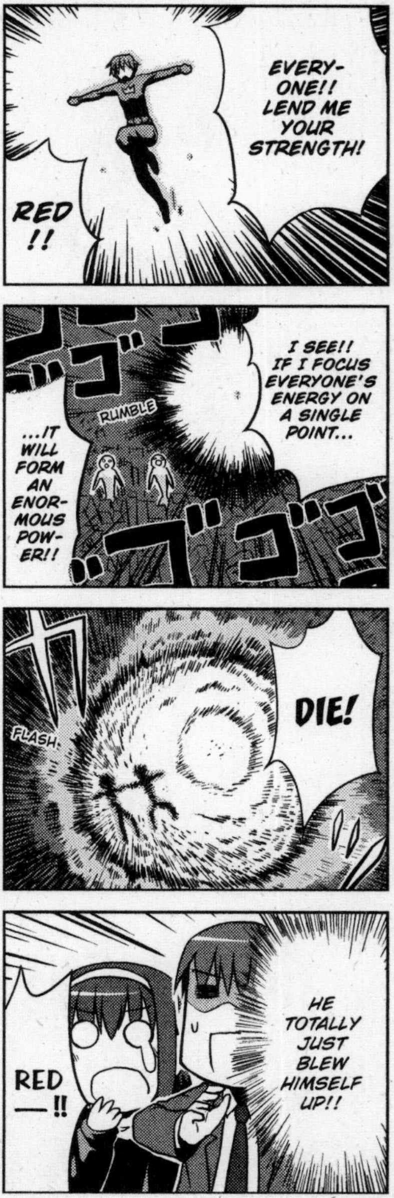
EVERYONE!! LEND ME YOUR STRENGTH!
RED !!
I SEE!! IF I FOCUS EVERYONE'S ENERGY ON A SINGLE POINT...
RUMBLE
...IT WILL FORM AN ENORMOUS POWER!!
DIE!
FLASH
HE TOTALLY JUST BLEW HIMSELF UP!!
RED—!!

NEXT THING YOU KNOW...

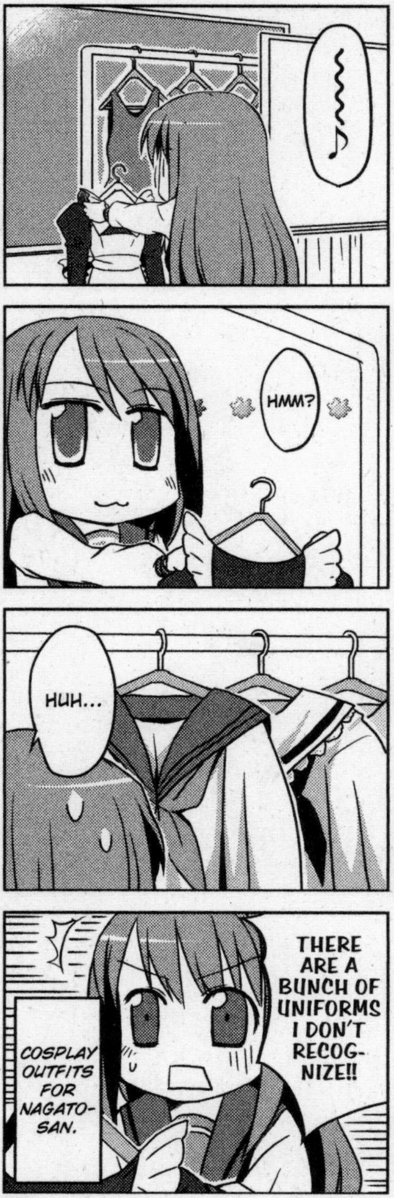
HMM?
HUH...
THERE ARE A BUNCH OF UNIFORMS I DON'T RECOGNIZE!!
COSPLAY OUTFITS FOR NAGATO-SAN.

BACK IN ACTION

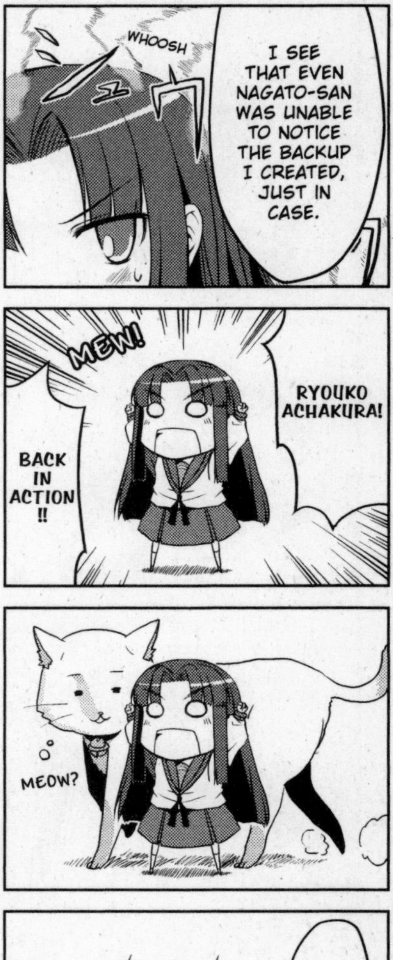
I SEE THAT EVEN NAGATO-SAN WAS UNABLE TO NOTICE THE BACKUP I CREATED, JUST IN CASE.
WHOOSH
MEW!
RYOUKO ACHAKURA!
BACK IN ACTION!!
MEOW?
...
ちーん。
SILENCE
DENIED.

CAPTURE

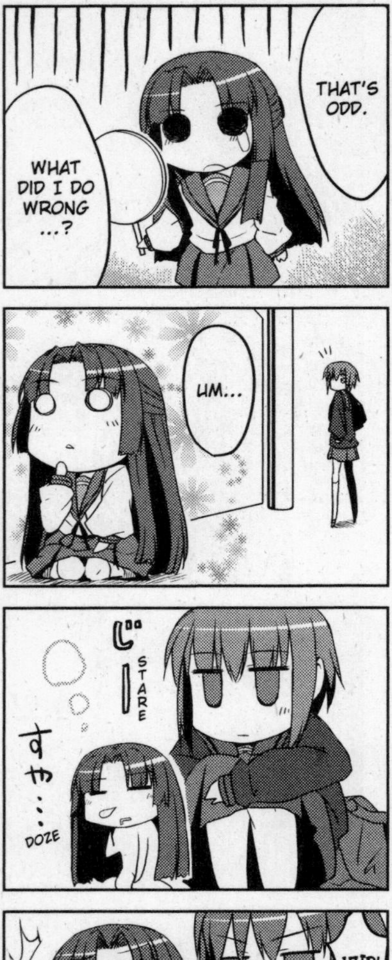
THAT'S ODD.
WHAT DID I DO WRONG ...?
UM...
じー
STARE
すや…
DOZE
HUP!
GRAB
!?

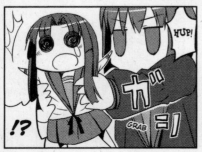

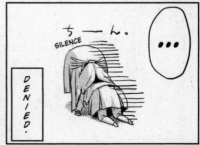

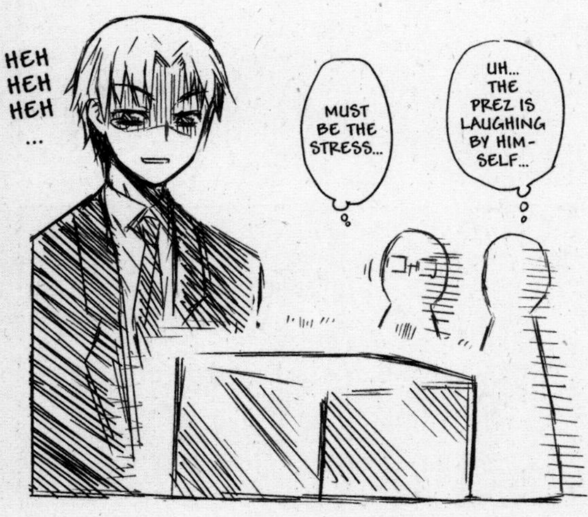
UH... THE PREZ IS LAUGHING BY HIM-SELF...
MUST BE THE STRESS...
HEH HEH HEH ...

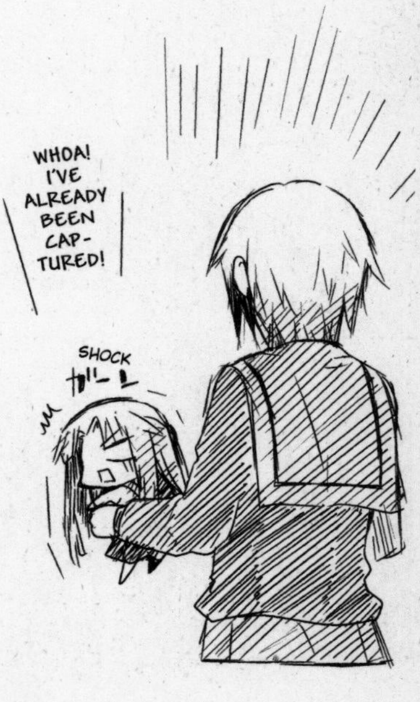
WHOA! I'VE ALREADY BEEN CAP-TURED!
SHOCK

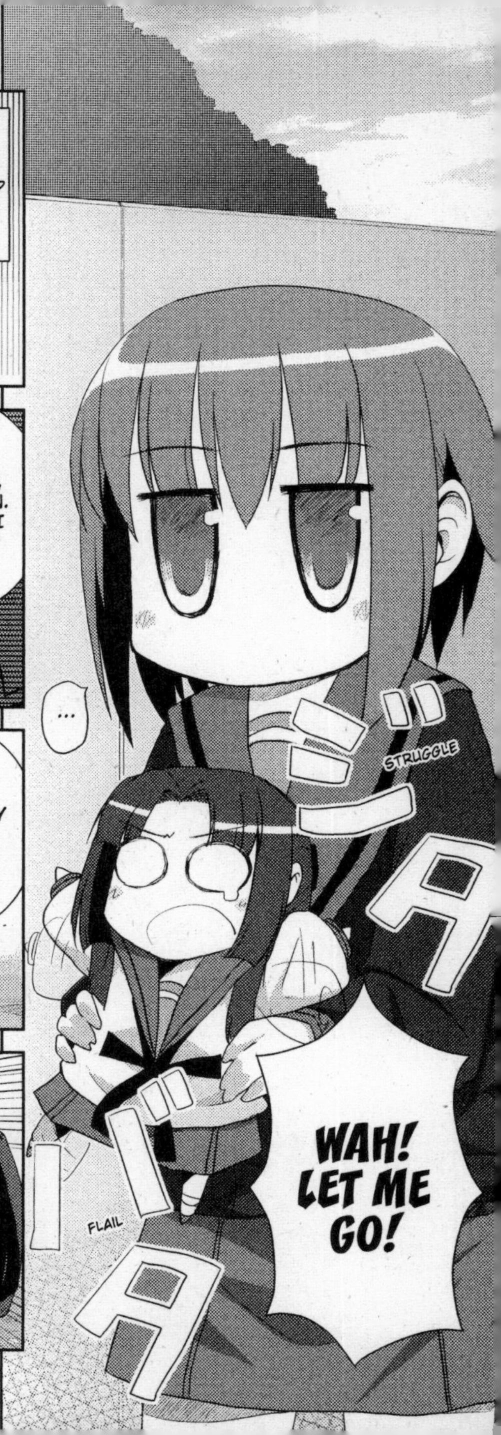
...
STRUGGLE
WAH! LET ME GO!
FLAIL

STASH AWAY

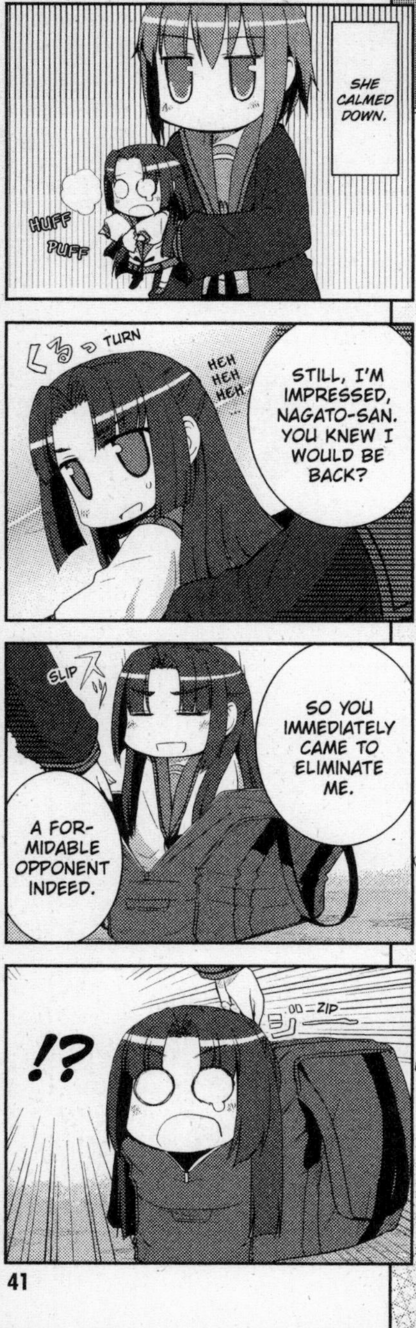
SHE CALMED DOWN.
HUFF
PUFF
STILL, I'M IMPRESSED, NAGATO-SAN. YOU KNEW I WOULD BE BACK?
HEH HEH HEH...
くるっ TURN
SO YOU IMMEDIATELY CAME TO ELIMINATE ME.
A FOR-MIDABLE OPPONENT INDEED.
SLIP
ZIP
!?

ASSISTANT

AND SO.

I SHALL SHOW YOU WHAT I HAVE ACHIEVED AFTER DAYS OF HARD WORK.

GLOOM

SO THIS IS HER FAULT.

...TSURUYA-SAN!

HEYA!

I ALSO WANT TO INTRODUCE MY ASSISTANT, WHO PROVIDED VALUABLE MATERIALS...

BLACK MAGIC FOR DUMMIES

1

AND THIS IS ASSISTANT #2.

GLOOM

ずううん

SUZUMIYA! WE'RE ALL READY!!

GOOD WORK.

TANI-GUCHI!?

2

HEH HEH, APPRECIATE IT.

PANT PANT

A BRIBE!?

AND AS PROMISED, HERE'S A DATA CARD FEATURING MIKURU CHANGING.

2

SCHEDULE

THAT'S HOW VALUABLE TIME IS.

PLAN EVERYTHING AHEAD. THE ADULT MANNER OF CONDUCTING BUSINESS.

...FOR RE-EVALUATING YOUR DAILY ROUTINE.

LOOK.

AND SO, YOU CAN USE MY FLAWLESS SCHEDULE AS A REFERENCE...

BAM

19:00	BREAK
20:00	TUTORING
21:00	STUDY
22:00	BLACK MAGIC
23:00	MEDITATE
24:00	SUMMONING

SLIP

WHAT THE HELL DOES SHE DO AT HOME!!?

• Haruhi-chan •SOS Brigade brigade chief. Apparently keeps busy at home.

• Kyon •Supposed to be the main character in this story. His life is one riposte after another.

• Nagato •A taciturn alien who's always reading. As of late, she's acquired an interest in games and cosplay in addition to reading.

42

#3 SACRIFICE

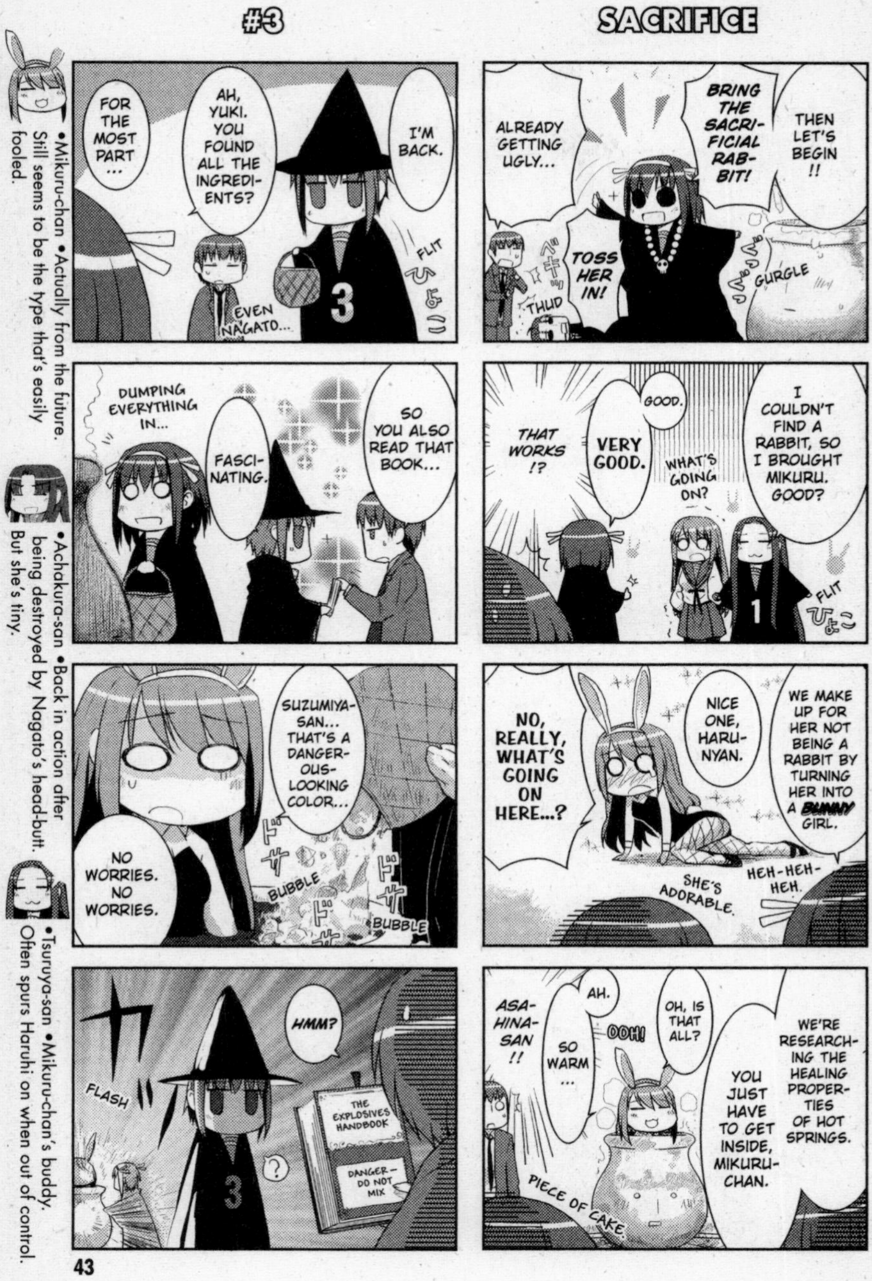
THEN LET'S BEGIN!!
BRING THE SACRIFICIAL RABBIT!
ALREADY GETTING UGLY...
TOSS HER IN!
GURGLE
THUD
I COULDN'T FIND A RABBIT, SO I BROUGHT MIKURU. GOOD?
FLIT
GOOD.
VERY GOOD.
WHAT'S GOING ON?
THAT WORKS!?
WE MAKE UP FOR HER NOT BEING A RABBIT BY TURNING HER INTO A BUNNY GIRL.
NICE ONE, HARUNYAN.
HEH-HEH-HEH.
SHE'S ADORABLE.
NO, REALLY, WHAT'S GOING ON HERE...?
WE'RE RESEARCHING THE HEALING PROPERTIES OF HOT SPRINGS.
YOU JUST HAVE TO GET INSIDE, MIKURU-CHAN.
OH, IS THAT ALL?
AH.
OOH!
SO WARM...
ASAHINA-SAN!!
PIECE OF CAKE.
I'M BACK.
FLIT
AH, YUKI. YOU FOUND ALL THE INGREDIENTS?
FOR THE MOST PART...
EVEN NAGATO...
SO YOU ALSO READ THAT BOOK...
FASCINATING.
DUMPING EVERYTHING IN...
SUZUMIYA-SAN... THAT'S A DANGEROUS-LOOKING COLOR...
BUBBLE
BUBBLE
NO WORRIES. NO WORRIES.
HMM?
THE EXPLOSIVES HANDBOOK
DANGER—DO NOT MIX
FLASH

•Mikuru-chan •Actually from the future. Still seems to be the type that's easily fooled.

•Achakura-san •Back in action after being destroyed by Nagato's head-butt. But she's tiny.

•Tsuruya-san •Mikuru-chan's buddy. Often spurs Haruhi on when out of control.

RUDE

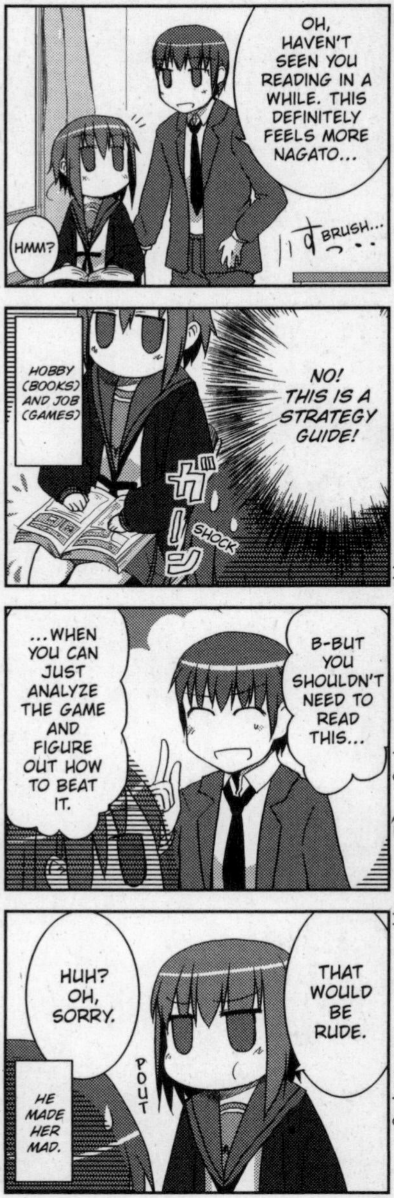
OH, HAVEN'T SEEN YOU READING IN A WHILE. THIS DEFINITELY FEELS MORE NAGATO...
HMM?
BRUSH...
NO! THIS IS A STRATEGY GUIDE!
HOBBY (BOOKS) AND JOB (GAMES)
ガーン
SHOCK
B-BUT YOU SHOULDN'T NEED TO READ THIS...
...WHEN YOU CAN JUST ANALYZE THE GAME AND FIGURE OUT HOW TO BEAT IT.
THAT WOULD BE RUDE.
HUH? OH, SORRY.
POUT
HE MADE HER MAD.

DIFFICULTY

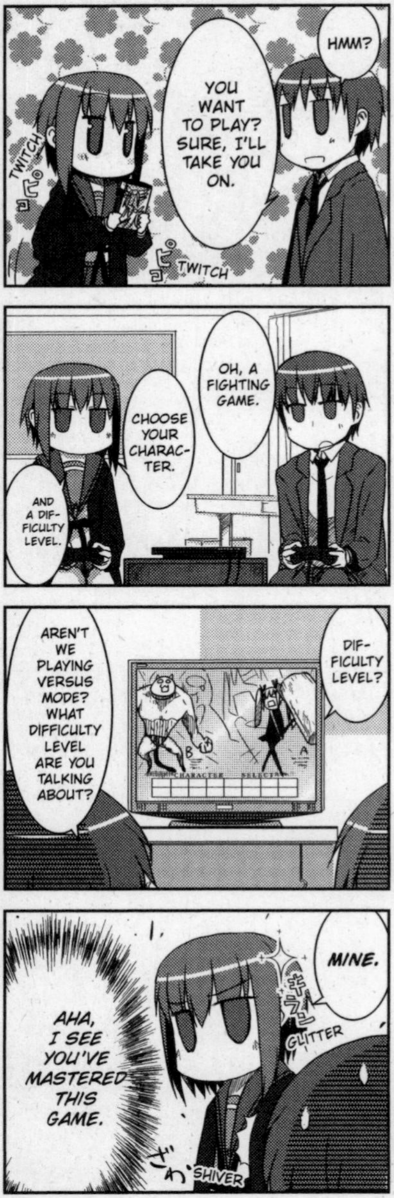
HMM?
YOU WANT TO PLAY? SURE, I'LL TAKE YOU ON.
TWITCH
TWITCH
OH, A FIGHTING GAME.
CHOOSE YOUR CHARACTER.
AND A DIFFICULTY LEVEL.
DIFFICULTY LEVEL?
AREN'T WE PLAYING VERSUS MODE? WHAT DIFFICULTY LEVEL ARE YOU TALKING ABOUT?
CHARACTER SELECT
MINE.
GLITTER
AHA, I SEE YOU'VE MASTERED THIS GAME.
SHIVER

•Taniguchi •Kyon's useless friend. Apparently bribed by Haruhi.

•Kunikida •Kyon's friend. Doesn't stand out, but he's a good guy. Makes an appearance on the next page.

•Kyon's sister •The person responsible for Kyon's nickname sticking. Makes her first appearance on the next page.

OPENING CEREMONY

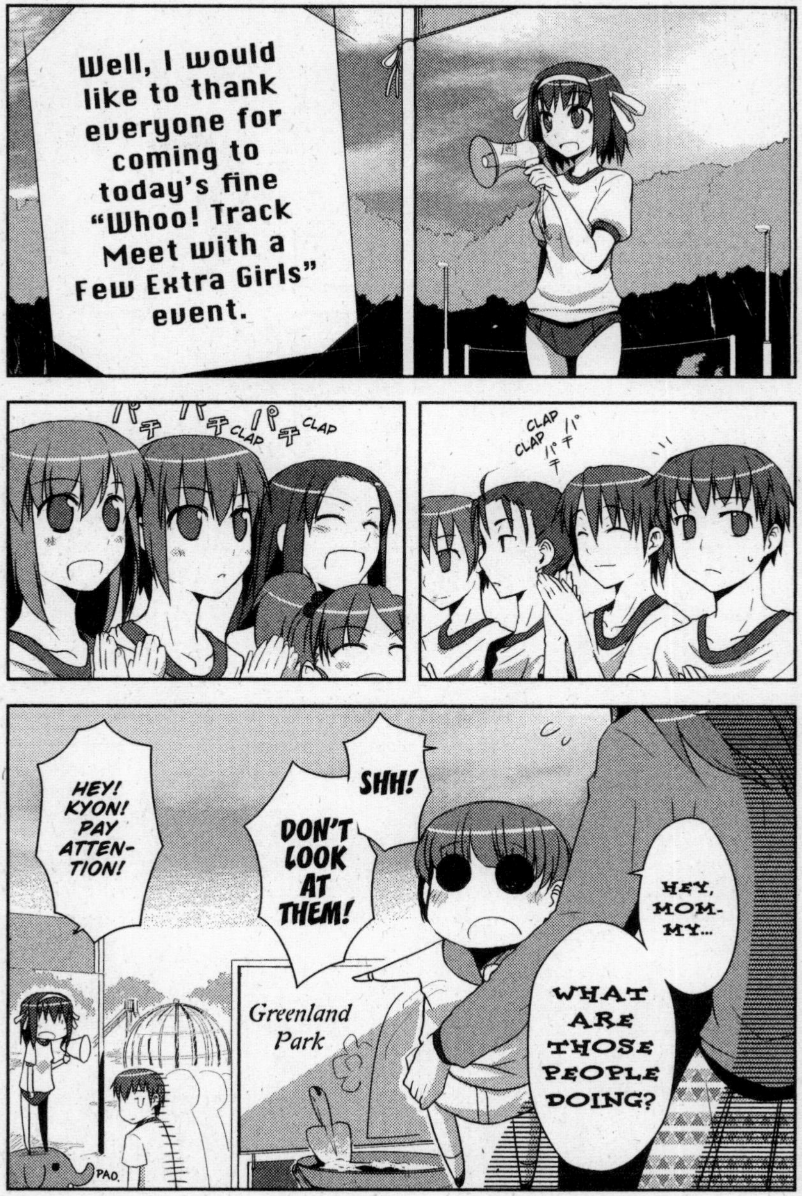
Well, I would like to thank everyone for coming to today's fine "Whoo! Track Meet with a Few Extra Girls" event.
CLAP CLAP パチパチ
パチパチパチ CLAP CLAP
HEY, MOMMY...
WHAT ARE THOSE PEOPLE DOING?
SHH!
DON'T LOOK AT THEM!
Greenland Park
HEY! KYON! PAY ATTENTION!
PAO.

MAKING TEAMS

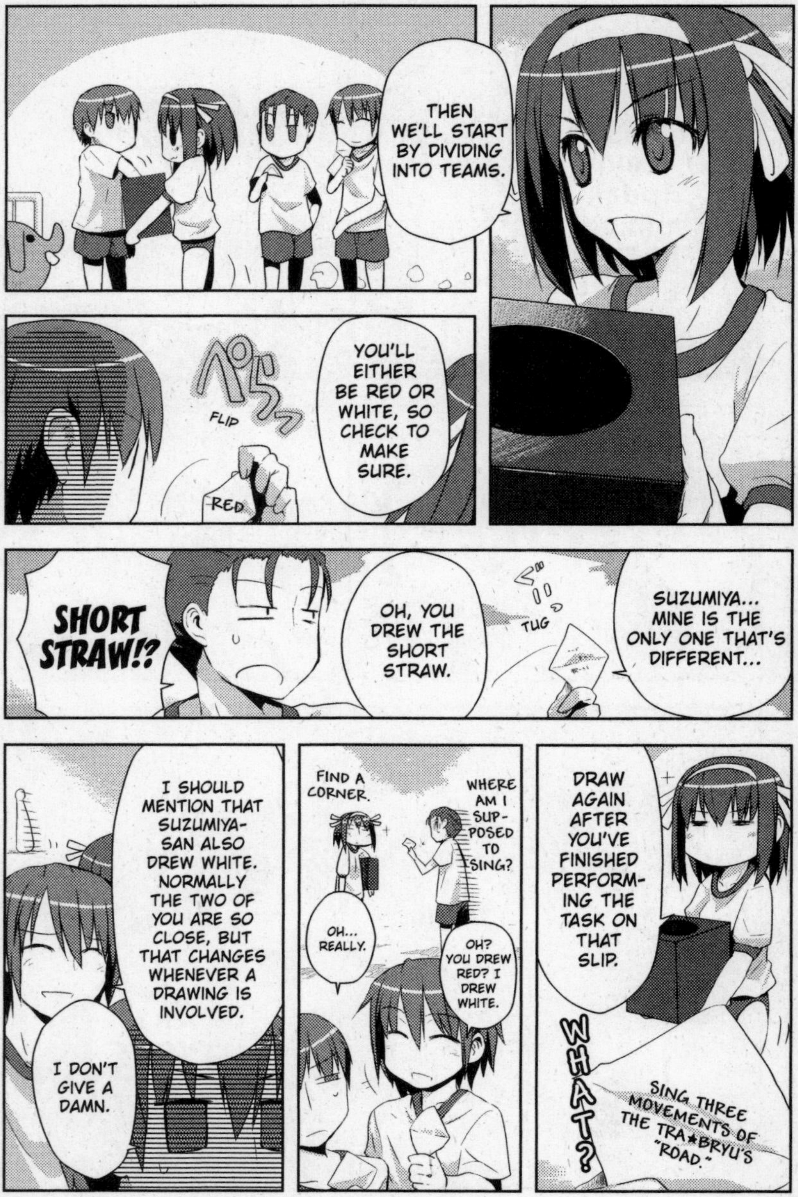
THEN WE'LL START BY DIVIDING INTO TEAMS.
YOU'LL EITHER BE RED OR WHITE, SO CHECK TO MAKE SURE.
ぺらっ
FLIP
RED
SUZUMIYA... MINE IS THE ONLY ONE THAT'S DIFFERENT...
TUG
OH, YOU DREW THE SHORT STRAW.
SHORT STRAW!?
DRAW AGAIN AFTER YOU'VE FINISHED PERFORMING THE TASK ON THAT SLIP.
WHAT?
SING THREE MOVEMENTS OF THE TRA★BRYU'S "ROAD."
WHERE AM I SUPPOSED TO SING?
FIND A CORNER.
OH? YOU DREW RED? I DREW WHITE.
OH... REALLY.
I SHOULD MENTION THAT SUZUMIYA-SAN ALSO DREW WHITE. NORMALLY THE TWO OF YOU ARE SO CLOSE, BUT THAT CHANGES WHENEVER A DRAWING IS INVOLVED.
I DON'T GIVE A DAMN.

SCAVENGER HUNT

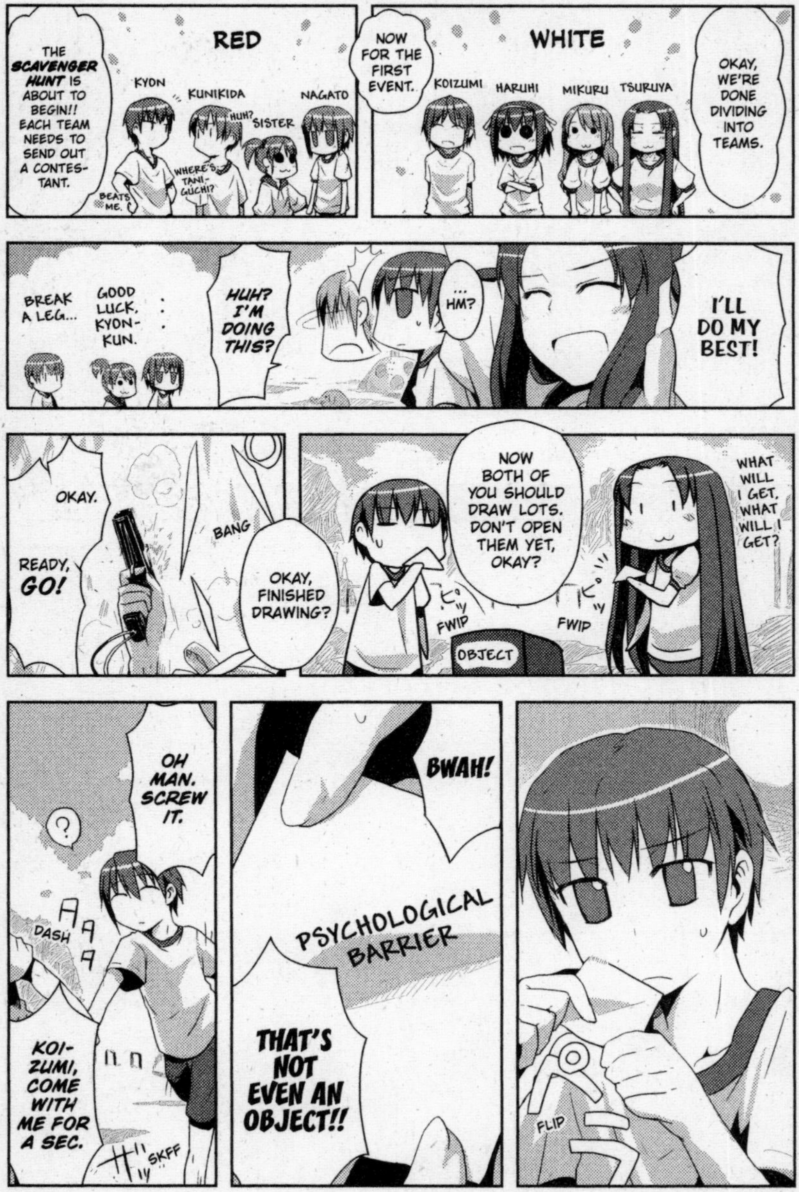

OKAY, WE'RE DONE DIVIDING INTO TEAMS.
WHITE
TSURUYA
MIKURU
HARUHI
KOIZUMI
NOW FOR THE FIRST EVENT.
RED
NAGATO
SISTER
HUH?
KUNIKIDA
KYON
THE SCAVENGER HUNT IS ABOUT TO BEGIN!! EACH TEAM NEEDS TO SEND OUT A CONTESTANT.
WHERE'S TANI-GUCHI?
BEATS ME.
I'LL DO MY BEST!
... HM?
HUH? I'M DOING THIS?
GOOD LUCK, KYON-KUN.
BREAK A LEG...
WHAT WILL I GET, WHAT WILL I GET?
NOW BOTH OF YOU SHOULD DRAW LOTS. DON'T OPEN THEM YET, OKAY?
FWIP
FWIP
OBJECT
OKAY, FINISHED DRAWING?
BANG
OKAY.
READY, GO!
FLIP
BWAH!
PSYCHOLOGICAL BARRIER
THAT'S NOT EVEN AN OBJECT!!
OH MAN. SCREW IT.
?
DASH
KOI-ZUMI, COME WITH ME FOR A SEC.
SKFF

PSYCHOLOGICAL BARRIER

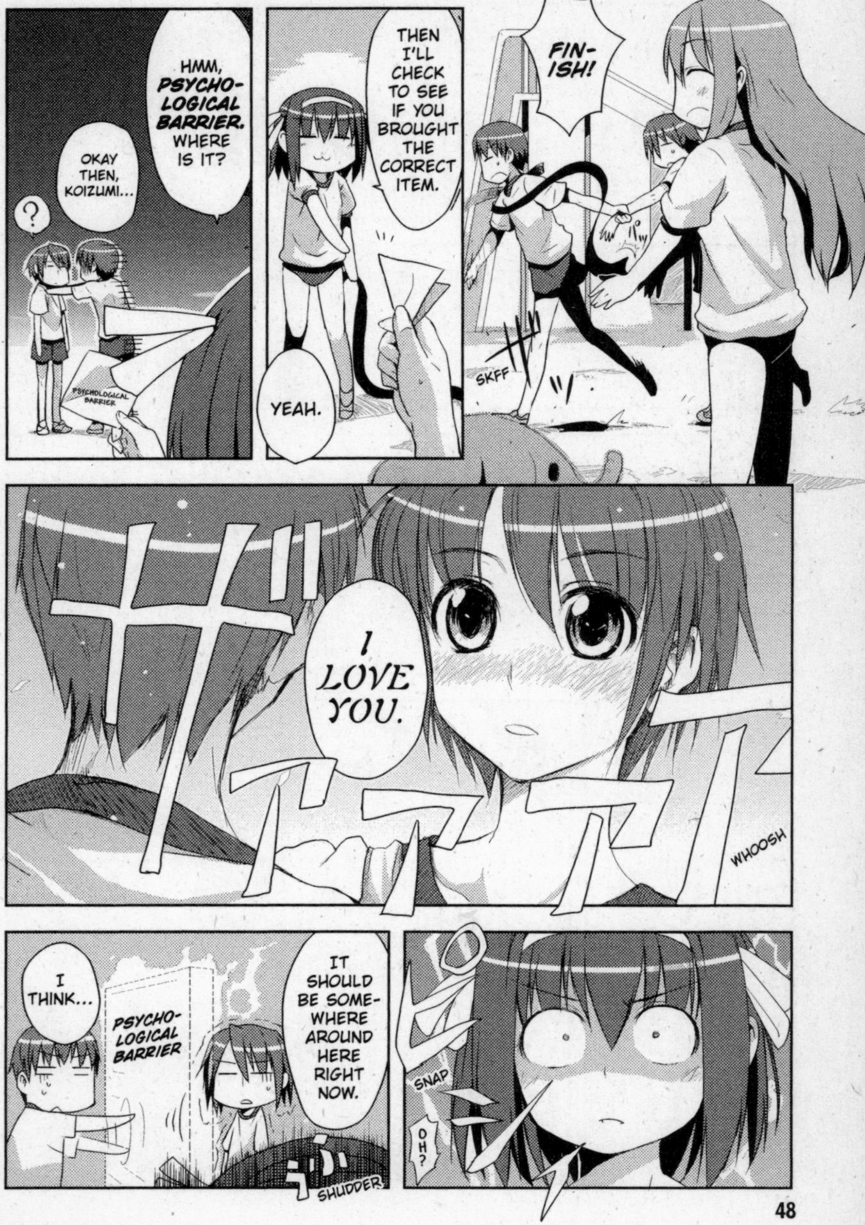

FIN-ISH!
SKFF
THEN I'LL CHECK TO SEE IF YOU BROUGHT THE CORRECT ITEM.
YEAH.
HMM, PSYCHOLOGICAL BARRIER. WHERE IS IT?
OKAY THEN, KOIZUMI...
?
PSYCHOLOGICAL BARRIER
I LOVE YOU.
WHOOSH
SNAP
OH?
IT SHOULD BE SOMEWHERE AROUND HERE RIGHT NOW.
I THINK...
PSYCHOLOGICAL BARRIER
SHUDDER

POOR TANIGUCHI

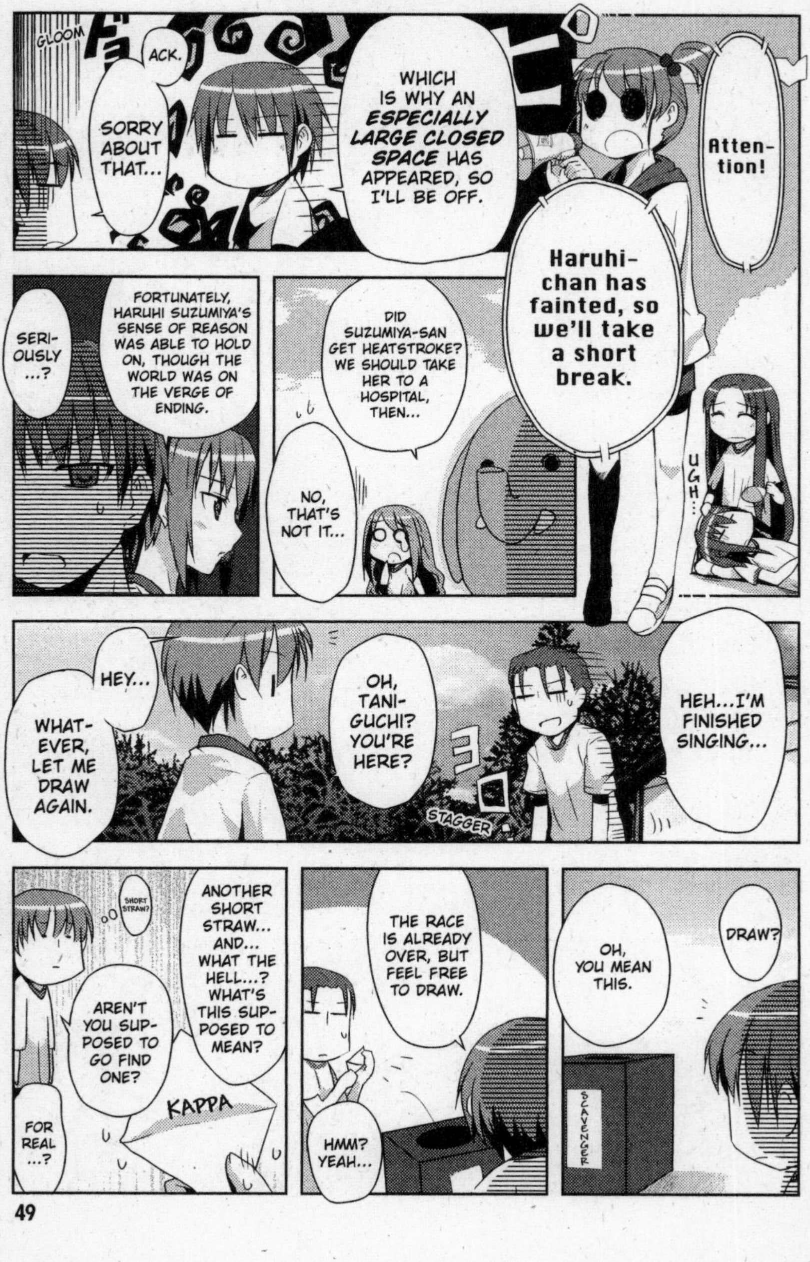
Attention!
Haruhi-chan has fainted, so we'll take a short break.
UGH...
WHICH IS WHY AN ESPECIALLY LARGE CLOSED SPACE HAS APPEARED, SO I'LL BE OFF.
ACK.
SORRY ABOUT THAT...
GLOOM
DID SUZUMIYA-SAN GET HEATSTROKE? WE SHOULD TAKE HER TO A HOSPITAL, THEN...
NO, THAT'S NOT IT...
FORTUNATELY, HARUHI SUZUMIYA'S SENSE OF REASON WAS ABLE TO HOLD ON, THOUGH THE WORLD WAS ON THE VERGE OF ENDING.
SERIOUSLY ...?
HEH...I'M FINISHED SINGING...
STAGGER
OH, TANIGUCHI? YOU'RE HERE?
HEY...
WHATEVER, LET ME DRAW AGAIN.
DRAW?
OH, YOU MEAN THIS.
SCAVENGER
THE RACE IS ALREADY OVER, BUT FEEL FREE TO DRAW.
HMM? YEAH...
ANOTHER SHORT STRAW... AND... WHAT THE HELL...? WHAT'S THIS SUPPOSED TO MEAN?
SHORT STRAW?
AREN'T YOU SUPPOSED TO GO FIND ONE?
KAPPA
FOR REAL ...?

THE NEXT EVENT

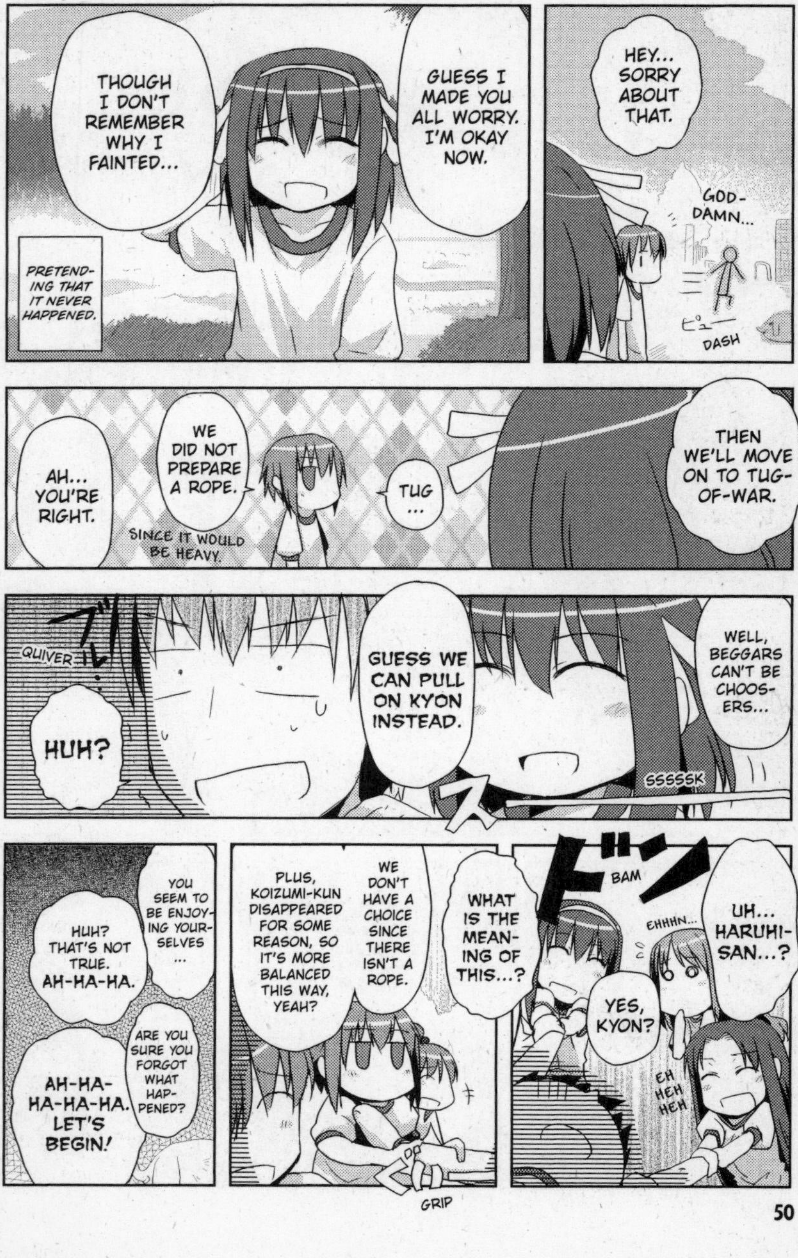
HEY... SORRY ABOUT THAT.
GOD-DAMN...
DASH
GUESS I MADE YOU ALL WORRY. I'M OKAY NOW.
THOUGH I DON'T REMEMBER WHY I FAINTED...
PRETENDING THAT IT NEVER HAPPENED.
THEN WE'LL MOVE ON TO TUG-OF-WAR.
TUG...
WE DID NOT PREPARE A ROPE.
SINCE IT WOULD BE HEAVY.
AH... YOU'RE RIGHT.
WELL, BEGGARS CAN'T BE CHOOSERS...
SSSSSK
GUESS WE CAN PULL ON KYON INSTEAD.
QUIVER
HUH?
BAM
UH... HARUHI-SAN...?
EHHHN...
WHAT IS THE MEANING OF THIS...?
YES, KYON?
EH HEH HEH
WE DON'T HAVE A CHOICE SINCE THERE ISN'T A ROPE.
PLUS, KOIZUMI-KUN DISAPPEARED FOR SOME REASON, SO IT'S MORE BALANCED THIS WAY, YEAH?
GRIP
YOU SEEM TO BE ENJOYING YOURSELVES...
HUH? THAT'S NOT TRUE. AH-HA-HA.
ARE YOU SURE YOU FORGOT WHAT HAPPENED?
AH-HA-HA-HA-HA. LET'S BEGIN!

JUDGMENT OF SOLOMON

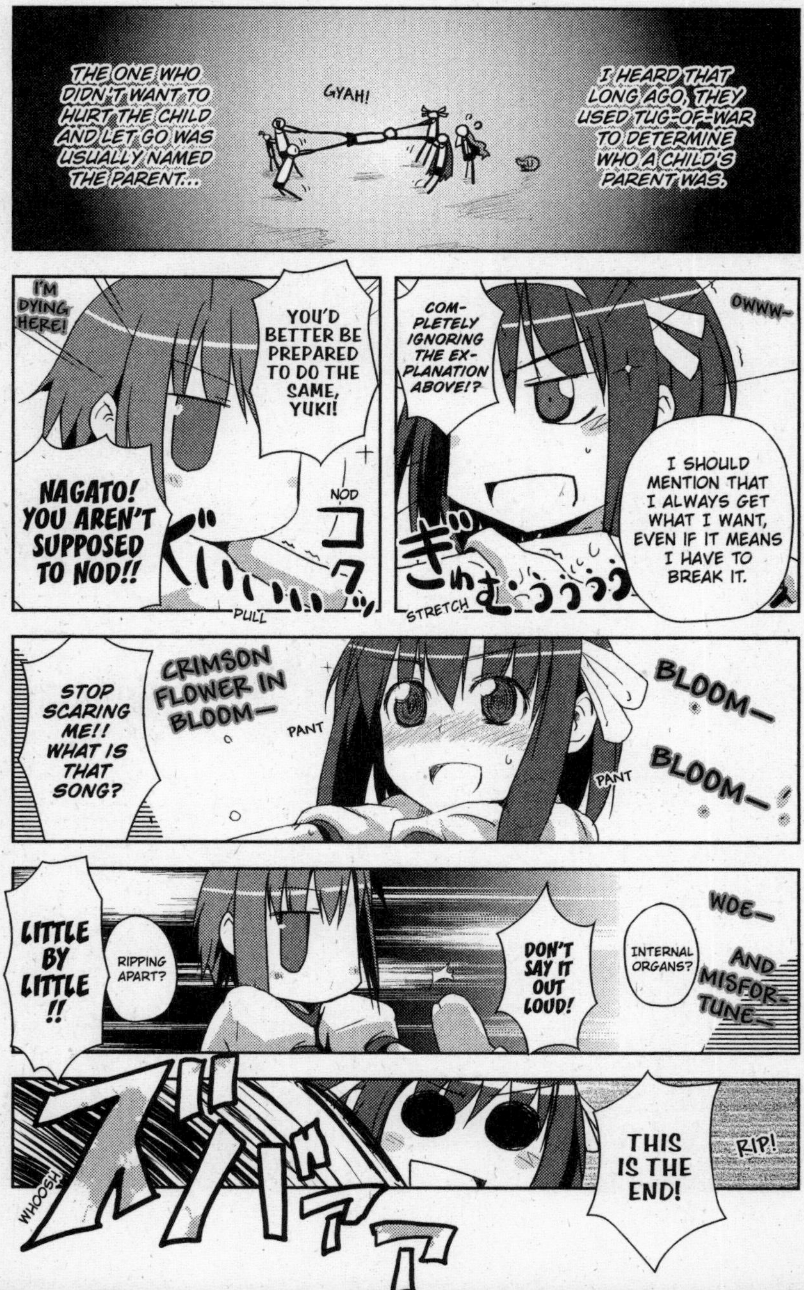
I HEARD THAT LONG AGO, THEY USED TUG-OF-WAR TO DETERMINE WHO A CHILD'S PARENT WAS.
GYAH!
THE ONE WHO DIDN'T WANT TO HURT THE CHILD AND LET GO WAS USUALLY NAMED THE PARENT...
OWWW-
COMPLETELY IGNORING THE EXPLANATION ABOVE!?
I SHOULD MENTION THAT I ALWAYS GET WHAT I WANT, EVEN IF IT MEANS I HAVE TO BREAK IT.
STRETCH
YOU'D BETTER BE PREPARED TO DO THE SAME, YUKI!
I'M DYING HERE!
NOD
NAGATO! YOU AREN'T SUPPOSED TO NOD!!
PULL
BLOOM—
BLOOM—!
PANT
CRIMSON FLOWER IN BLOOM—
PANT
STOP SCARING ME!! WHAT IS THAT SONG?
WOE—
AND MISFORTUNE—
INTERNAL ORGANS?
DON'T SAY IT OUT LOUD!
RIPPING APART?
LITTLE BY LITTLE!!
RIP!
THIS IS THE END!
WHOOSH

BLOOM

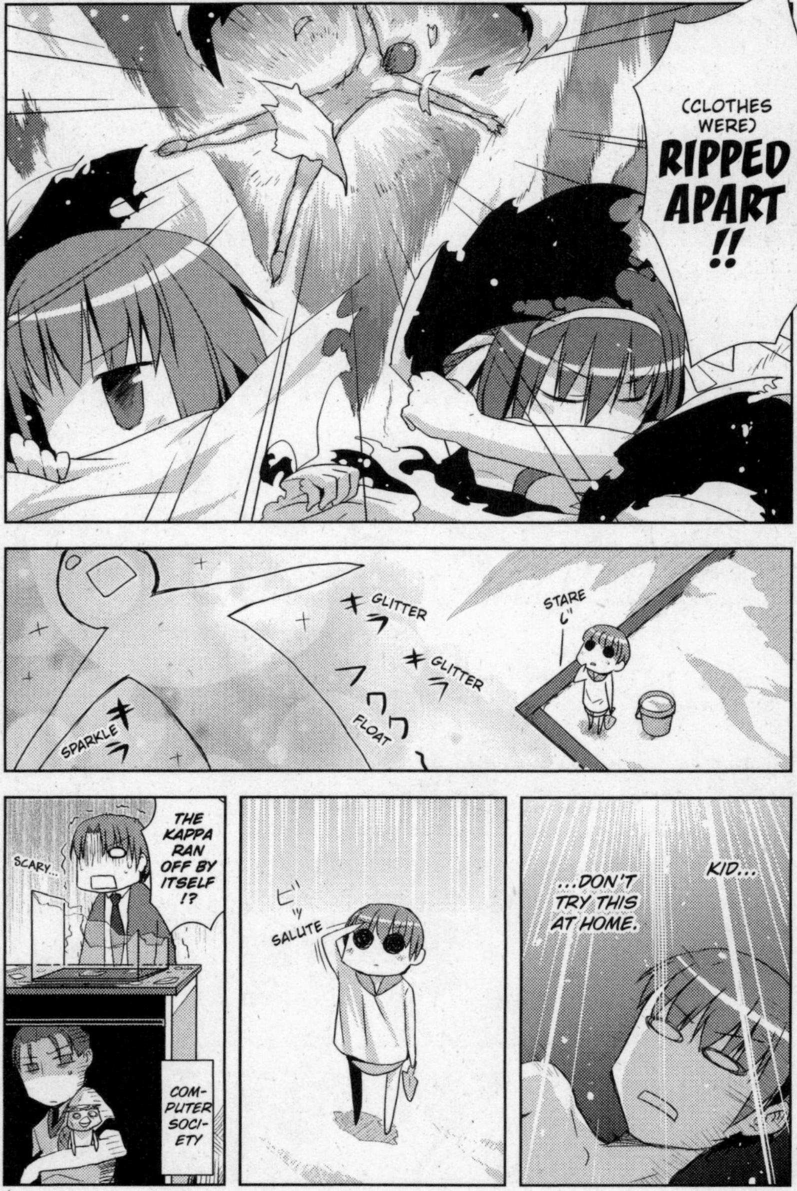
(CLOTHES WERE) RIPPED APART !!
STARE じ
キラ GLITTER
キラ GLITTER
フワフワ FLOAT
キラ SPARKLE
KID...
...DON'T TRY THIS AT HOME.
ビッ SALUTE
THE KAPPA RAN OFF BY ITSELF !?
SCARY...
COMPUTER SOCIETY

JUST FINE

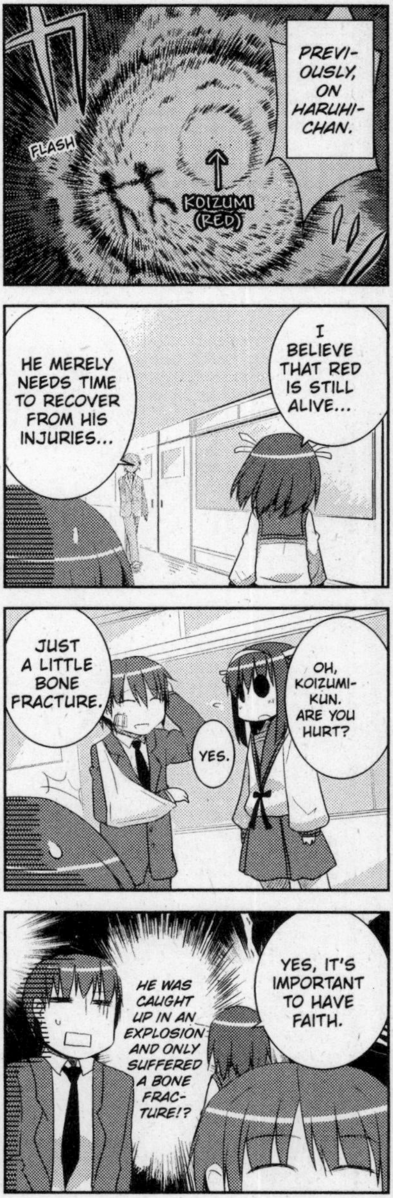
PREVIOUSLY, ON HARUHI-CHAN.
FLASH
KOIZUMI (RED)
I BELIEVE THAT RED IS STILL ALIVE...
HE MERELY NEEDS TIME TO RECOVER FROM HIS INJURIES...
OH, KOIZUMI-KUN. ARE YOU HURT?
YES.
JUST A LITTLE BONE FRACTURE.
YES, IT'S IMPORTANT TO HAVE FAITH.
HE WAS CAUGHT UP IN AN EXPLOSION AND ONLY SUFFERED A BONE FRACTURE!?

JUST FINE

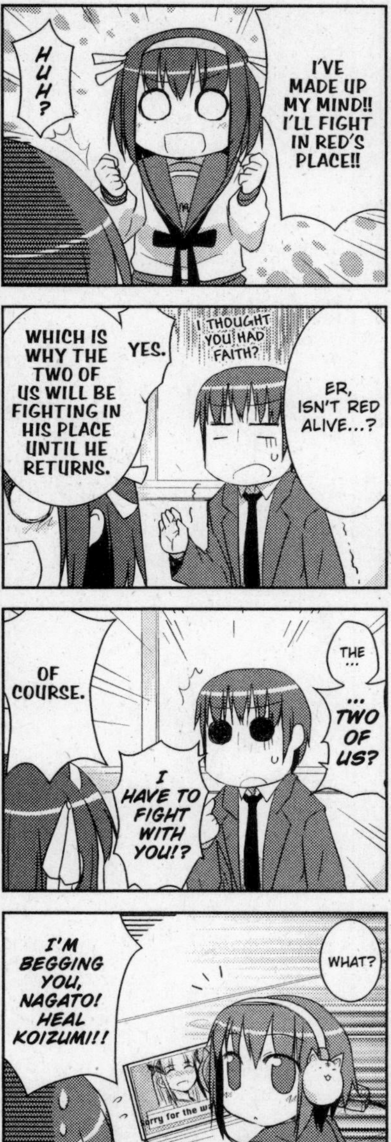
I'VE MADE UP MY MIND!! I'LL FIGHT IN RED'S PLACE!!
HUH?
ER, ISN'T RED ALIVE...?
I THOUGHT YOU HAD FAITH?
YES.
WHICH IS WHY THE TWO OF US WILL BE FIGHTING IN HIS PLACE UNTIL HE RETURNS.
THE ...
... TWO OF US?
OF COURSE.
I HAVE TO FIGHT WITH YOU!?
WHAT?
I'M BEGGING YOU, NAGATO! HEAL KOIZUMI!!

•Koizumi •An enigmatic transfer student who happens to be an esper. He's always smiling, but he may actually be mean at heart.

•Little sister heroine •Heroine in the game Nagato is playing. Her smile is absolutely adorable.

RELIEF

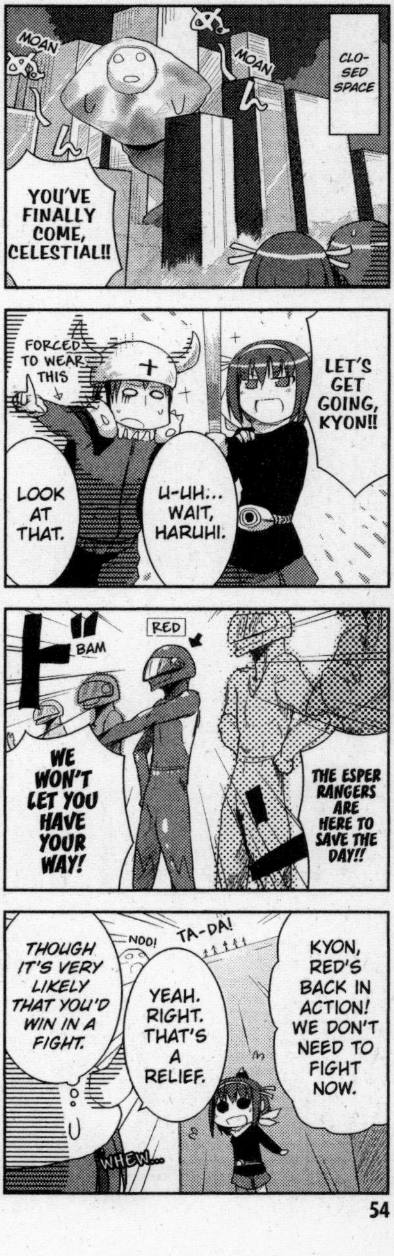
CLO-SED SPACE
MOAN
MOAN
YOU'VE FINALLY COME, CELESTIAL!!
LET'S GET GOING, KYON!!
U-UH... WAIT, HARUHI.
FORCED TO WEAR THIS
LOOK AT THAT.
THE ESPER RANGERS ARE HERE TO SAVE THE DAY!!
RED
BAM
WE WON'T LET YOU HAVE YOUR WAY!
KYON, RED'S BACK IN ACTION! WE DON'T NEED TO FIGHT NOW.
TA-DA!
YEAH. RIGHT. THAT'S A RELIEF.
NOO!
THOUGH IT'S VERY LIKELY THAT YOU'D WIN IN A FIGHT.
WHEW...

SENSING DANGER

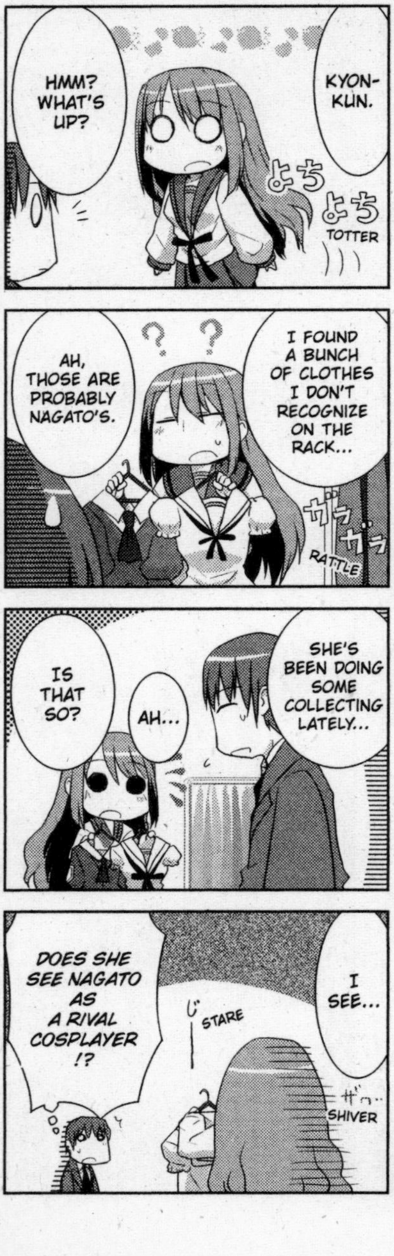
KYON-KUN.
よち よち
TOTTER
HMM? WHAT'S UP?
I FOUND A BUNCH OF CLOTHES I DON'T RECOGNIZE ON THE RACK...
RATTLE
AH, THOSE ARE PROBABLY NAGATO'S.
SHE'S BEEN DOING SOME COLLECTING LATELY...
AH...
IS THAT SO?
I SEE...
STARE
SHIVER
DOES SHE SEE NAGATO AS A RIVAL COSPLAYER!?

COMPETITION

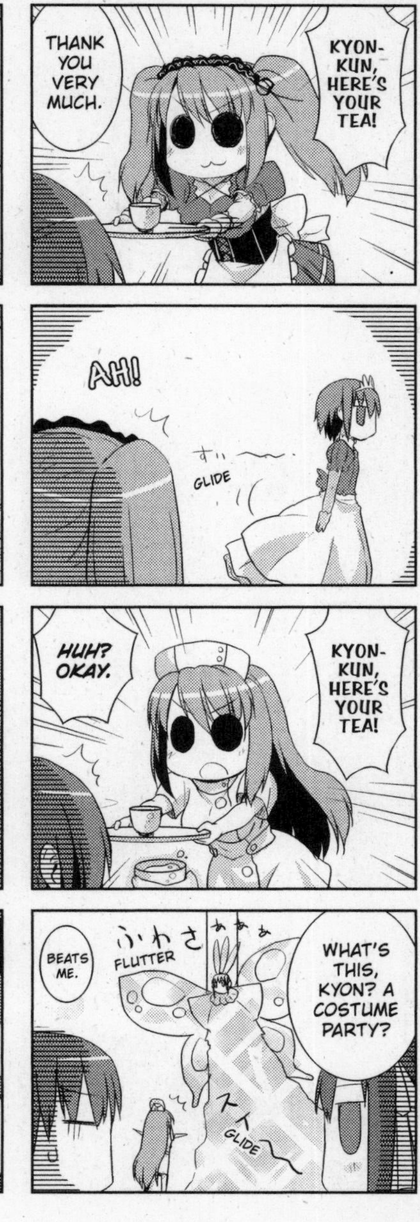
KYON-KUN, HERE'S YOUR TEA!
THANK YOU VERY MUCH.
AH!
すぃ〜
GLIDE
KYON-KUN, HERE'S YOUR TEA!
HUH? OKAY.
WHAT'S THIS, KYON? A COSTUME PARTY?
ふわさ
FLUTTER
BEATS ME.
GLIDE

DON'T LAUGH

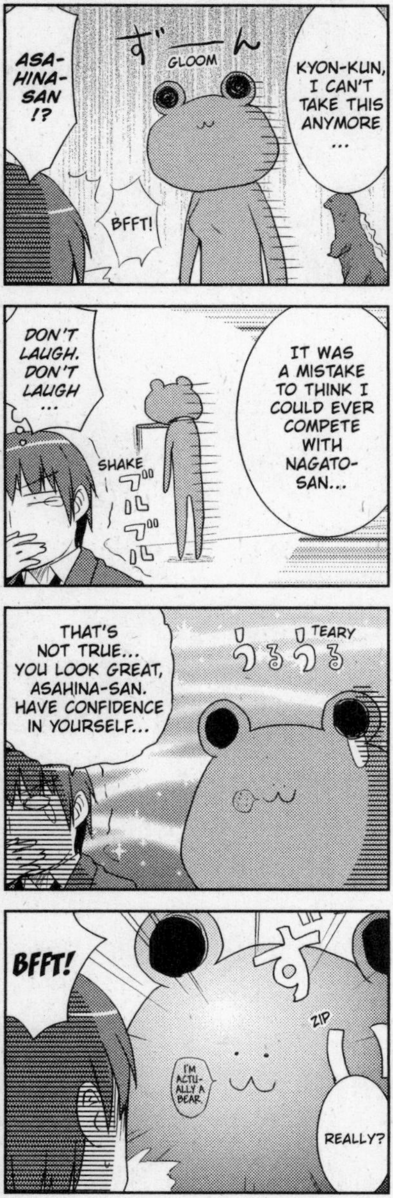
KYON-KUN, I CAN'T TAKE THIS ANYMORE ...
ずーん
GLOOM
ASA-HINA-SAN !?
BFFT!
IT WAS A MISTAKE TO THINK I COULD EVER COMPETE WITH NAGATO-SAN...
DON'T LAUGH. DON'T LAUGH ...
SHAKE
ブルブル
うるうる
TEARY
THAT'S NOT TRUE... YOU LOOK GREAT, ASAHINA-SAN. HAVE CONFIDENCE IN YOURSELF...
ず
ZIP
REALLY?
I'M ACTUALLY A BEAR.
BFFT!

A SECOND ENEMY

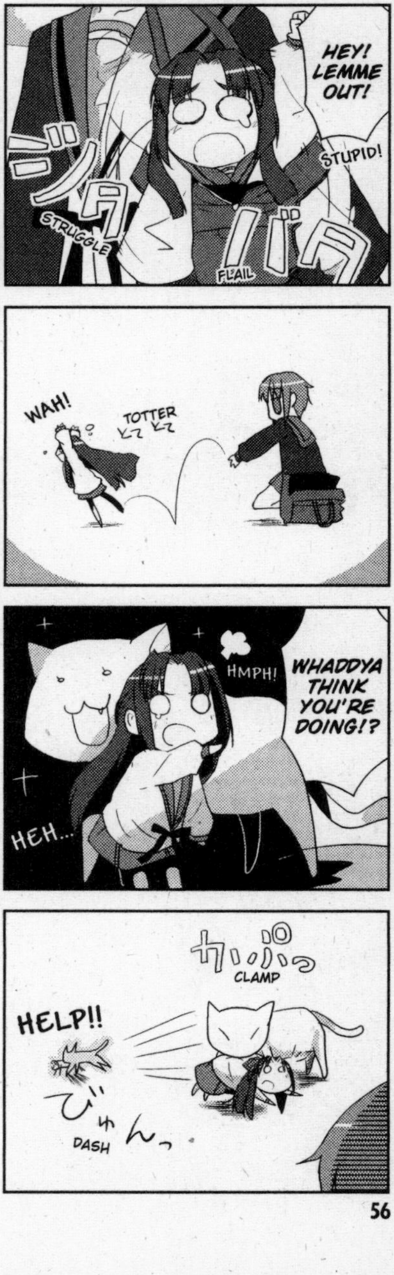
HEY! LEMME OUT!
STUPID!
ジタ
STRUGGLE
バタ
FLAIL
WAH!
TOTTER
...
HMPH!
WHADDYA THINK YOU'RE DOING!?
HEH...
かぷっ
CLAMP
HELP!!
びゅんっ
DASH

IN THE END

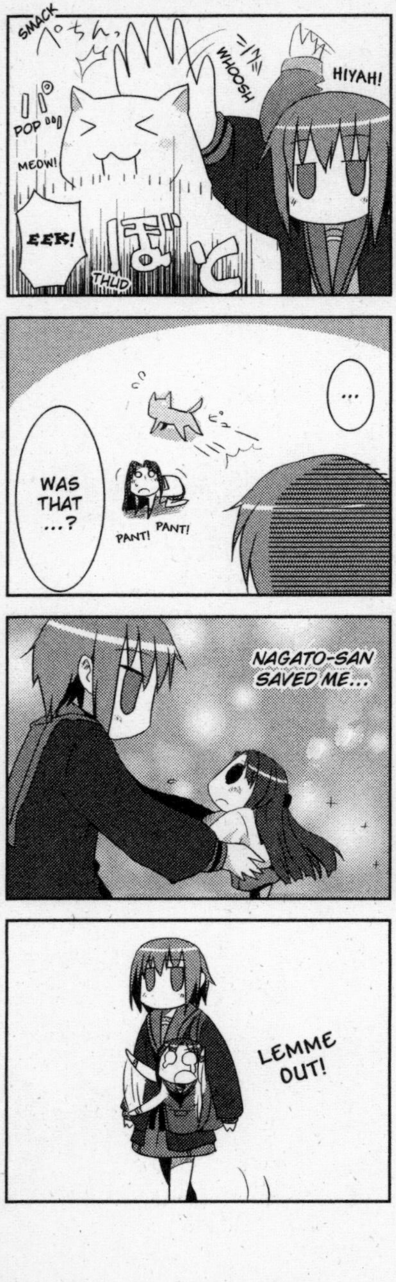
ぺちんっ
SMACK
HIYAH!
WHOOSH
POP
MEOW!
EEK!
THUD
...
WAS THAT ...?
PANT! PANT!
NAGATO-SAN SAVED ME...
LEMME OUT!

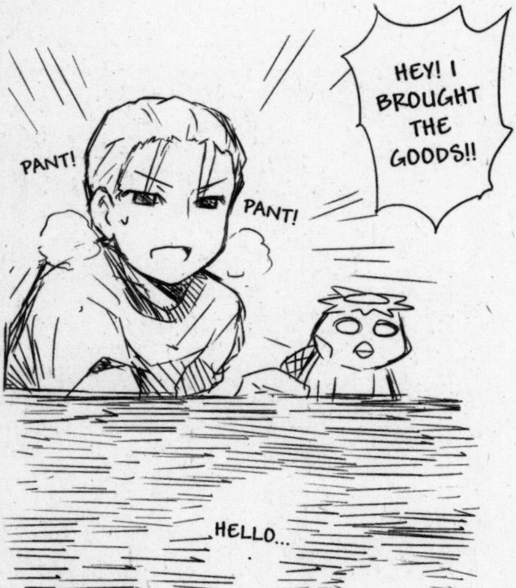
HEY! I BROUGHT THE GOODS!!
PANT!
PANT!
HELLO...
KAW!
KAW!

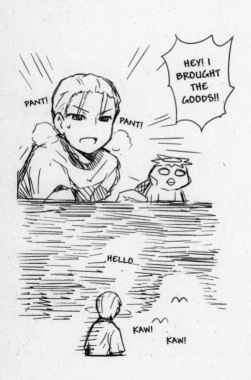

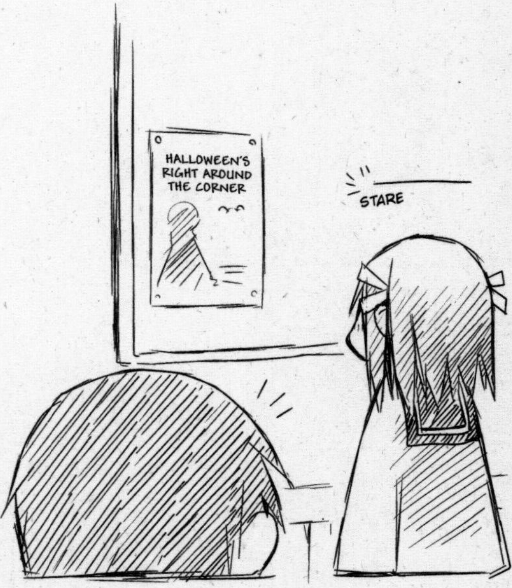
HALLOWEEN'S RIGHT AROUND THE CORNER
STARE

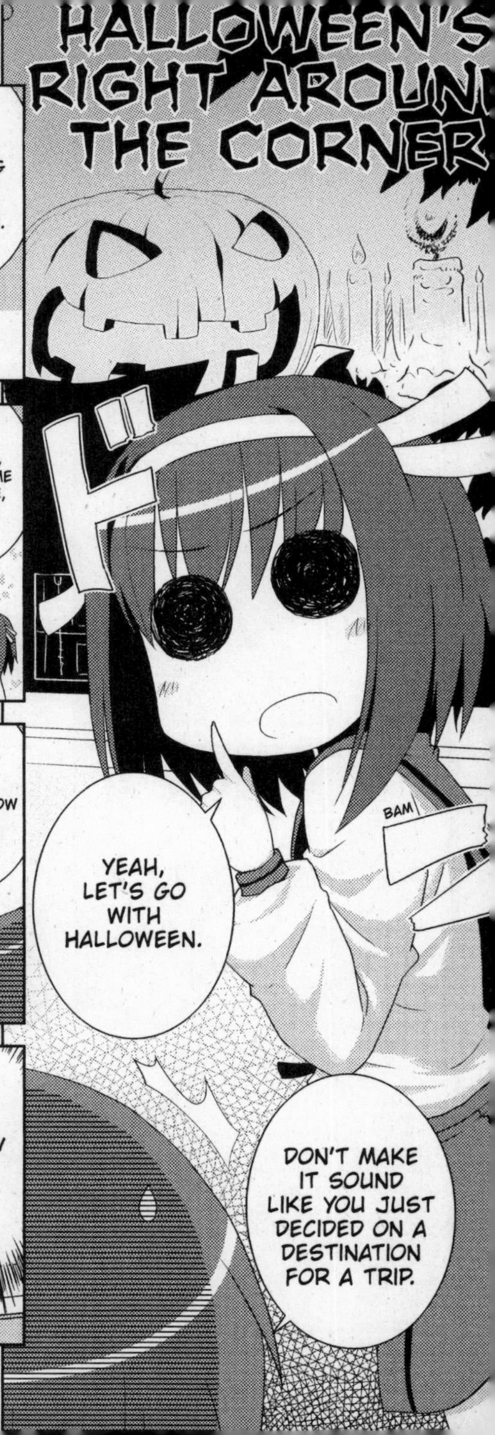
HALLOWEEN'S RIGHT AROUN THE CORNER
YEAH, LET'S GO WITH HALLOWEEN.
BAM
DON'T MAKE IT SOUND LIKE YOU JUST DECIDED ON A DESTINATION FOR A TRIP.

RESEARCH

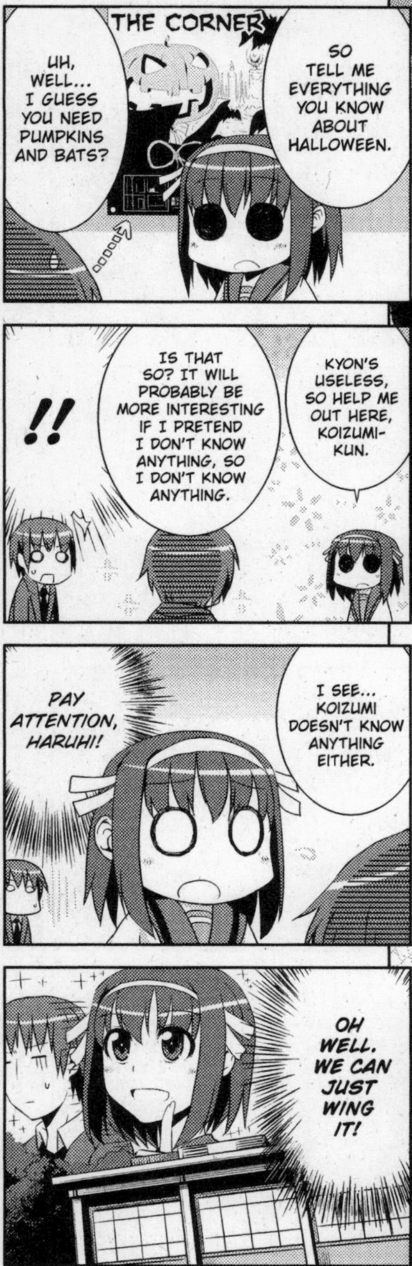
THE CORNER
SO TELL ME EVERYTHING YOU KNOW ABOUT HALLOWEEN.
UH, WELL... I GUESS YOU NEED PUMPKINS AND BATS?
KYON'S USELESS, SO HELP ME OUT HERE, KOIZUMI-KUN.
IS THAT SO? IT WILL PROBABLY BE MORE INTERESTING IF I PRETEND I DON'T KNOW ANYTHING, SO I DON'T KNOW ANYTHING.
!!
I SEE... KOIZUMI DOESN'T KNOW ANYTHING EITHER.
PAY ATTENTION, HARUHI!
OH WELL. WE CAN JUST WING IT!

IMAGE

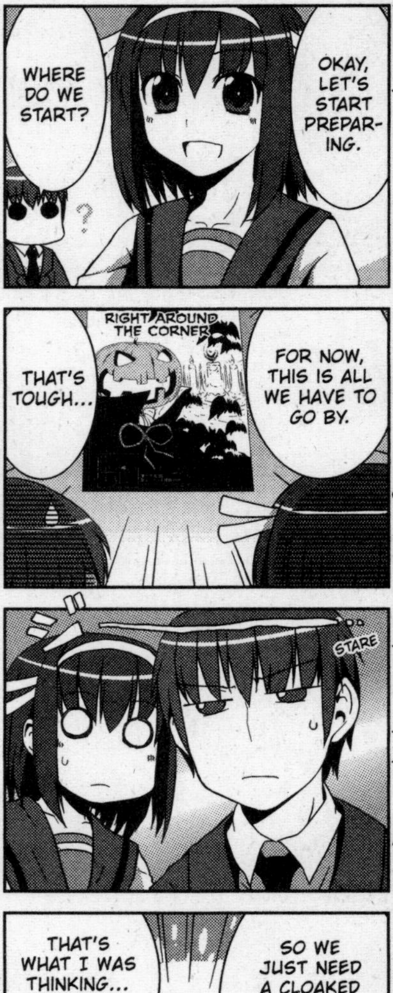

OKAY, LET'S START PREPAR-ING.
WHERE DO WE START?
?
FOR NOW, THIS IS ALL WE HAVE TO GO BY.
RIGHT AROUND THE CORNER
THAT'S TOUGH...
STARE
SO WE JUST NEED A CLOAKED GUY WEARING A PUMPKIN ON HIS HEAD WITH BATS FLYING AROUND?
THAT'S WHAT I WAS THINKING... BUT IT'S PROBABLY WRONG.
DING

•Haruhi-chan •SOS Brigade brigade chief. Very interested in Halloween activities.

•Kyon •Supposed to be the main character in this story. It's rough when he has to play straight man for so many different people.

•Nagato •Actually an alien. She always appears to be deep in thought, but she isn't. Likes games.

RAW

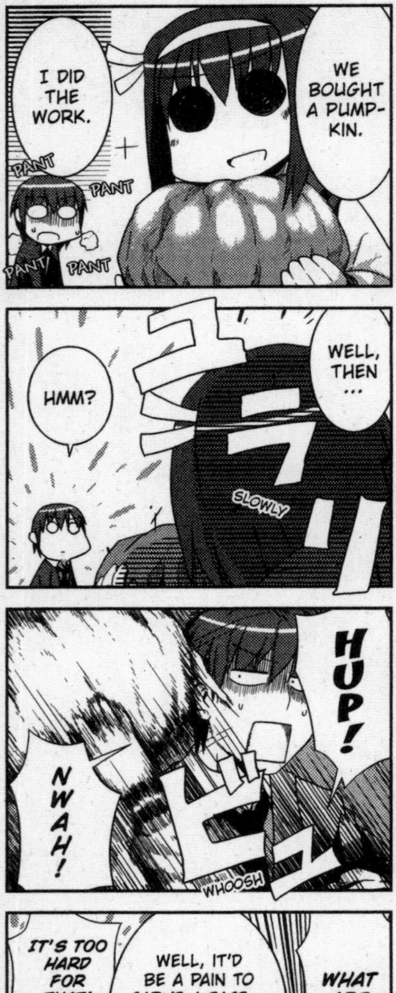

WE BOUGHT A PUMP-KIN.
I DID THE WORK.
PANT
PANT
PANT
PANT
WELL, THEN...
SLOWLY
HMM?
HUP!
NWAH!
WHOOSH
WHAT ARE YOU DOING!?
WELL, IT'D BE A PAIN TO CARVE A FACE... SO I FIGURED I'D JUST GET AN IMPRESSION OF YOUR FACE.
IT'S TOO HARD FOR THAT! DON'T UNDER-ESTI-MATE RAW PUMP-KINS!

SFX: SQUISH

EXACT

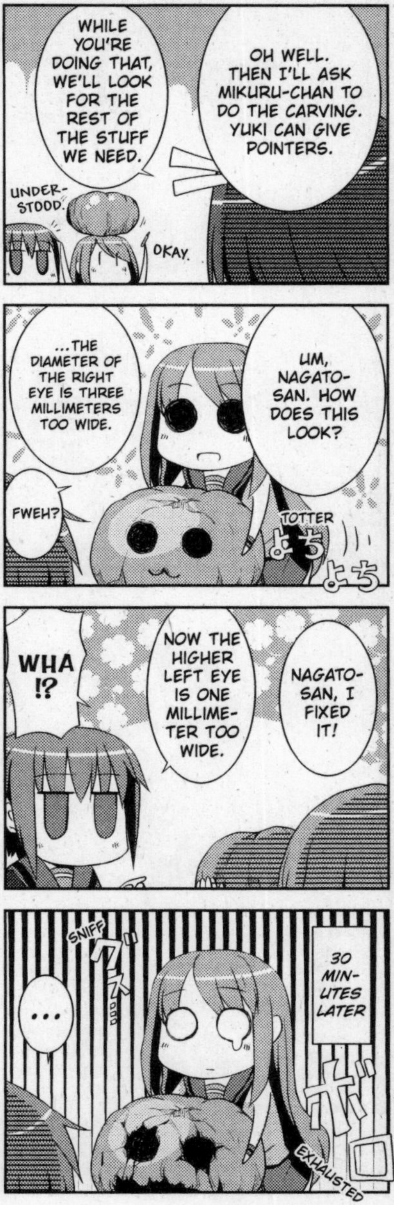
OH WELL. THEN I'LL ASK MIKURU-CHAN TO DO THE CARVING. YUKI CAN GIVE POINTERS.
WHILE YOU'RE DOING THAT, WE'LL LOOK FOR THE REST OF THE STUFF WE NEED.
UNDERSTOOD.
OKAY.
UM, NAGATO-SAN. HOW DOES THIS LOOK?
...THE DIAMETER OF THE RIGHT EYE IS THREE MILLIMETERS TOO WIDE.
TOTTER
よちよち
FWEH?
NAGATO-SAN, I FIXED IT!
NOW THE HIGHER LEFT EYE IS ONE MILLIMETER TOO WIDE.
WHA!?
30 MINUTES LATER
SNIFF
グス
...
ボロ
EXHAUSTED

SORE THUMB

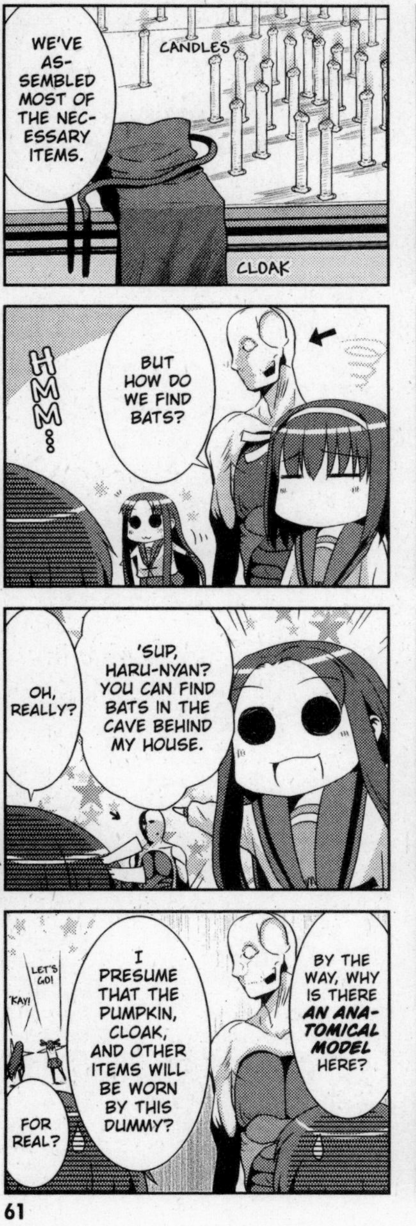
WE'VE ASSEMBLED MOST OF THE NECESSARY ITEMS.
CANDLES
CLOAK
BUT HOW DO WE FIND BATS?
HMM...
'SUP, HARU-NYAN? YOU CAN FIND BATS IN THE CAVE BEHIND MY HOUSE.
OH, REALLY?
BY THE WAY, WHY IS THERE AN ANATOMICAL MODEL HERE?
I PRESUME THAT THE PUMPKIN, CLOAK, AND OTHER ITEMS WILL BE WORN BY THIS DUMMY?
LET'S GO!
'KAY!
FOR REAL?

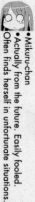

•Mikuru-chan •Actually from the future. Easily fooled. Often finds herself in unfortunate situations.

•Koizumi •An enigmatic transfer student who happens to be an esper. Doesn't show up much this time.

•Tsuruya-san •Mikuru-chan's buddy. The situation tends to worsen when she's around.

COMPLETION

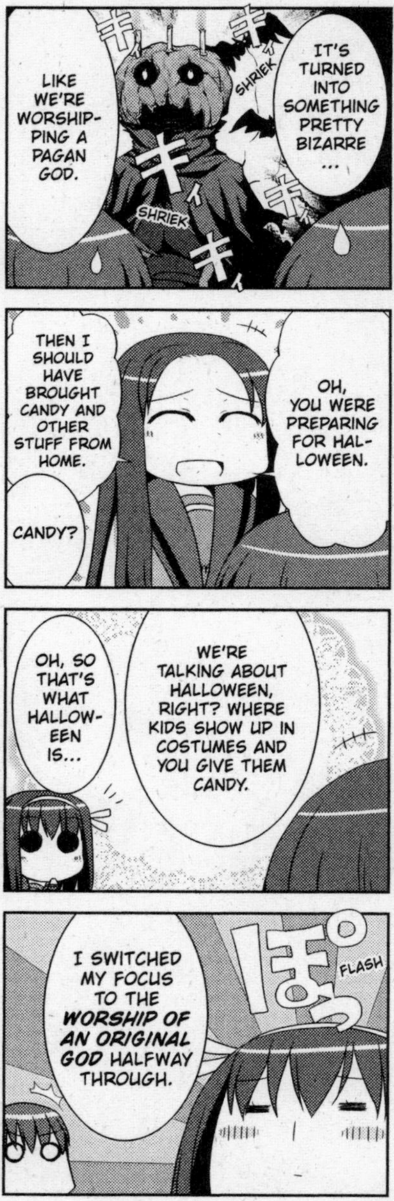

IT'S TURNED INTO SOMETHING PRETTY BIZARRE ...
LIKE WE'RE WORSHIPPING A PAGAN GOD.
SHRIEK
SHRIEK
OH, YOU WERE PREPARING FOR HALLOWEEN.
THEN I SHOULD HAVE BROUGHT CANDY AND OTHER STUFF FROM HOME.
CANDY?
WE'RE TALKING ABOUT HALLOWEEN, RIGHT? WHERE KIDS SHOW UP IN COSTUMES AND YOU GIVE THEM CANDY.
OH, SO THAT'S WHAT HALLOWEEN IS...
FLASH
I SWITCHED MY FOCUS TO THE WORSHIP OF AN ORIGINAL GOD HALFWAY THROUGH.

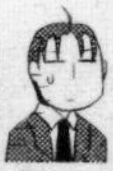

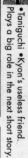

•Taniguchi •Kyon's useless friend. Plays a big role in the next short story.

HALLOWEEN PARTY

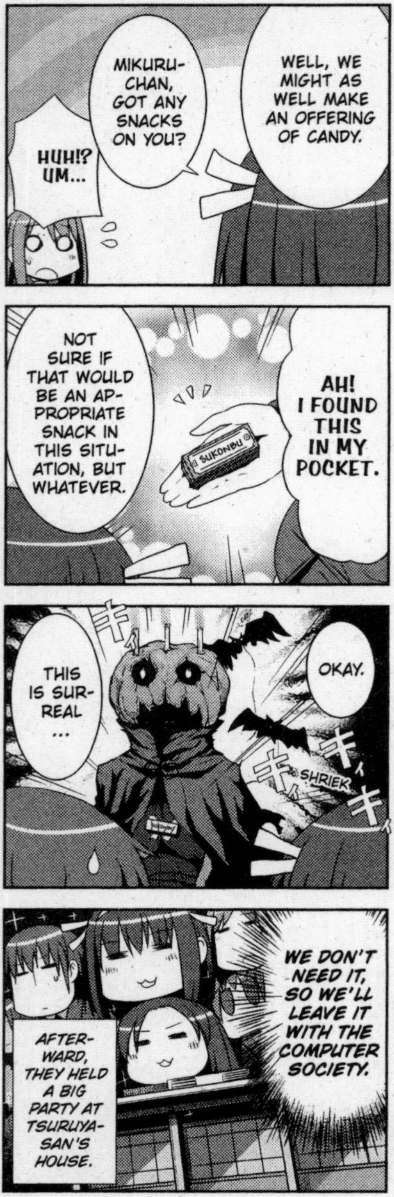

WELL, WE MIGHT AS WELL MAKE AN OFFERING OF CANDY.
MIKURU-CHAN, GOT ANY SNACKS ON YOU?
HUH!? UM...
AH! I FOUND THIS IN MY POCKET.
SUKONBU
NOT SURE IF THAT WOULD BE AN APPROPRIATE SNACK IN THIS SITUATION, BUT WHATEVER.
OKAY.
SHRIEK
THIS IS SURREAL ...
WE DON'T NEED IT, SO WE'LL LEAVE IT WITH THE COMPUTER SOCIETY.
AFTERWARD, THEY HELD A BIG PARTY AT TSURUYA-SAN'S HOUSE.

THE EVERYDAY OF HARUHI-CHAN

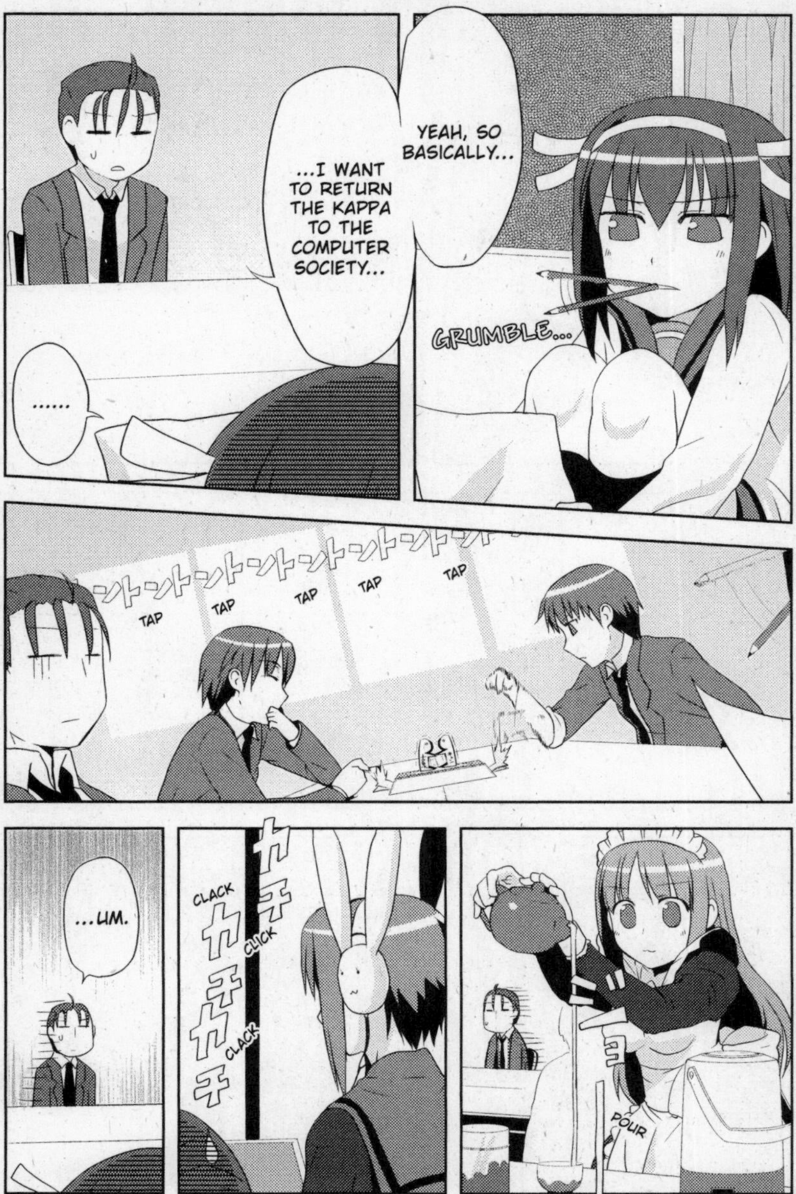
YEAH, SO BASICALLY...
GRUMBLE...
...I WANT TO RETURN THE KAPPA TO THE COMPUTER SOCIETY...
......
TAP
TAP
TAP
TAP
TAP
POUR
CLACK
CLICK
CLACK
...UM.

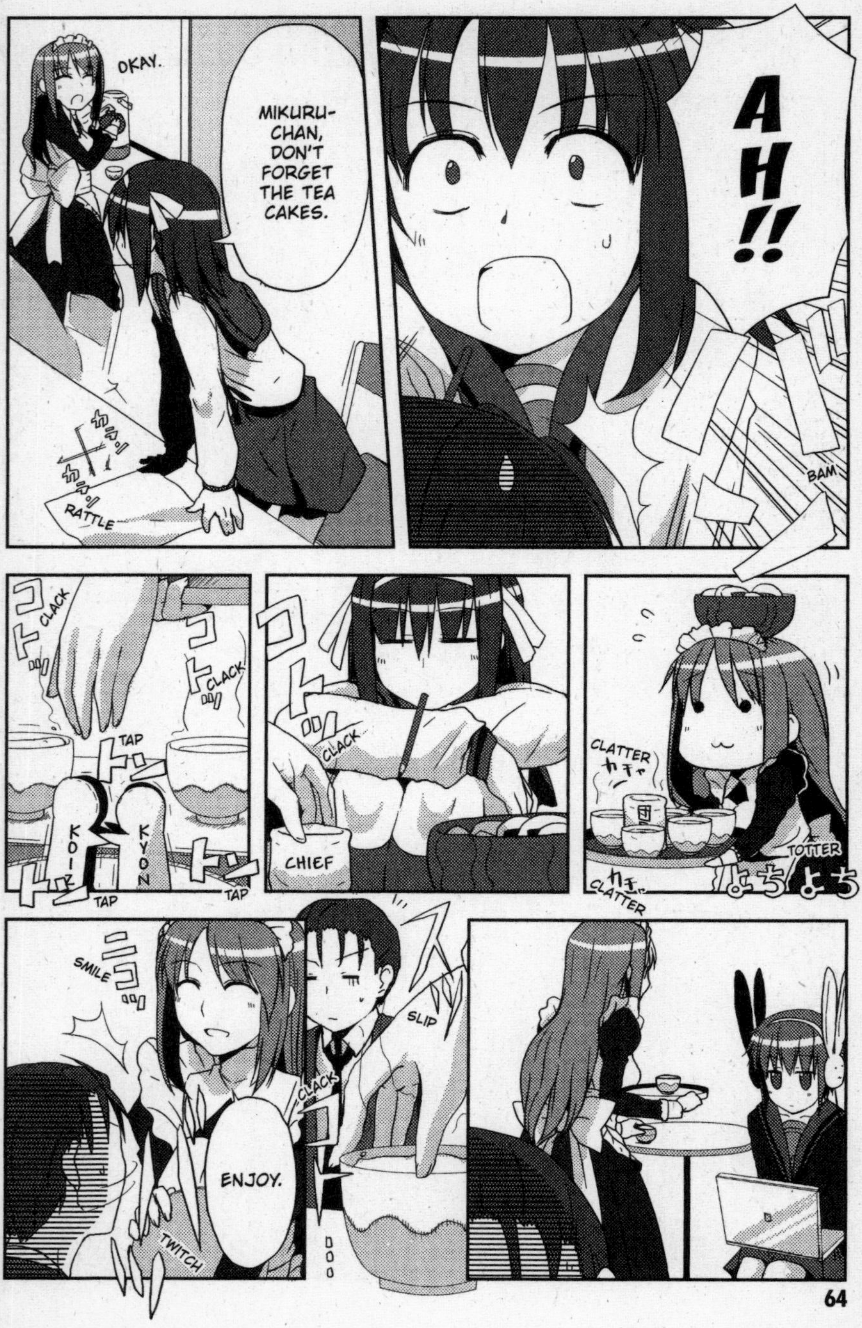
AH!!
BAM
MIKURU-CHAN, DON'T FORGET THE TEA CAKES.
OKAY.
RATTLE
CLATTER
カチャ
TOTTER
よちよち
CLATTER
CLACK
CHIEF
CLACK
CLACK
TAP
KYON
TAP
TAP
SMILE
SLIP
CLACK
ENJOY.
TWITCH

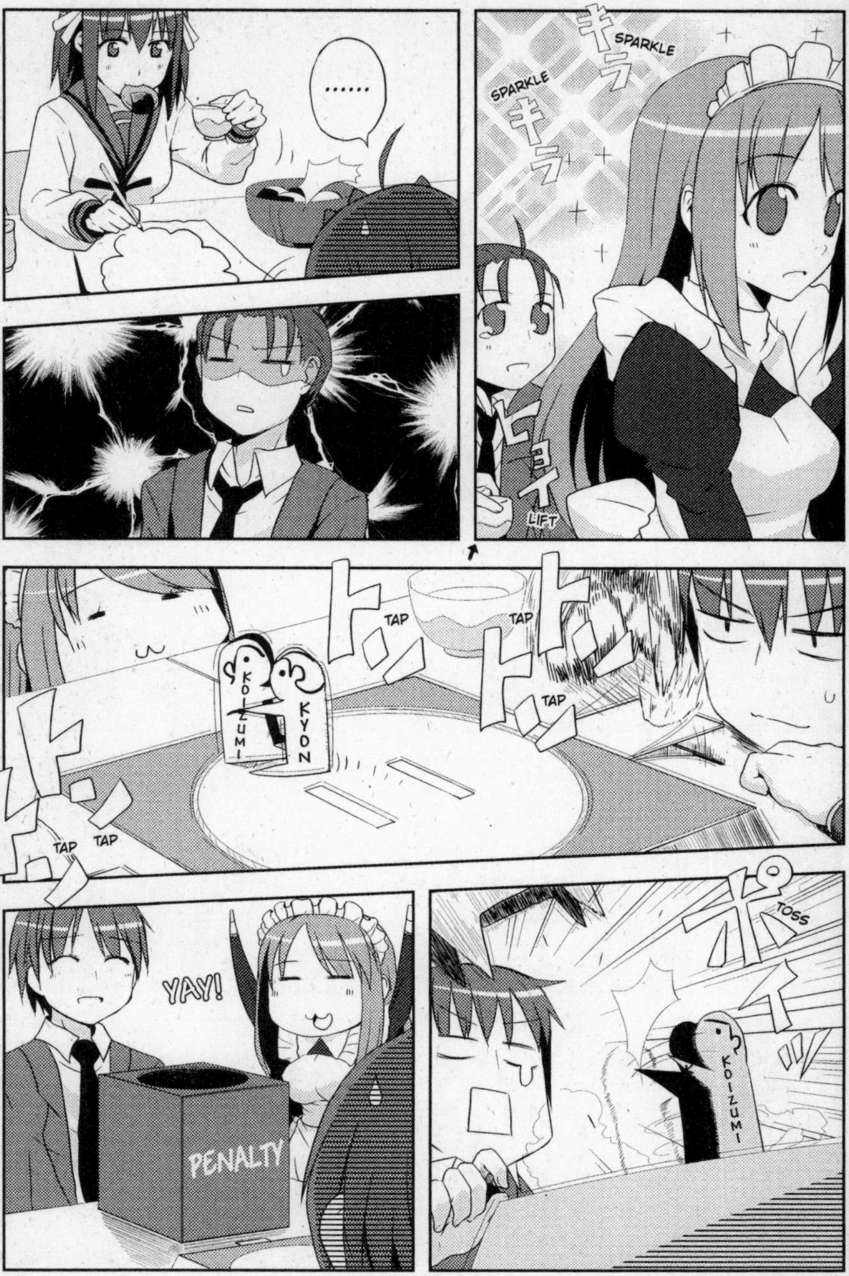

キラ
SPARKLE
キラ
SPARKLE
ヒョイ
LIFT
....
TAP
TAP
TAP
KOIZUMI
KYON
TAP
TAP
ポイ
TOSS
KOIZUMI
YAY!
PENALTY

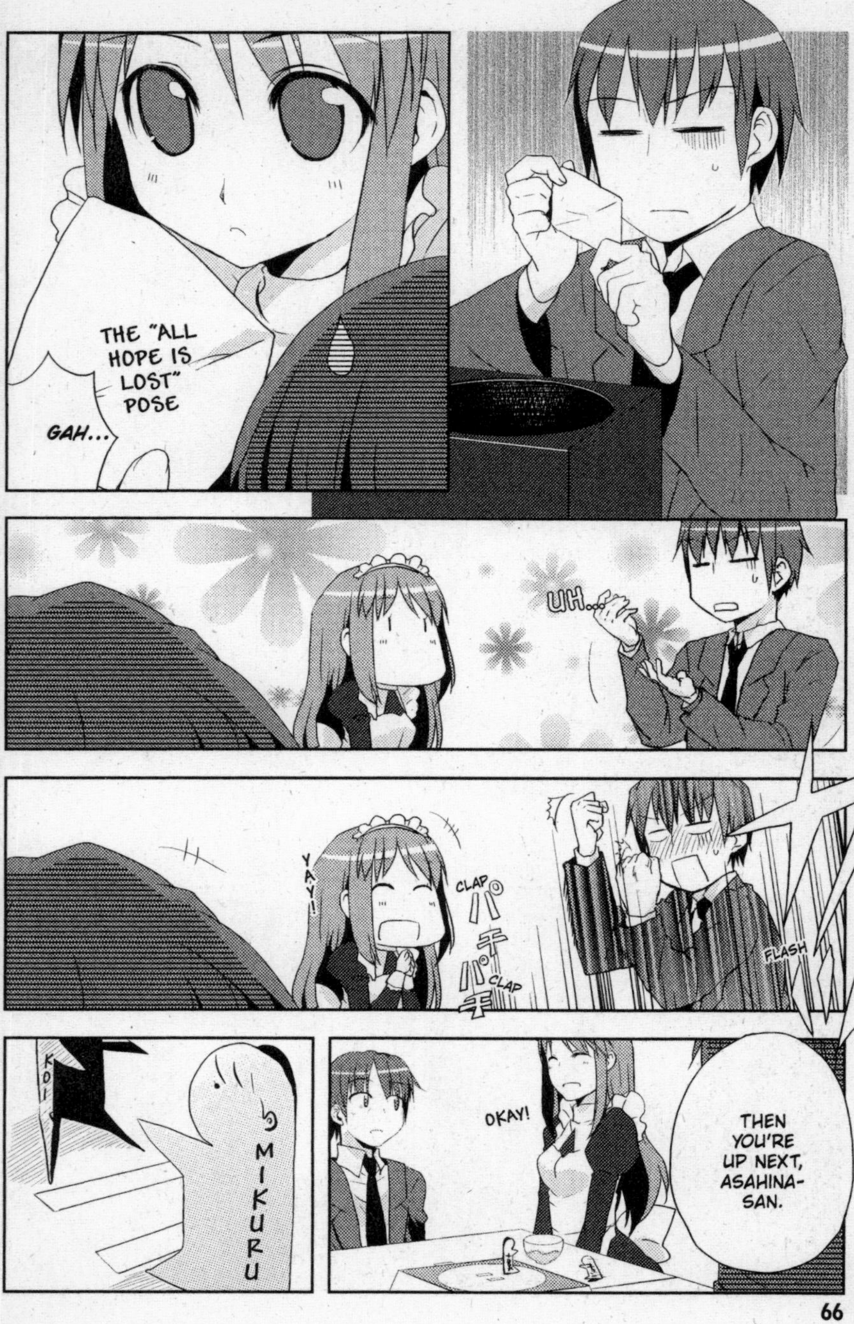

THE "ALL HOPE IS LOST" POSE
GAH...
UH...
FLASH
CLAP
CLAP
YAY!
THEN YOU'RE UP NEXT, ASAHINA-SAN.
OKAY!
KOI
MIKURU

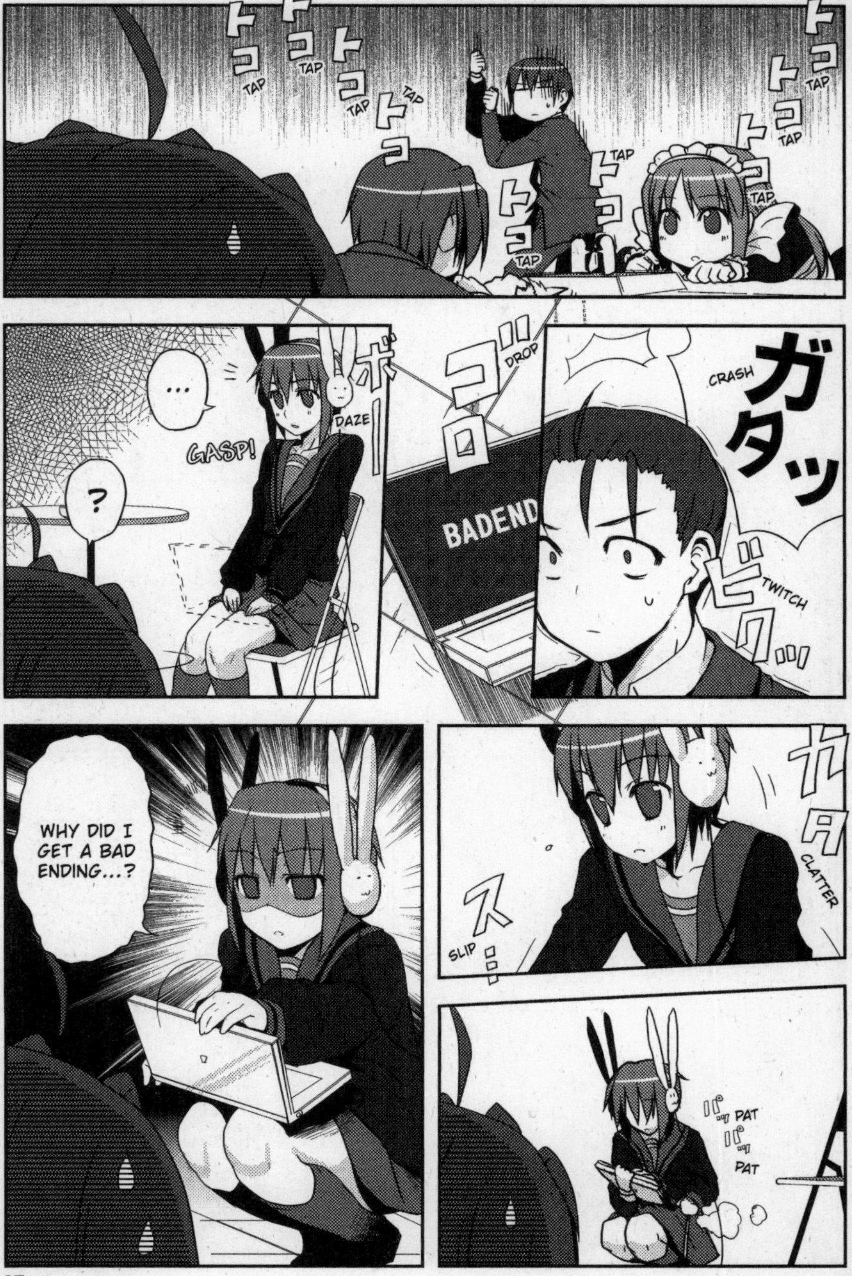
トコ TAP
トコ TAP
トコ TAP
トコ TAP
トコ TAP
トコ TAP
トコ TAP
トコ TAP
トコ TAP
ガタッ CRASH
ビク… TWITCH
ゴロ DROP
BADEND
ボー DAZE
...
GASP!
?
カタ CLATTER
ス… SLIP
パッ PAT
パッ PAT
WHY DID I GET A BAD ENDING...?

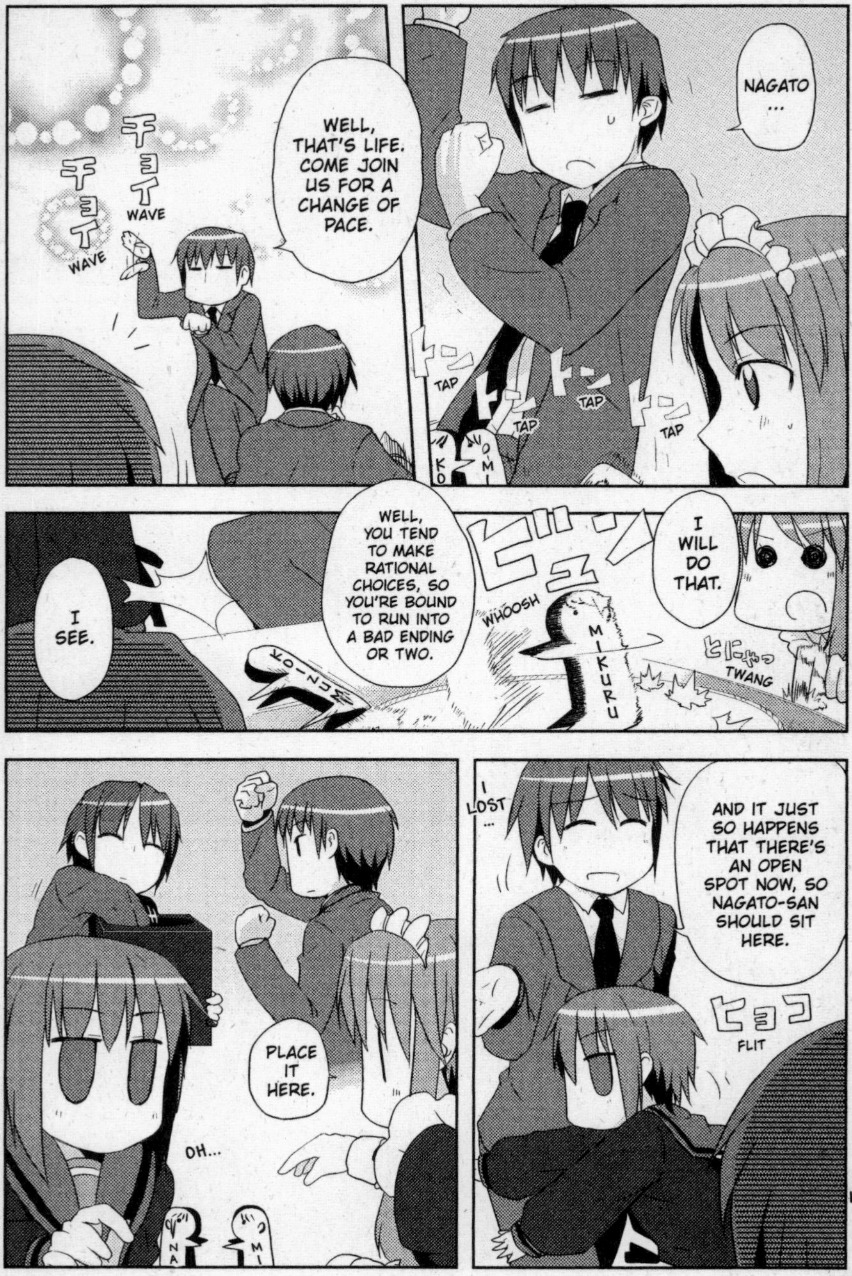
NAGATO ...
トン
TAP
トン
TAP
トン
TAP
トン
TAP
KO
MI
WELL, THAT'S LIFE. COME JOIN US FOR A CHANGE OF PACE.
チョイ
WAVE
チョイ
WAVE
I WILL DO THAT.
とにゃっ
TWANG
ビュン
WHOOSH
MIKURU
WELL, YOU TEND TO MAKE RATIONAL CHOICES, SO YOU'RE BOUND TO RUN INTO A BAD ENDING OR TWO.
I SEE.
AND IT JUST SO HAPPENS THAT THERE'S AN OPEN SPOT NOW, SO NAGATO-SAN SHOULD SIT HERE.
I LOST ...
ヒョコ
FLIT
PLACE IT HERE.
OH...
NA
MI
SO YOU LOST ...

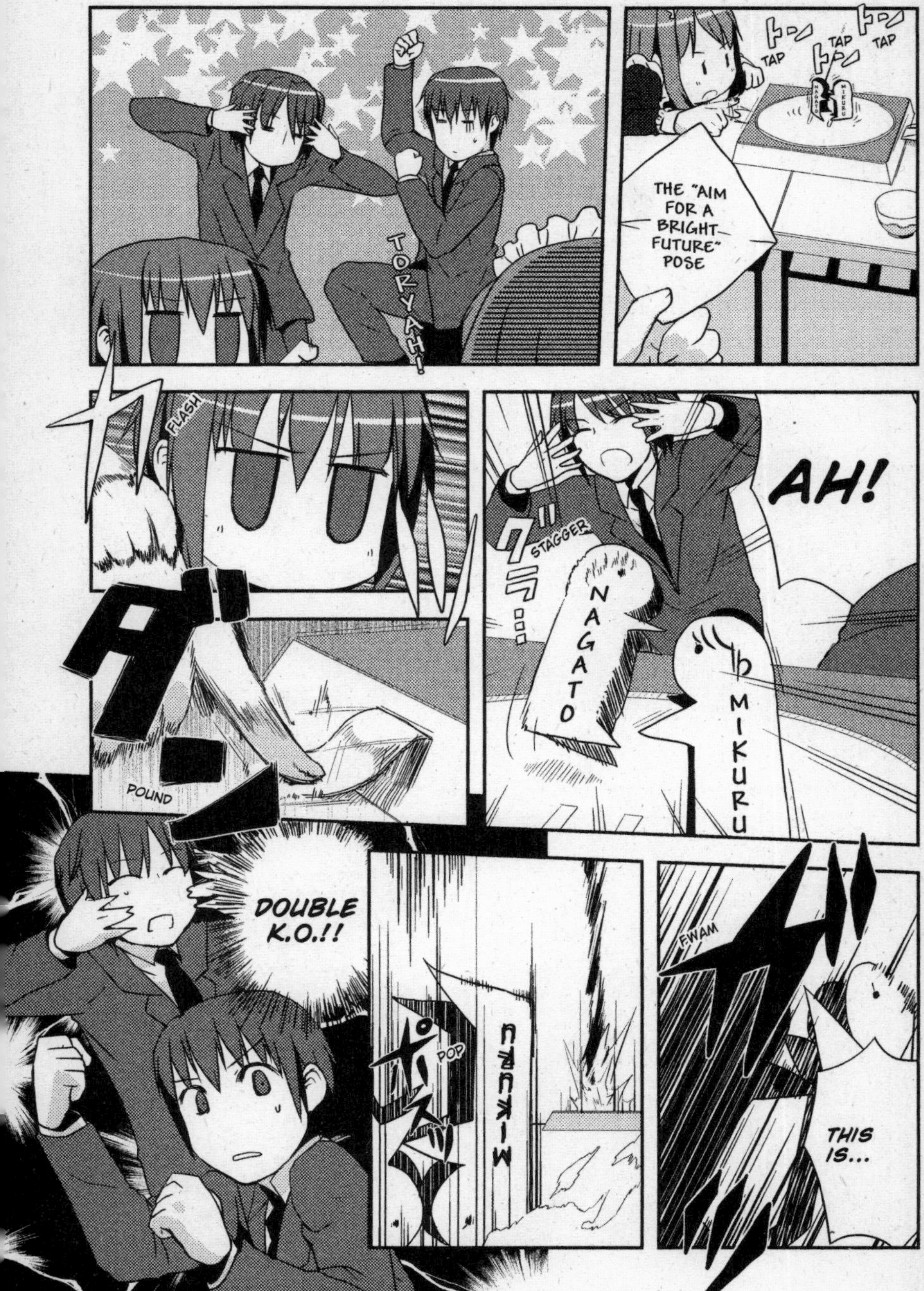

TAP
TAP
TAP
TAP
THE "AIM FOR A BRIGHT FUTURE" POSE
TORYAH!
AH!
STAGGER
NAGATO
MIKURU
FLASH
POUND
F-WAM
THIS IS...
POP
DOUBLE K.O.!!

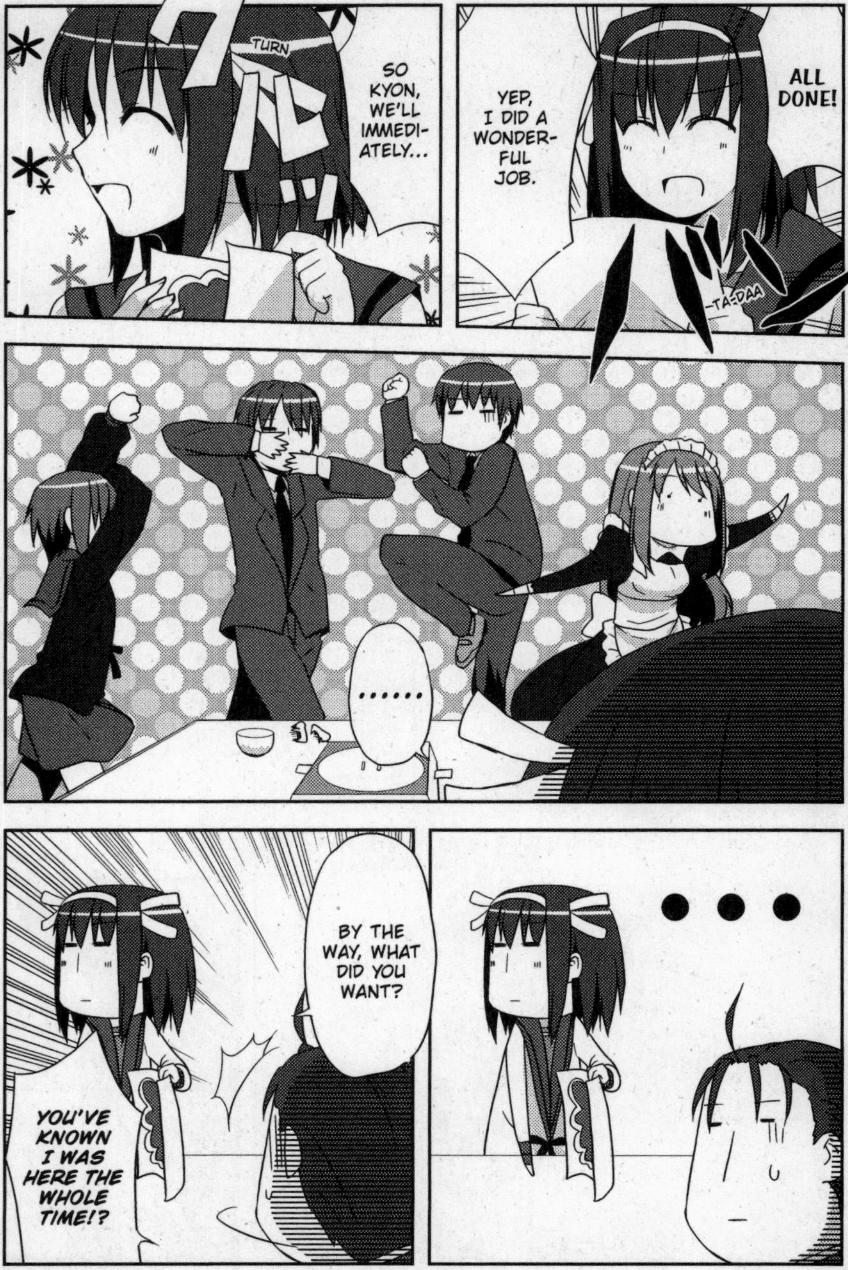
ALL DONE!
YEP, I DID A WONDERFUL JOB.
TA-DAA
TURN
SO KYON, WE'LL IMMEDIATELY...
......
• • •
BY THE WAY, WHAT DID YOU WANT?
YOU'VE KNOWN I WAS HERE THE WHOLE TIME!?

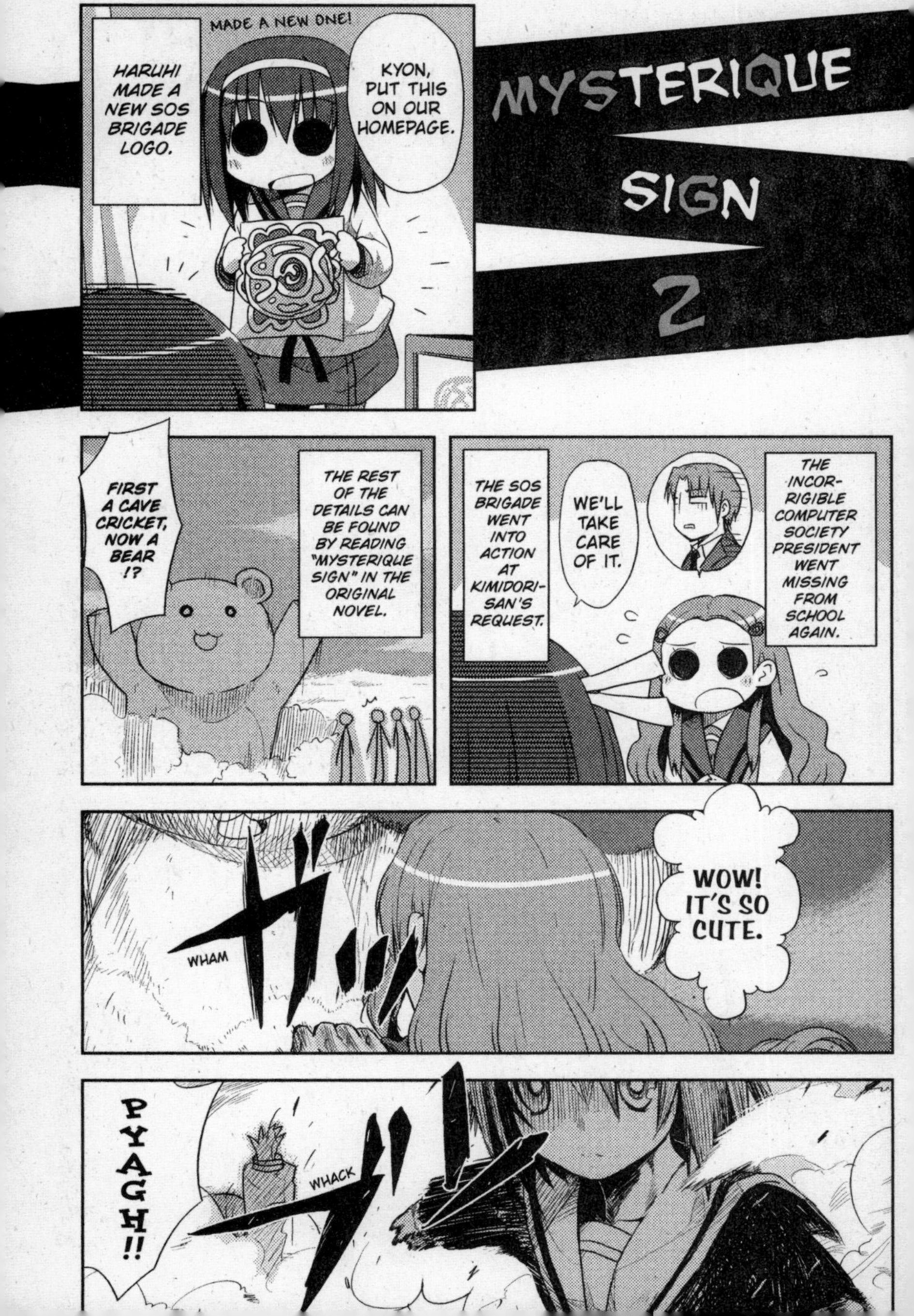
MYSTERIQUE SIGN 2
MADE A NEW ONE!
KYON, PUT THIS ON OUR HOMEPAGE.
HARUHI MADE A NEW SOS BRIGADE LOGO.
THE INCORRIGIBLE COMPUTER SOCIETY PRESIDENT WENT MISSING FROM SCHOOL AGAIN.
WE'LL TAKE CARE OF IT.
THE SOS BRIGADE WENT INTO ACTION AT KIMIDORI-SAN'S REQUEST.
THE REST OF THE DETAILS CAN BE FOUND BY READING "MYSTERIQUE SIGN" IN THE ORIGINAL NOVEL.
FIRST A CAVE CRICKET, NOW A BEAR!?
WOW! IT'S SO CUTE.
WHAM
WHACK
PYAGH!!

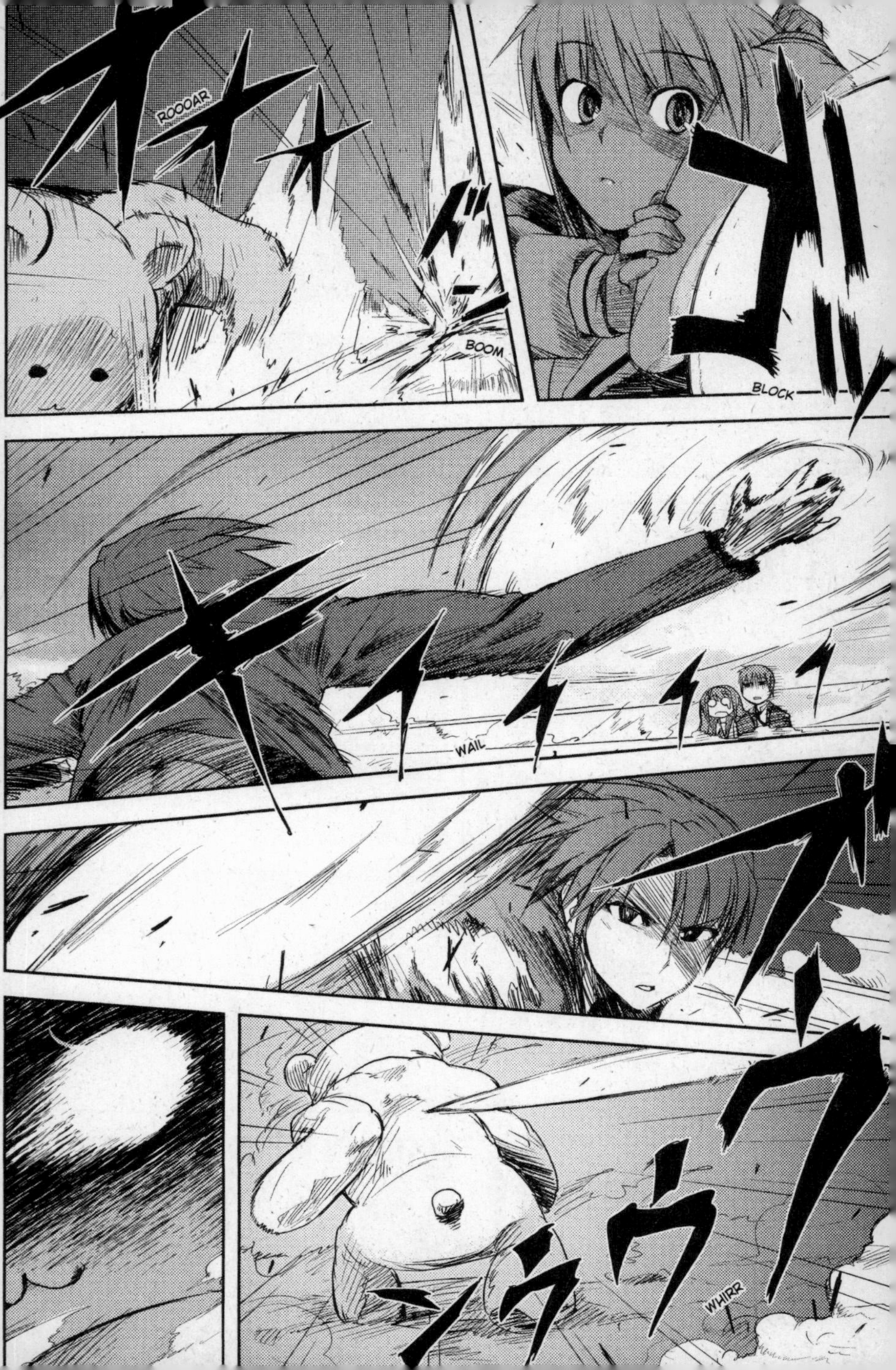

BLOCK
ROOOAR
BOOM
WAIL
WHIRR

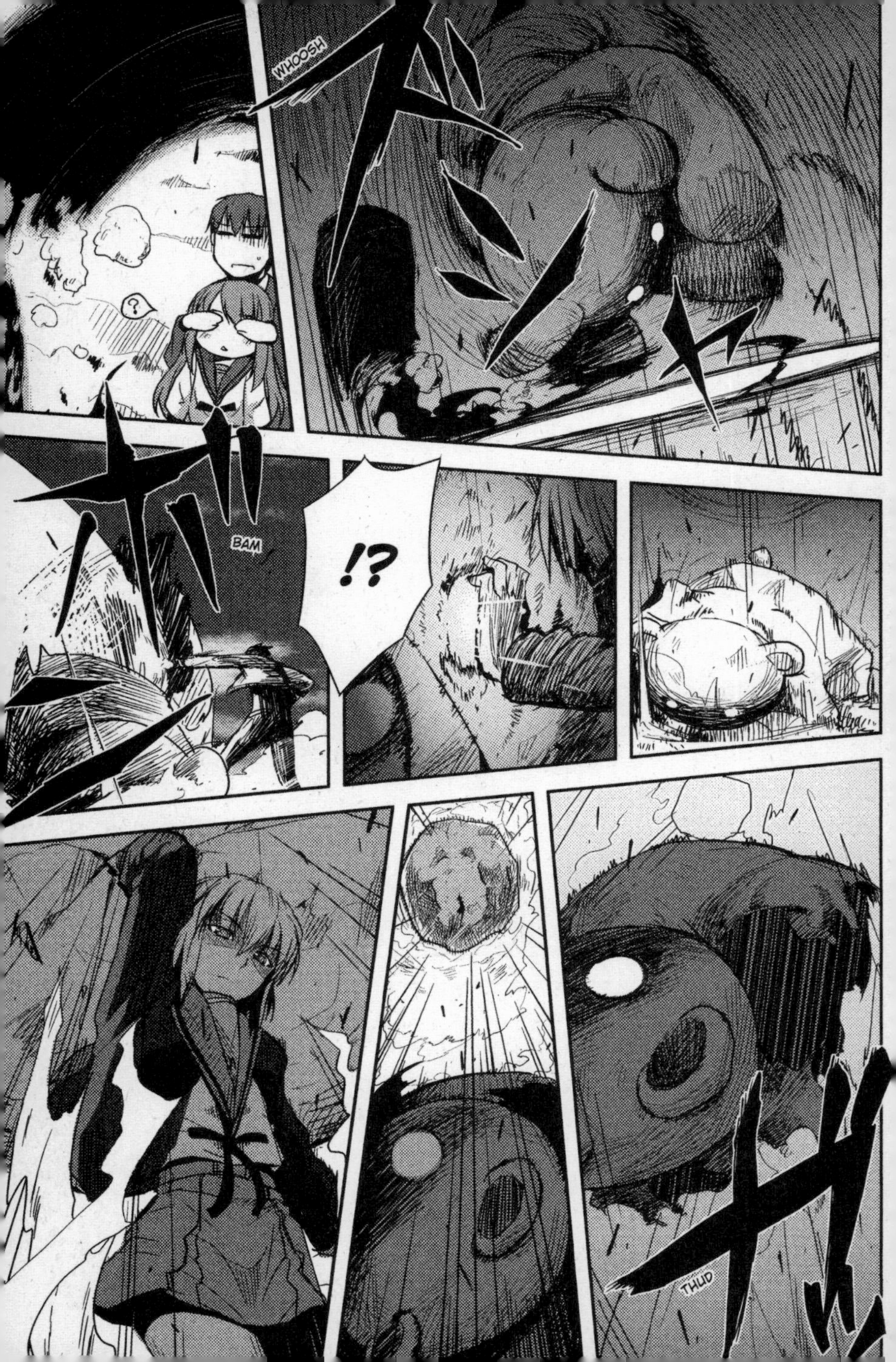

WHOOSH
?
!?
BAM
THUD

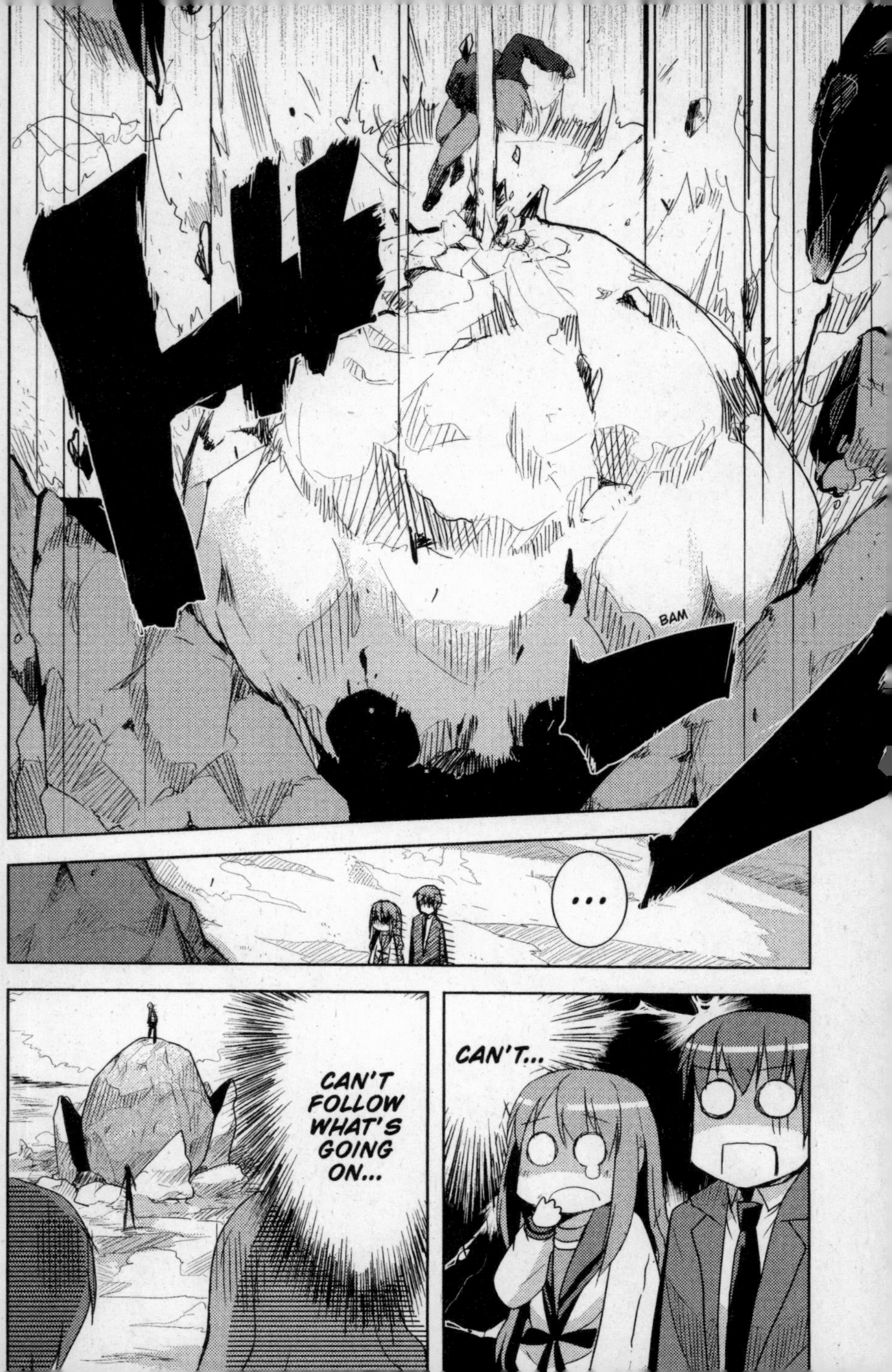
BAM
...
CAN'T...
CAN'T FOLLOW WHAT'S GOING ON...

COSTUME

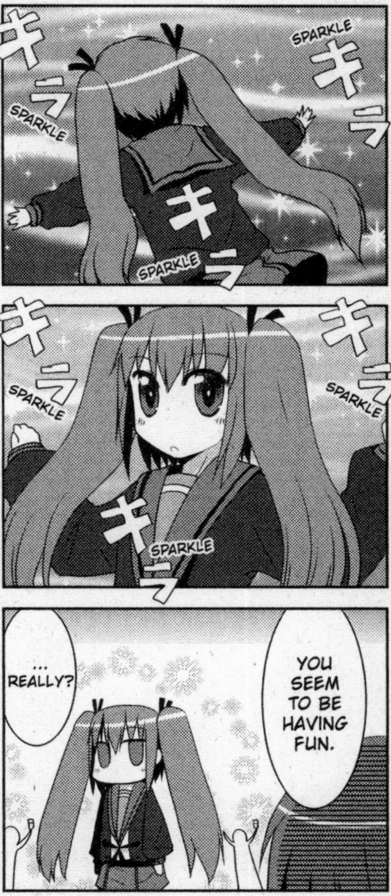
SPARKLE
キラ
SPARKLE
キラ
キラ
SPARKLE
キラ
キラ
SPARKLE
キラ
SPARKLE
YOU SEEM TO BE HAVING FUN.
... REALLY?
BUT YOU DO REALIZE THAT HALLOWEEN ISN'T A BIG COSPLAY PARTY?

CLEAR

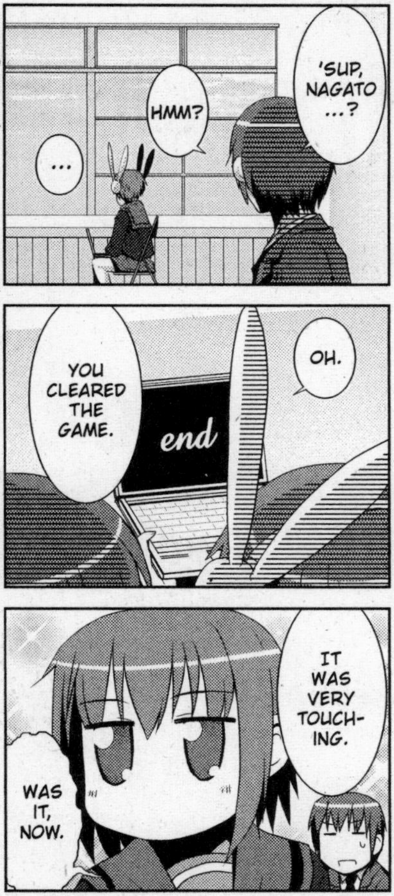
'SUP, NAGATO ...?
HMM?
...
OH.
YOU CLEARED THE GAME.
end
IT WAS VERY TOUCHING.
WAS IT, NOW.
I WILL LET YOU BORROW THE GAME, THE ANIME, THE COMIC ADAPTATION, AND THE LIGHT NOVEL ADAPTATION.
THANKS ...

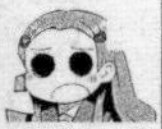

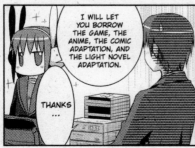

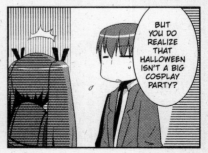

•Kimidori-san
•Claims to be the computer society president's girlfriend...? Snuck in her first appearance.

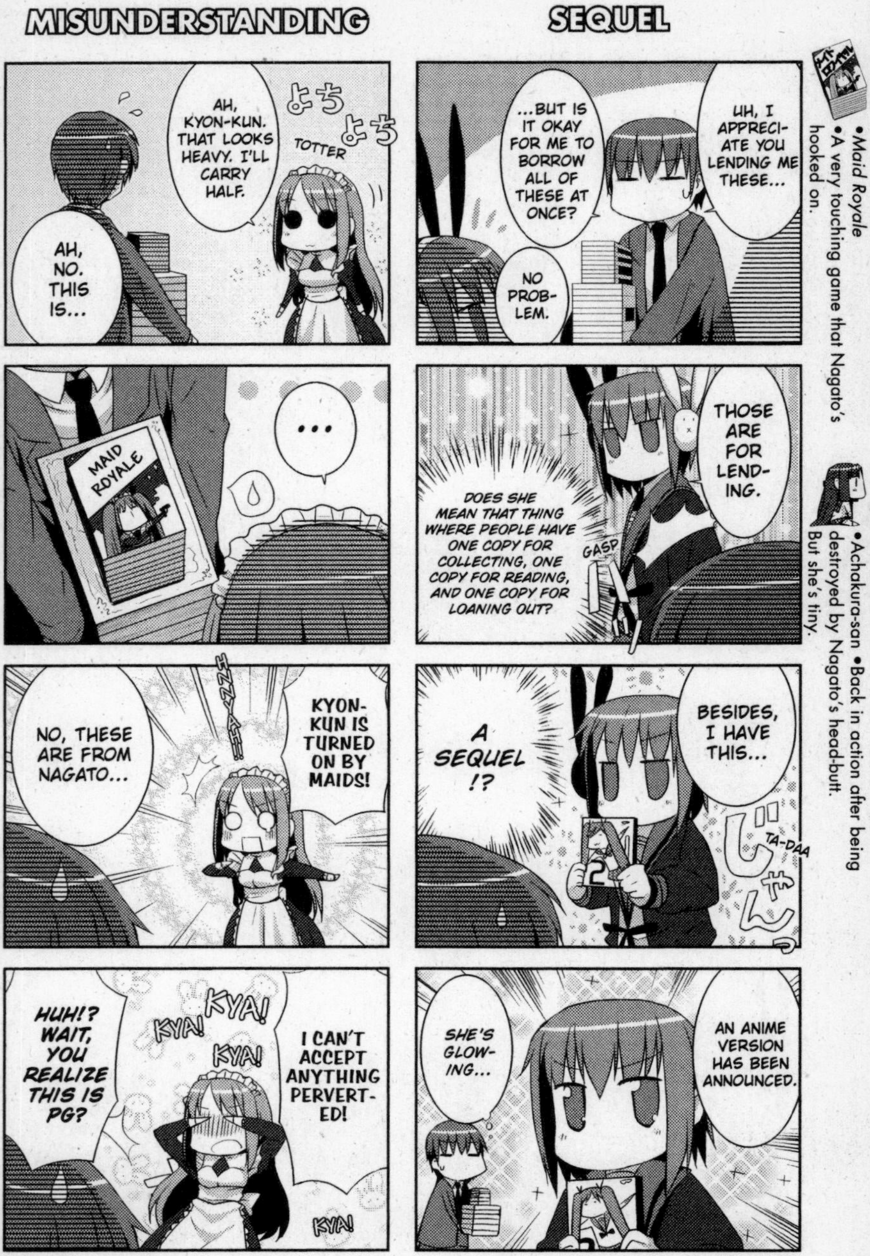
SEQUEL
UH, I APPRECIATE YOU LENDING ME THESE...
...BUT IS IT OKAY FOR ME TO BORROW ALL OF THESE AT ONCE?
NO PROBLEM.
THOSE ARE FOR LENDING.
GASP
DOES SHE MEAN THAT THING WHERE PEOPLE HAVE ONE COPY FOR COLLECTING, ONE COPY FOR READING, AND ONE COPY FOR LOANING OUT?
BESIDES, I HAVE THIS...
じゃん
TA-DAA
A SEQUEL!?
AN ANIME VERSION HAS BEEN ANNOUNCED.
SHE'S GLOWING...
•Maid Royale •A very touching game that Nagato's hooked on.
•Achakura-san •Back in action after being destroyed by Nagato's head-butt. But she's tiny.
MISUNDERSTANDING
AH, KYON-KUN. THAT LOOKS HEAVY. I'LL CARRY HALF.
よちよち
TOTTER
AH, NO. THIS IS...
...
MAID ROYALE
KYON-KUN IS TURNED ON BY MAIDS!
HNNYAH!!
NO, THESE ARE FROM NAGATO...
I CAN'T ACCEPT ANYTHING PERVERTED!
KYA!
KYA!
KYA!
KYA!
HUH!? WAIT, YOU REALIZE THIS IS PG?

FREELOADER

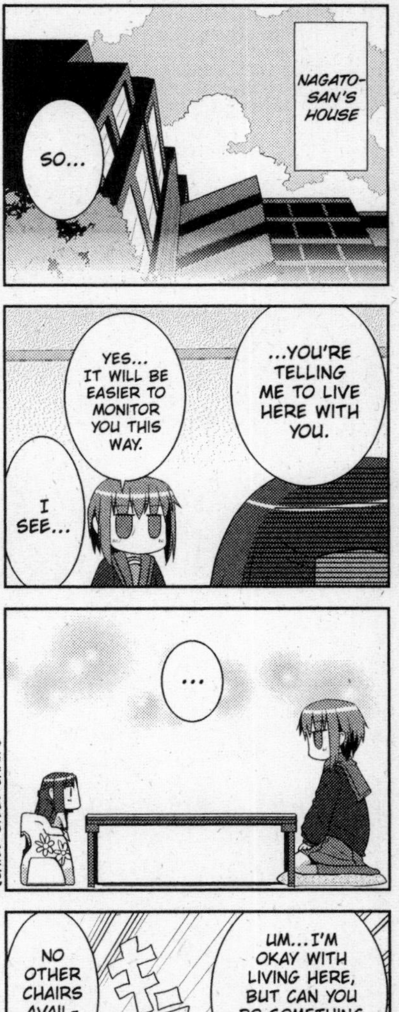
NAGATO-SAN'S HOUSE
SO...
...YOU'RE TELLING ME TO LIVE HERE WITH YOU.
YES... IT WILL BE EASIER TO MONITOR YOU THIS WAY.
I SEE...
...
(CHILD-SIZED CHAIR)
UM...I'M OKAY WITH LIVING HERE, BUT CAN YOU DO SOMETHING ABOUT THIS CHAIR?
GLINT
NO OTHER CHAIRS AVAIL-ABLE.

BOING

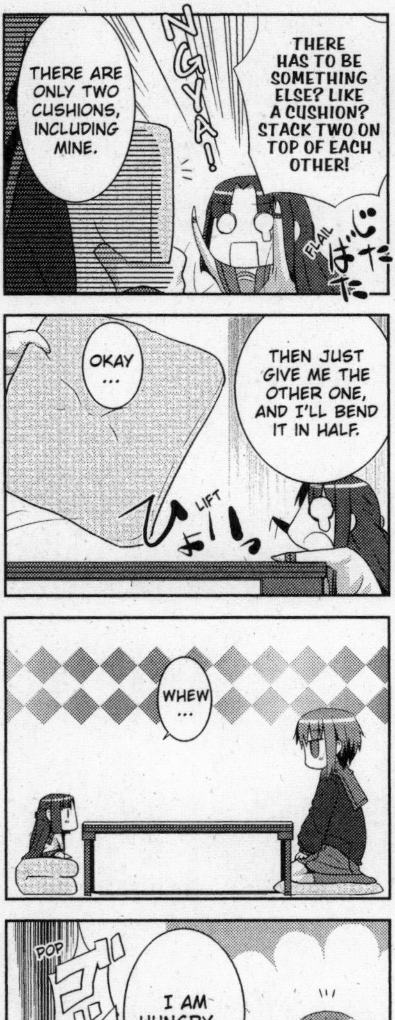
THERE HAS TO BE SOMETHING ELSE? LIKE A CUSHION? STACK TWO ON TOP OF EACH OTHER!
NGYAA!
FLAIL
THERE ARE ONLY TWO CUSHIONS, INCLUDING MINE.
THEN JUST GIVE ME THE OTHER ONE, AND I'LL BEND IT IN HALF.
OKAY ...
LIFT
WHEW ...
POP
I AM HUNGRY...
GRUMBLE

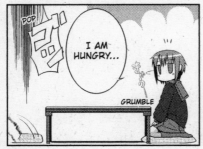

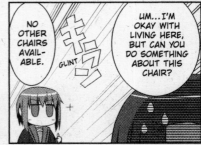

SETUP

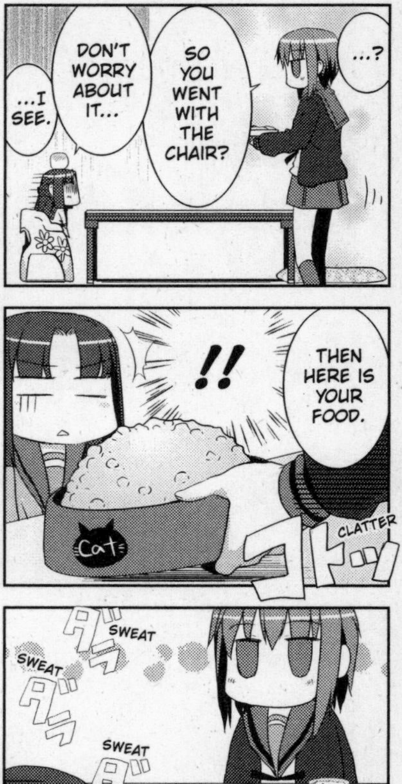
...?
SO YOU WENT WITH THE CHAIR?
DON'T WORRY ABOUT IT...
...I SEE.
THEN HERE IS YOUR FOOD.
!!
CLATTER
SWEAT
SWEAT
SWEAT
SAY SOME-THING ...
HUH? OH, THAT WAS A JOKE!?
SLIP

PUNCH LINE

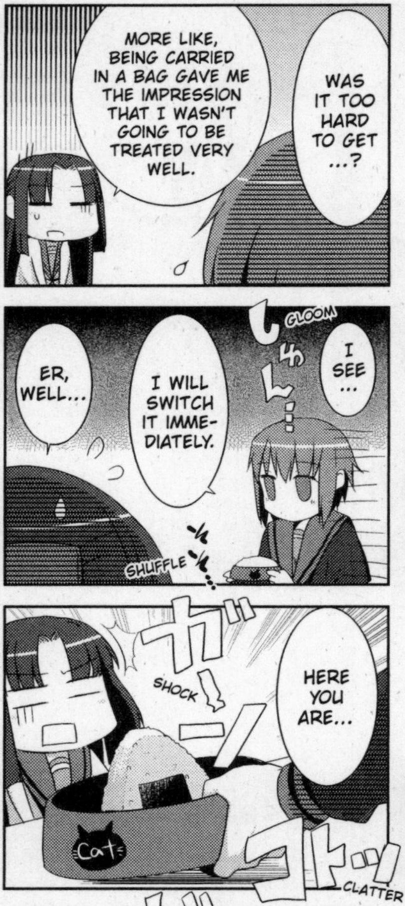
WAS IT TOO HARD TO GET ...?
MORE LIKE, BEING CARRIED IN A BAG GAVE ME THE IMPRESSION THAT I WASN'T GOING TO BE TREATED VERY WELL.
I SEE ...
GLOOM
I WILL SWITCH IT IMME-DIATELY.
ER, WELL...
SHUFFLE
HERE YOU ARE...
SHOCK
CLATTER
CAN YOU LOSE THE CAT DISH !?
CLATTER
OOH!!

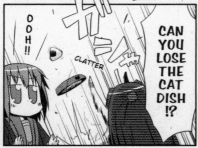

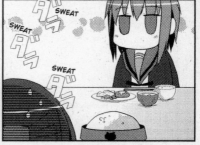

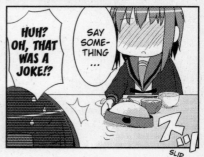

THE "I CAN FLY" POSE

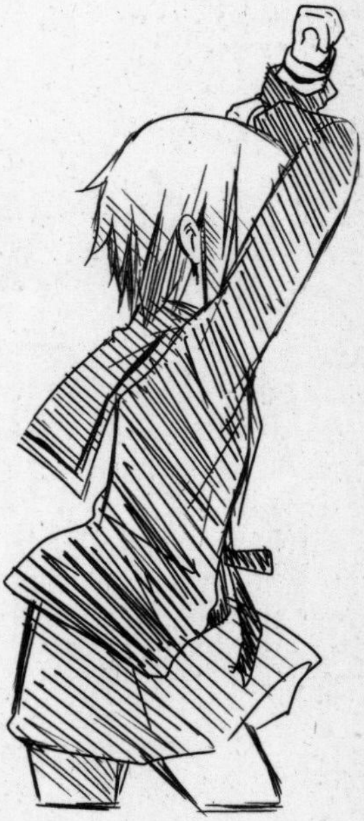

THE "MY BODY IS WIDE-OPEN" POSE

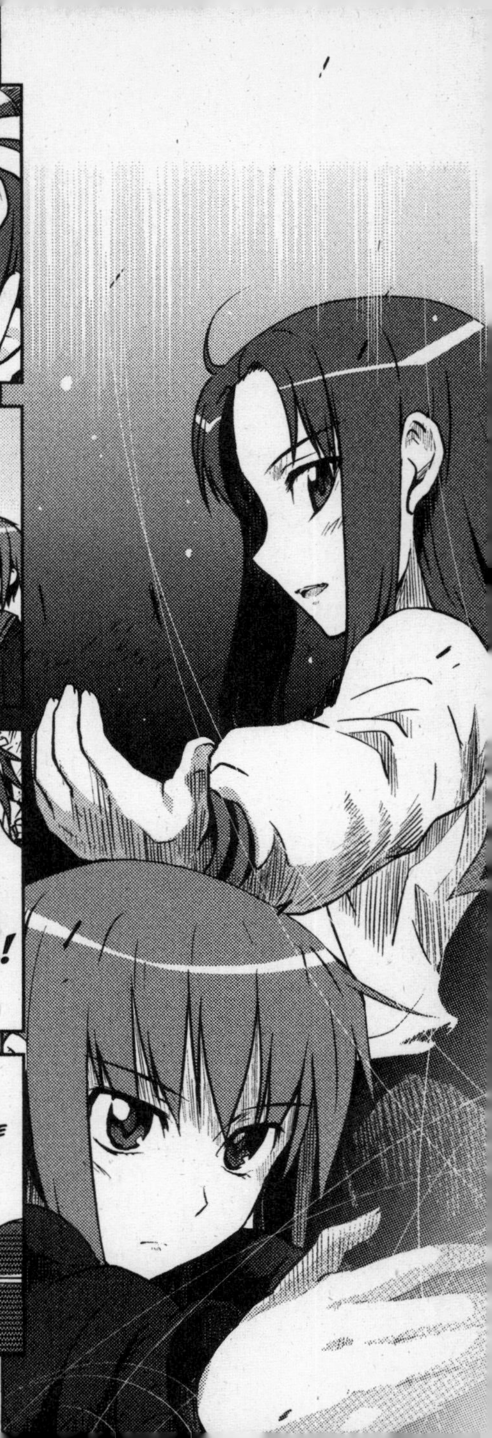

SINCE IT'S CHRISTMAS

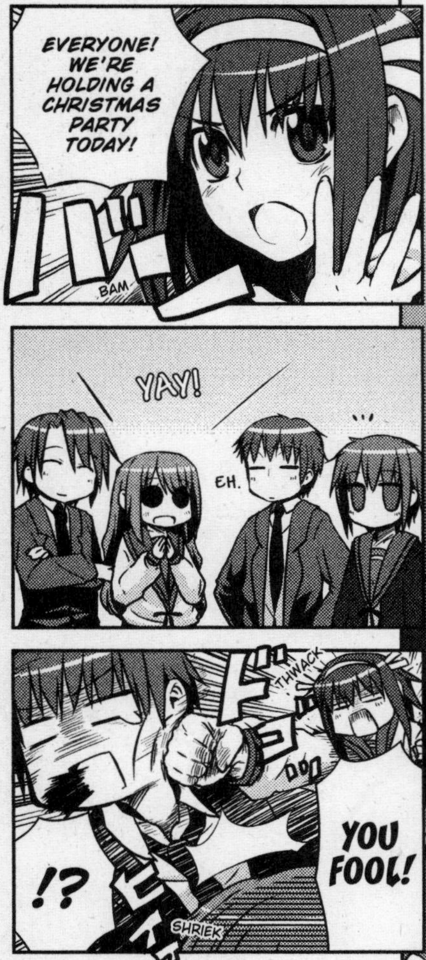
EVERYONE! WE'RE HOLDING A CHRISTMAS PARTY TODAY!
BAM
YAY!
EH.
THWACK
YOU FOOL!
DOO
!?
SHRIEK
IF YOU DON'T TAKE PARTYING SERIOUSLY, THOSE GUYS WILL HAVE NO TROUBLE KILLING YOU!
WHO IS SHE EVEN TALKING ABOUT!?

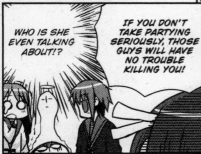

THOSE GUYS

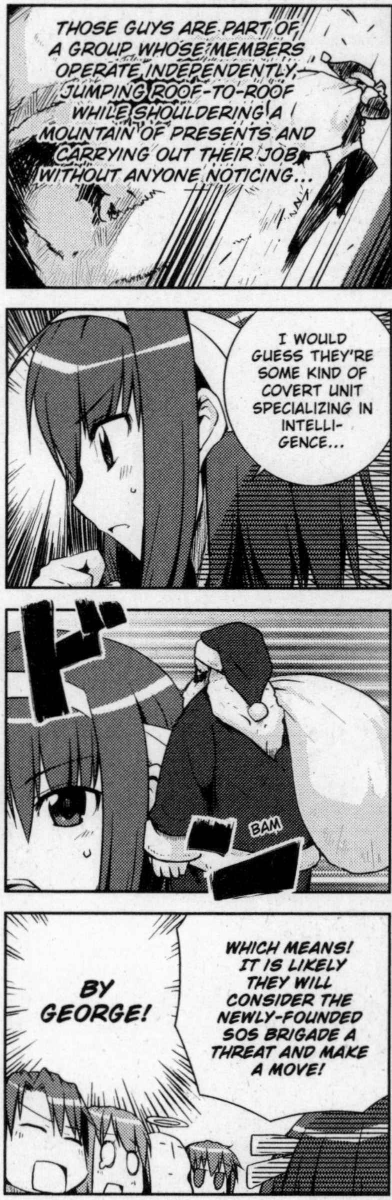
THOSE GUYS ARE PART OF A GROUP WHOSE MEMBERS OPERATE INDEPENDENTLY, JUMPING ROOF-TO-ROOF WHILE SHOULDERING A MOUNTAIN OF PRESENTS AND CARRYING OUT THEIR JOB WITHOUT ANYONE NOTICING...
I WOULD GUESS THEY'RE SOME KIND OF COVERT UNIT SPECIALIZING IN INTELLIGENCE...
BAM
WHICH MEANS! IT IS LIKELY THEY WILL CONSIDER THE NEWLY-FOUNDED SOS BRIGADE A THREAT AND MAKE A MOVE!
BY GEORGE!

PLAN

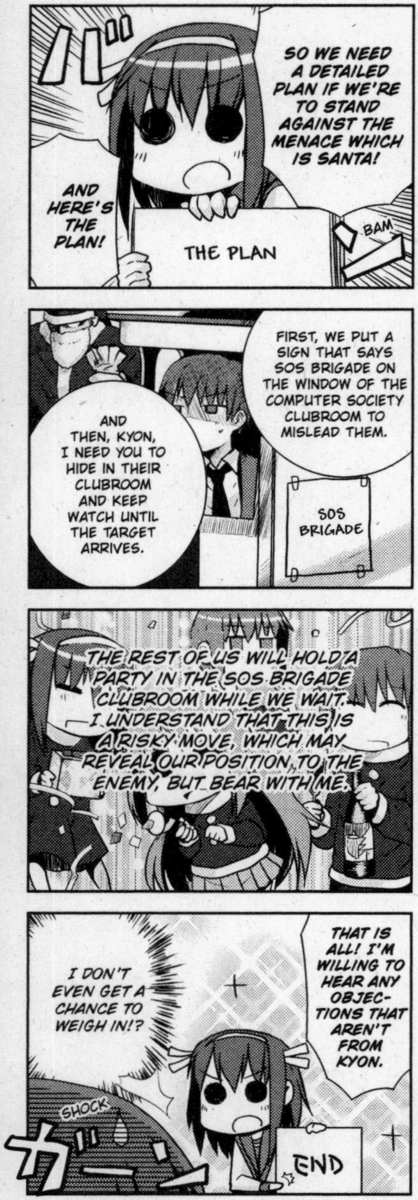
SO WE NEED A DETAILED PLAN IF WE'RE TO STAND AGAINST THE MENACE WHICH IS SANTA!
AND HERE'S THE PLAN!
THE PLAN
BAM
FIRST, WE PUT A SIGN THAT SAYS SOS BRIGADE ON THE WINDOW OF THE COMPUTER SOCIETY CLUBROOM TO MISLEAD THEM.
AND THEN, KYON, I NEED YOU TO HIDE IN THEIR CLUBROOM AND KEEP WATCH UNTIL THE TARGET ARRIVES.
SOS BRIGADE
THE REST OF US WILL HOLD A PARTY IN THE SOS BRIGADE CLUBROOM WHILE WE WAIT. I UNDERSTAND THAT THIS IS A RISKY MOVE, WHICH MAY REVEAL OUR POSITION TO THE ENEMY, BUT BEAR WITH ME.
THAT IS ALL! I'M WILLING TO HEAR ANY OBJECTIONS THAT AREN'T FROM KYON.
I DON'T EVEN GET A CHANCE TO WEIGH IN!?
SHOCK
END

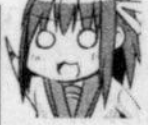
•Haruhi-chan •SOS Brigade brigade chief. Very interested in Christmas activities.

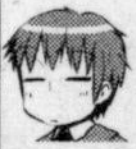
•Kyon •Supposed to be the main character in this story. Busy playing straight man for all comers.

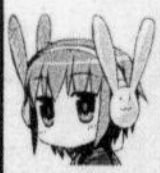
•Nagato •Actually an alien gamer. Recently picked up a new hobby of playing with Achakura-san.

REINFORCEMENTS

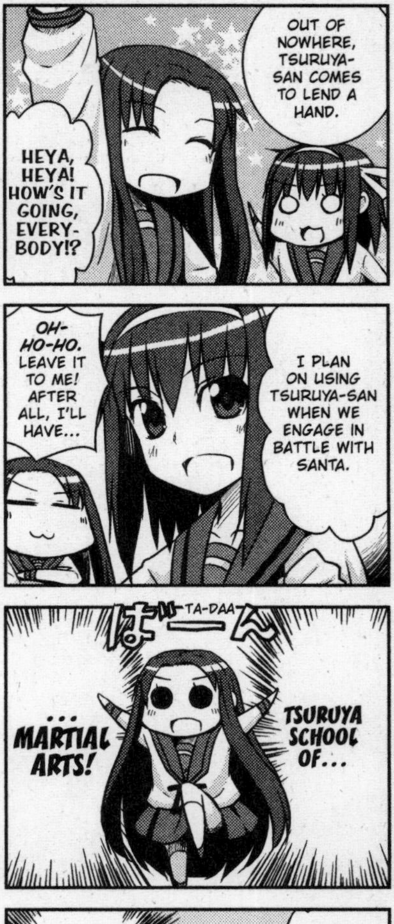
OUT OF NOWHERE, TSURUYA-SAN COMES TO LEND A HAND.
HEYA, HEYA! HOW'S IT GOING, EVERYBODY!?
I PLAN ON USING TSURUYA-SAN WHEN WE ENGAGE IN BATTLE WITH SANTA.
OH-HO-HO. LEAVE IT TO ME! AFTER ALL, I'LL HAVE...
ぱーん
TA-DAA
TSURUYA SCHOOL OF...
...MARTIAL ARTS!
...MASTERED AT THE YOUNG AGE OF NINETEEN, IF EVERYTHING GOES AS PLANNED.
"IF" !?

PROOF

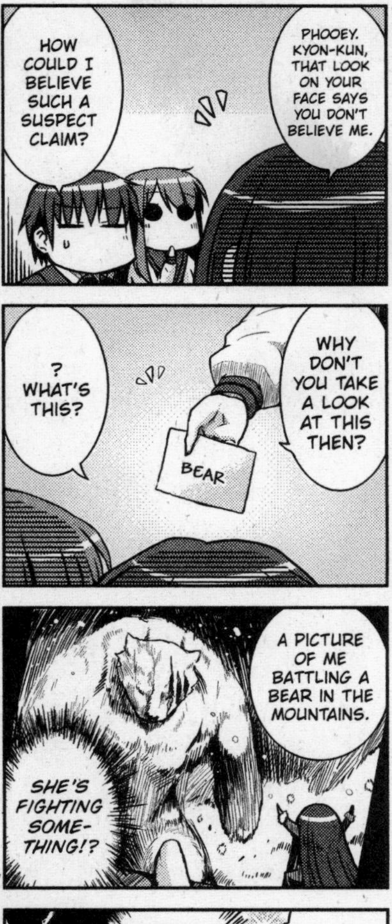
PHOOEY. KYON-KUN, THAT LOOK ON YOUR FACE SAYS YOU DON'T BELIEVE ME.
HOW COULD I BELIEVE SUCH A SUSPECT CLAIM?
WHY DON'T YOU TAKE A LOOK AT THIS THEN?
BEAR
? WHAT'S THIS?
A PICTURE OF ME BATTLING A BEAR IN THE MOUNTAINS.
SHE'S FIGHTING SOMETHING!?
WOW, THAT'S AMAZING!
WOW, THAT LOOKS FAKE!

•Mikuru-chan •Actually from the future. Frequently the attention of Haruhi's intense affection.

•Koizumi •An enigmatic transfer student who happens to be an esper. Sports a spiteful smile. Specializes in explanations and being funny man.

•Tsuruya-san •Mikuru-chan's buddy. The situation tends to worsen when she's around.

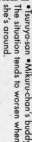

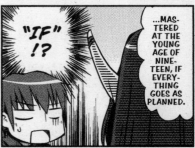

HIDING PLACE

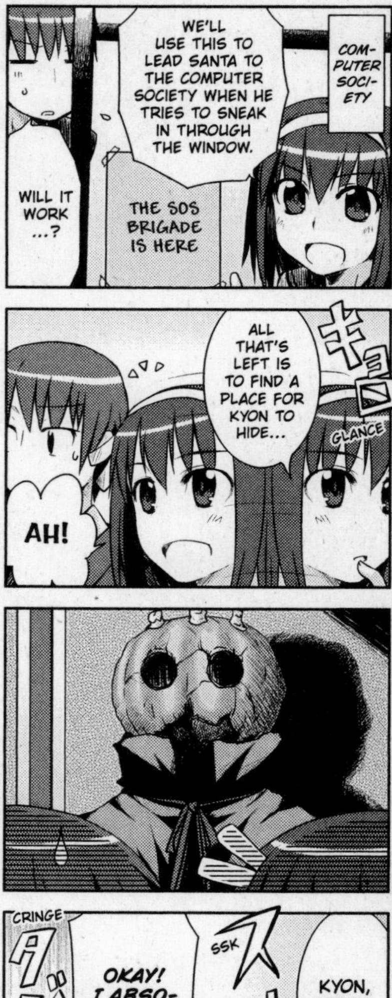
COMPUTER SOCIETY
WE'LL USE THIS TO LEAD SANTA TO THE COMPUTER SOCIETY WHEN HE TRIES TO SNEAK IN THROUGH THE WINDOW.
THE SOS BRIGADE IS HERE
WILL IT WORK ...?
ALL THAT'S LEFT IS TO FIND A PLACE FOR KYON TO HIDE...
GLANCE
AH!
KYON, HERE...
SSK
OKAY! I ABSOLUTELY REFUSE!
CRINGE

SETTLED

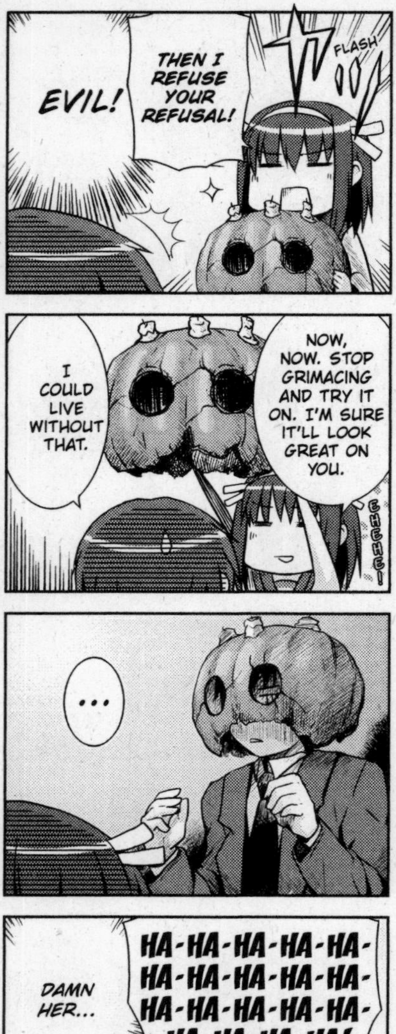
FLASH
THEN I REFUSE YOUR REFUSAL!
EVIL!
NOW, NOW. STOP GRIMACING AND TRY IT ON. I'M SURE IT'LL LOOK GREAT ON YOU.
EHEHE!
I COULD LIVE WITHOUT THAT.
...
HA-HA-HA-HA-HA-HA-HA-HA-HA-HA-HA-HA-HA-HA-HA-HA-HA-HA-HA!
DAMN HER...
POUND
POUND
POUND

•Halloween Pumpkin •After completion by the SOS Brigade, it was deemed too creepy and left in the computer society clubroom.

•Kyon's sister •Makes a brief appearance in the next short story. Has a surprising number of fans.

•Taniguchi •Kyon's useless friend. Gets another chance to shine in the next short story!!

TANIGUCHI AND THE KAPPA: FINAL EPISODE

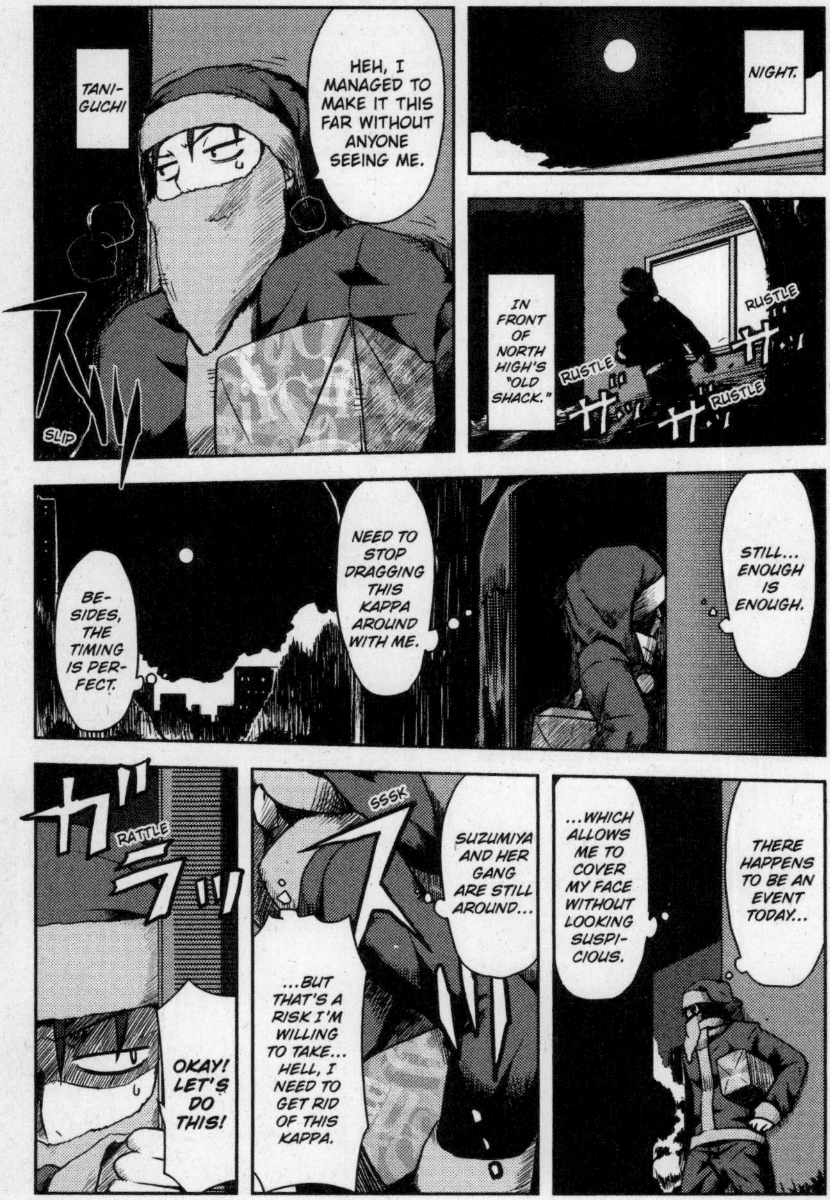
NIGHT.
IN FRONT OF NORTH HIGH'S "OLD SHACK."
RUSTLE
RUSTLE
RUSTLE
TANIGUCHI
HEH, I MANAGED TO MAKE IT THIS FAR WITHOUT ANYONE SEEING ME.
SLIP
STILL... ENOUGH IS ENOUGH.
NEED TO STOP DRAGGING THIS KAPPA AROUND WITH ME.
BESIDES, THE TIMING IS PERFECT.
THERE HAPPENS TO BE AN EVENT TODAY...
...WHICH ALLOWS ME TO COVER MY FACE WITHOUT LOOKING SUSPICIOUS.
SUZUMIYA AND HER GANG ARE STILL AROUND...
SSSK
...BUT THAT'S A RISK I'M WILLING TO TAKE... HELL, I NEED TO GET RID OF THIS KAPPA.
RATTLE
OKAY! LET'S DO THIS!

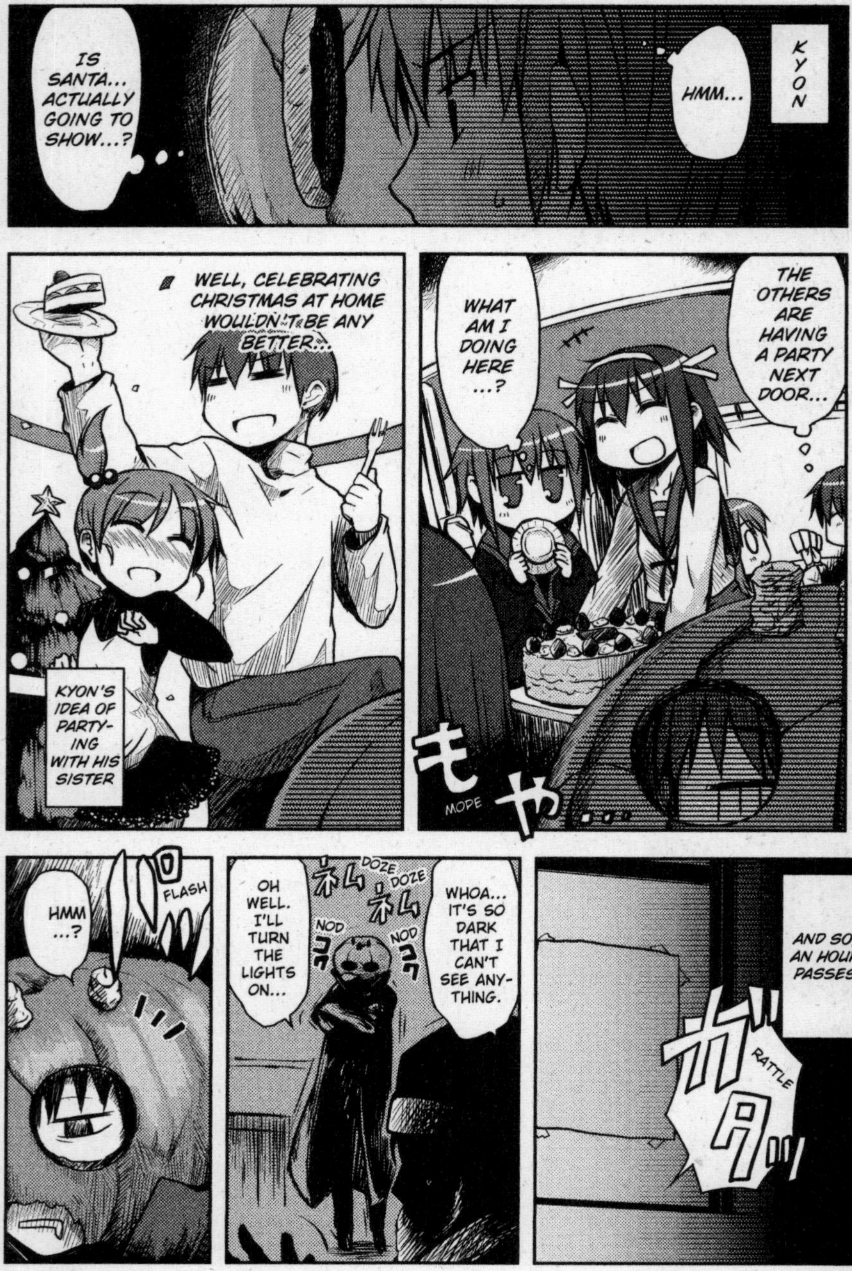
KYON
HMM...
IS SANTA... ACTUALLY GOING TO SHOW...?
THE OTHERS ARE HAVING A PARTY NEXT DOOR...
WHAT AM I DOING HERE ...?
MOPE
WELL, CELEBRATING CHRISTMAS AT HOME WOULDN'T BE ANY BETTER...
KYON'S IDEA OF PARTY-ING WITH HIS SISTER
AND SO, AN HOUR PASSES
RATTLE
WHOA... IT'S SO DARK THAT I CAN'T SEE ANY-THING.
DOZE
DOZE
NOD
NOD
OH WELL. I'LL TURN THE LIGHTS ON...
FLASH
HMM ...?

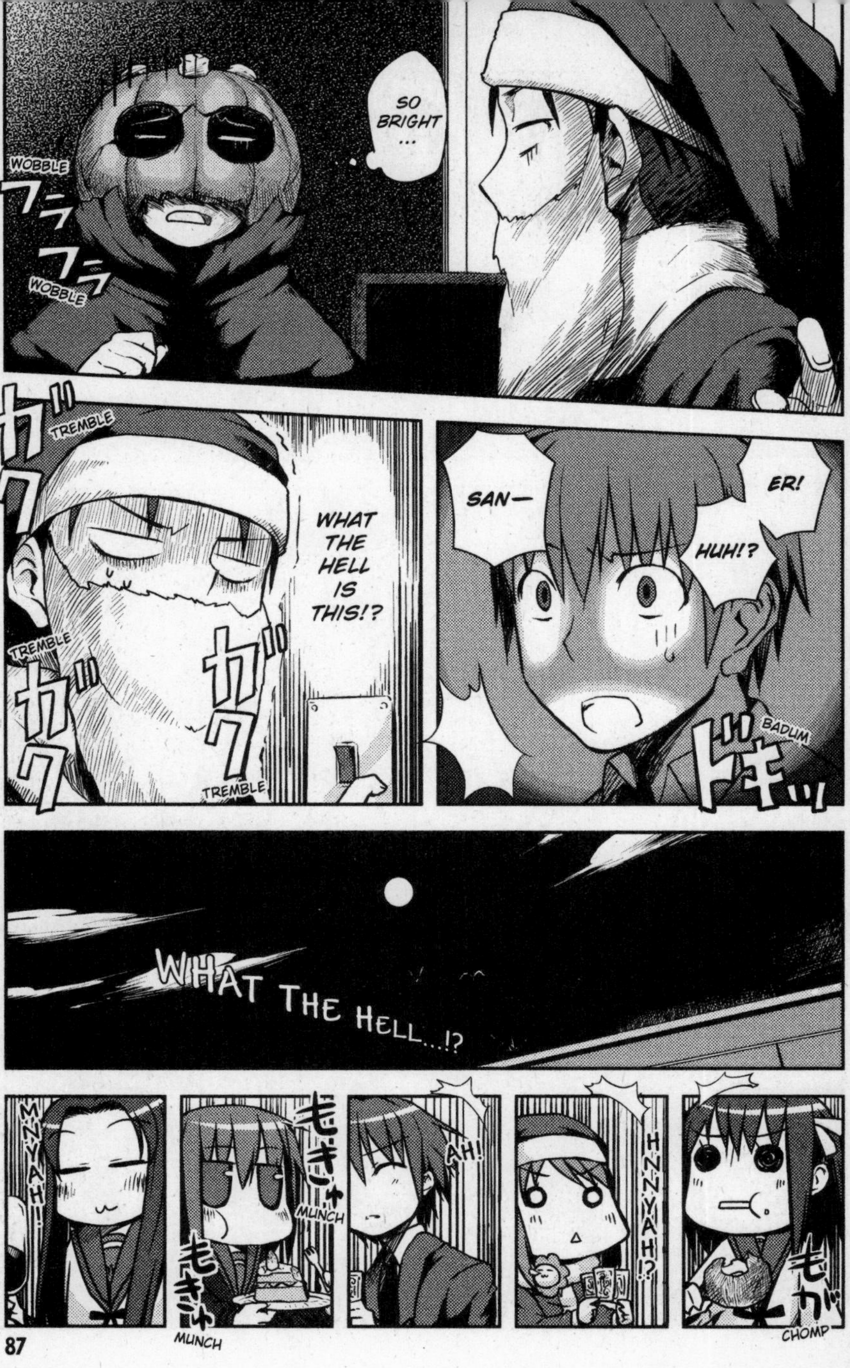
SO BRIGHT ...
フラフラ
WOBBLE
フラフラ
WOBBLE
SAN—
ER!
HUH!?
ドキッ
BADUM
ガクガク
TREMBLE
WHAT THE HELL IS THIS!?
ガクガク
TREMBLE
ガクガク
TREMBLE
WHAT THE HELL...!?
もが
CHOMP
HNNYAH!?
AH!
もきゅ
MUNCH
もきゅ
MUNCH
MNYAH!

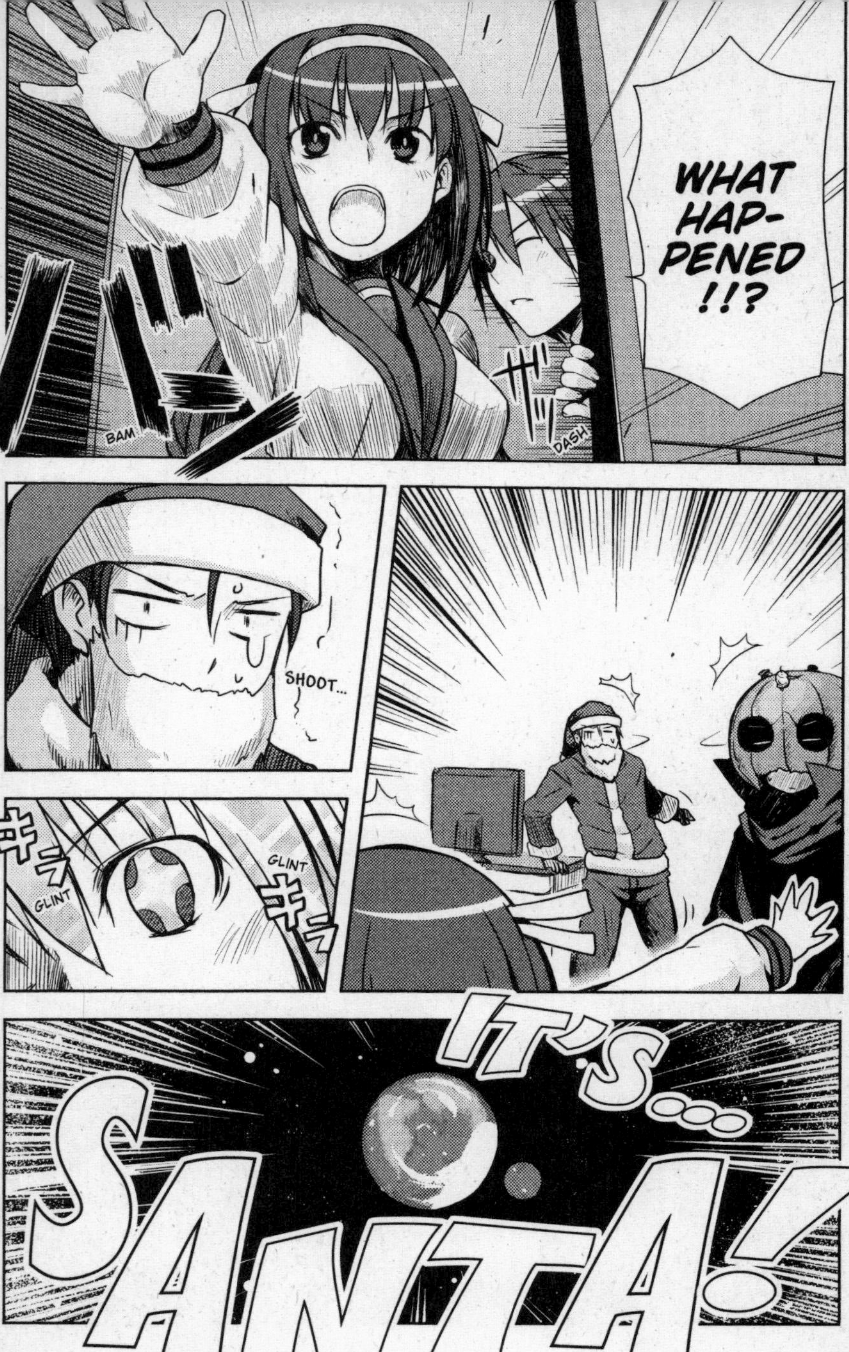

WHAT HAP-PENED!!?
DASH
BAM
SHOOT...
キラ
GLINT
GLINT
キラ
IT'S...
SANTA!

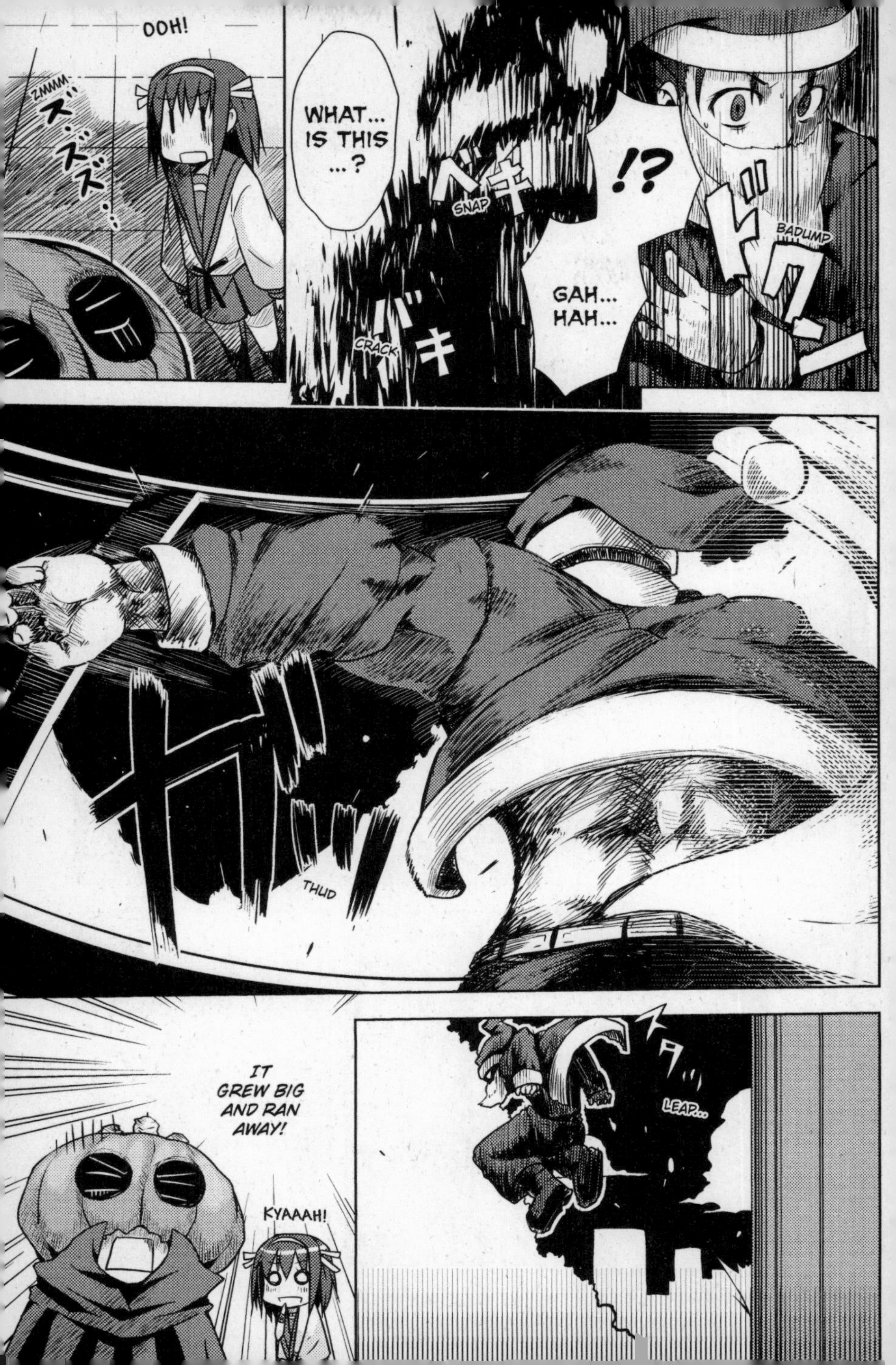

!?
BADUMP
GAH... HAH...
WHAT... IS THIS ...?
SNAP
CRACK
OOH!
ZMMM
THUD
LEAP...
IT GREW BIG AND RAN AWAY!
KYAAAH!

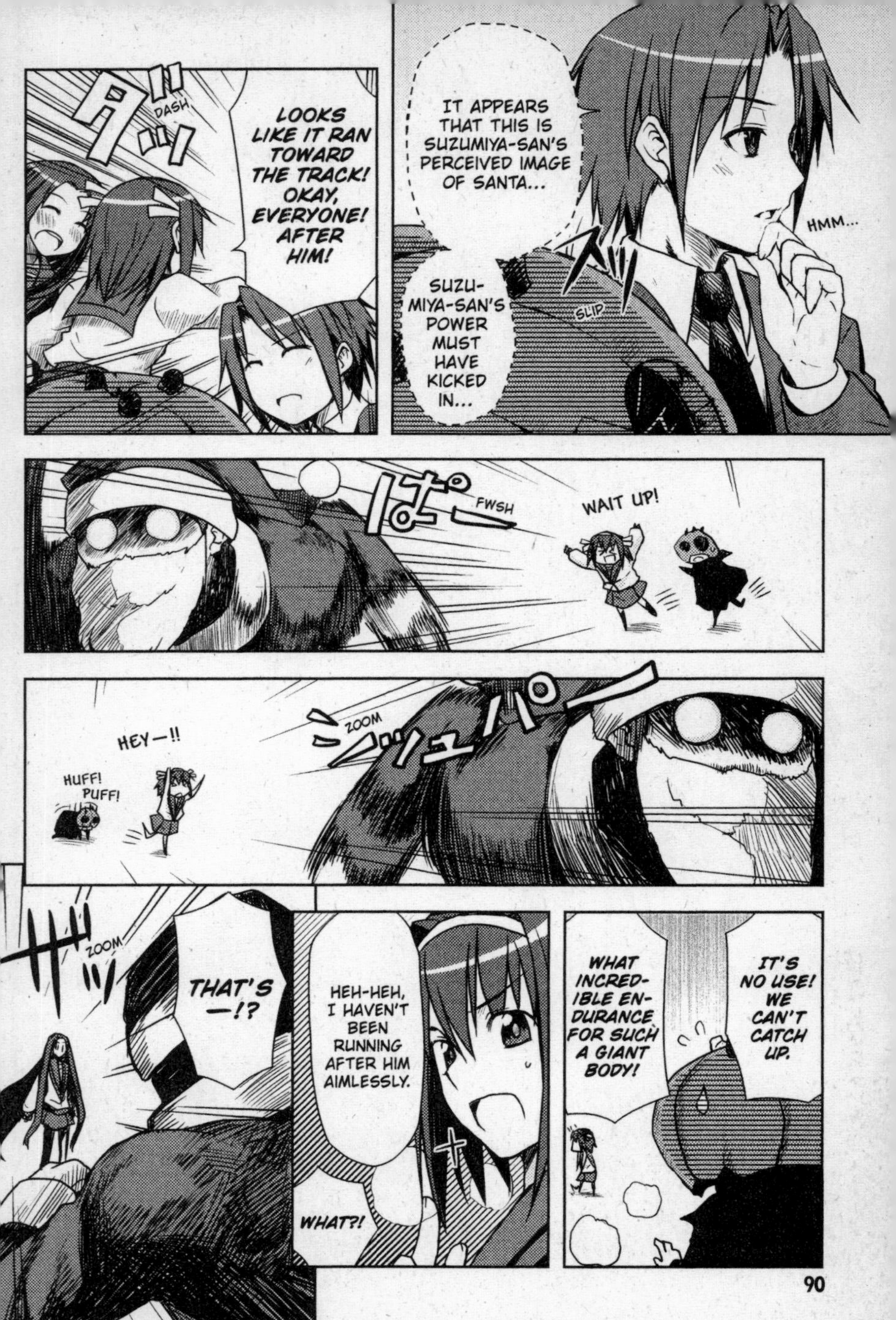
IT APPEARS THAT THIS IS SUZUMIYA-SAN'S PERCEIVED IMAGE OF SANTA...
HMM...
SLIP
SUZUMIYA-SAN'S POWER MUST HAVE KICKED IN...
DASH
LOOKS LIKE IT RAN TOWARD THE TRACK! OKAY, EVERYONE! AFTER HIM!
FWSH
WAIT UP!
ZOOM
HEY—!!
HUFF! PUFF!
IT'S NO USE! WE CAN'T CATCH UP.
WHAT INCREDIBLE ENDURANCE FOR SUCH A GIANT BODY!
HEH-HEH, I HAVEN'T BEEN RUNNING AFTER HIM AIMLESSLY.
WHAT?!
ZOOM
THAT'S—!?

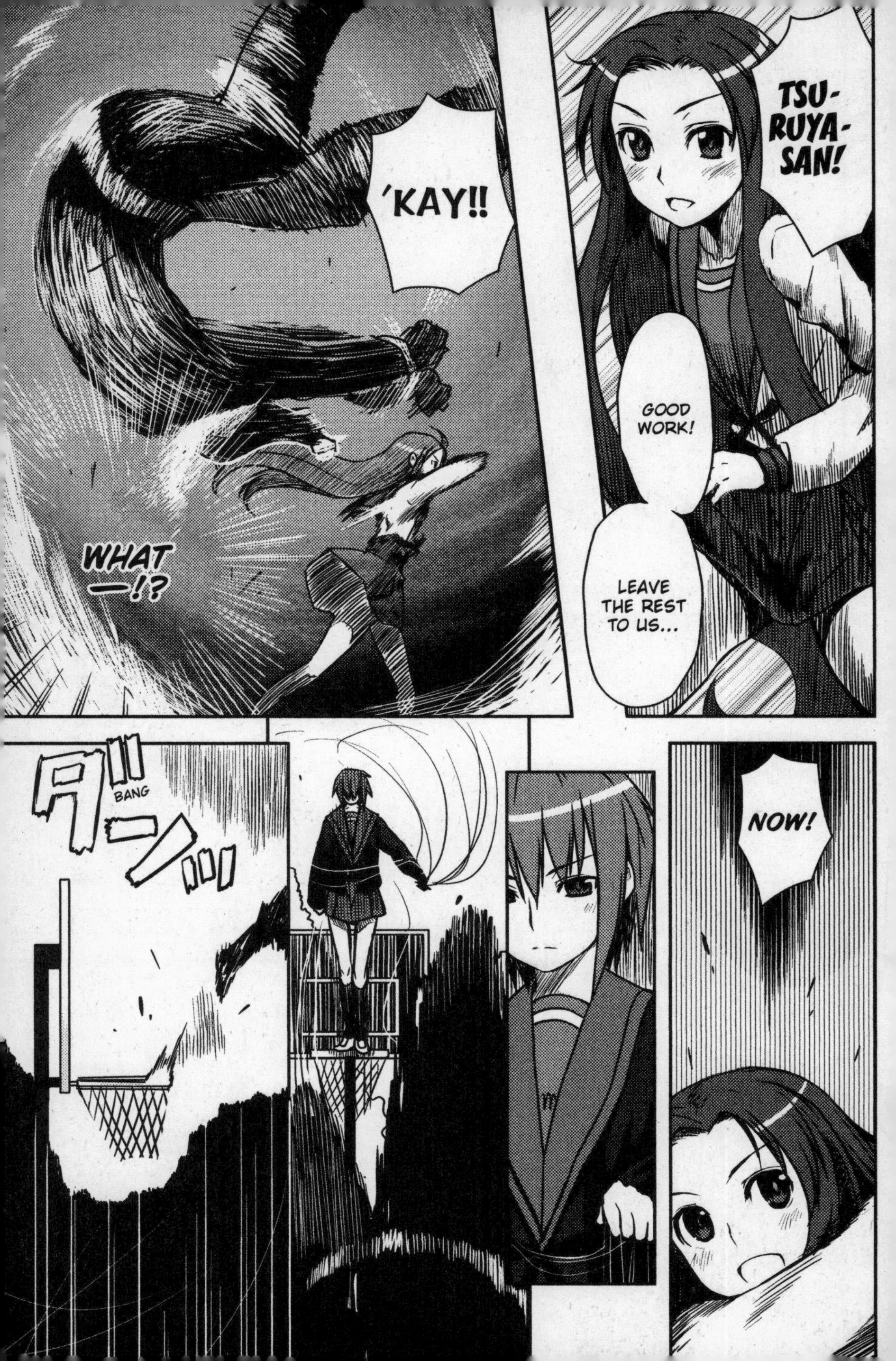
TSU-
RUYA-
SAN!
GOOD WORK!
LEAVE THE REST TO US...
'KAY!!
WHAT—!?
NOW!
ダーン
BANG

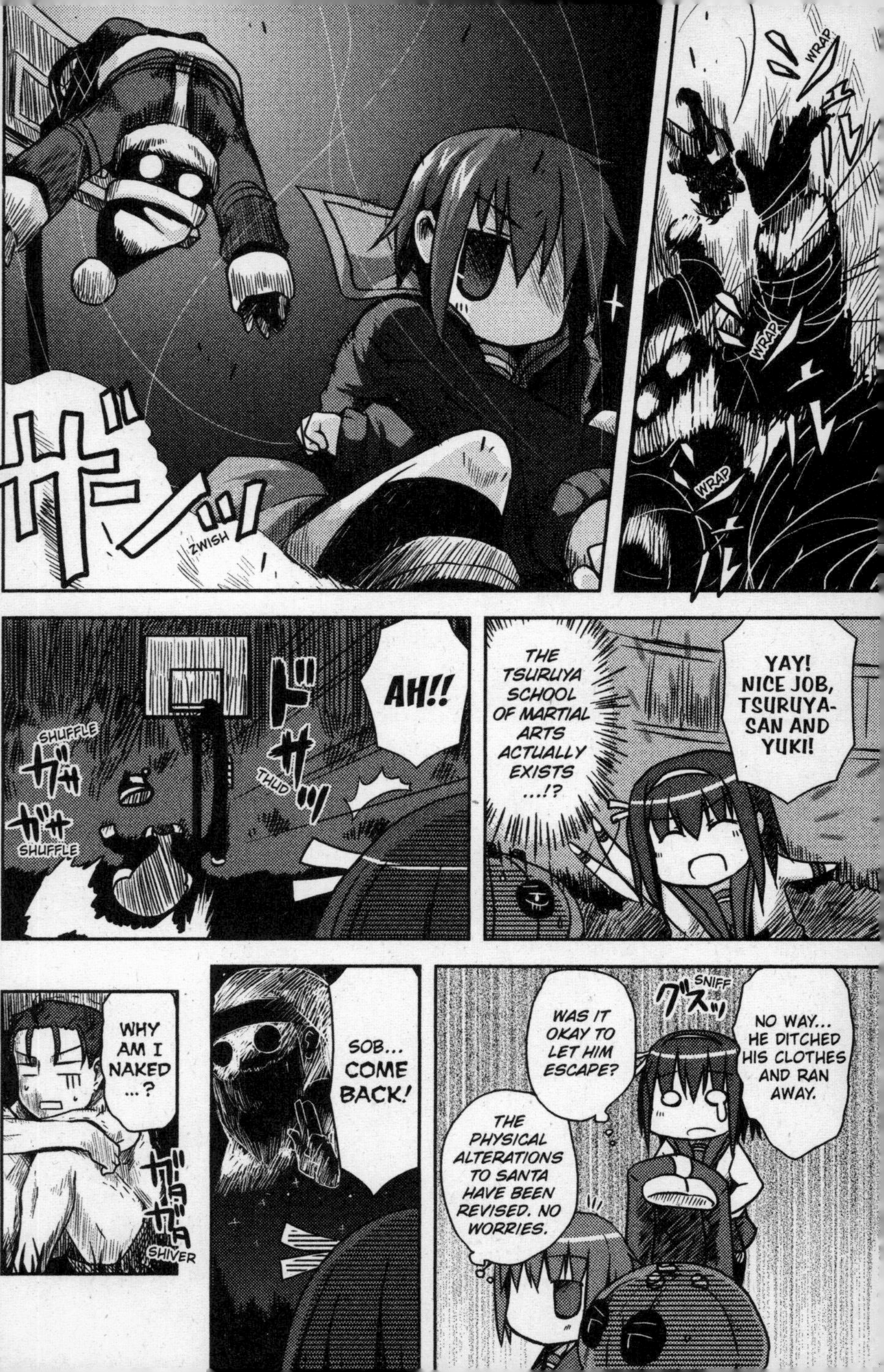
WRAP
WRAP
WRAP
ZWISH
YAY! NICE JOB, TSURUYA-SAN AND YUKI!
THE TSURUYA SCHOOL OF MARTIAL ARTS ACTUALLY EXISTS ...!?
AH!!
THUD
SHUFFLE
SHUFFLE
SNIFF
NO WAY... HE DITCHED HIS CLOTHES AND RAN AWAY.
WAS IT OKAY TO LET HIM ESCAPE?
THE PHYSICAL ALTERATIONS TO SANTA HAVE BEEN REVISED. NO WORRIES.
SOB... COME BACK!
WHY AM I NAKED ...?
SHIVER

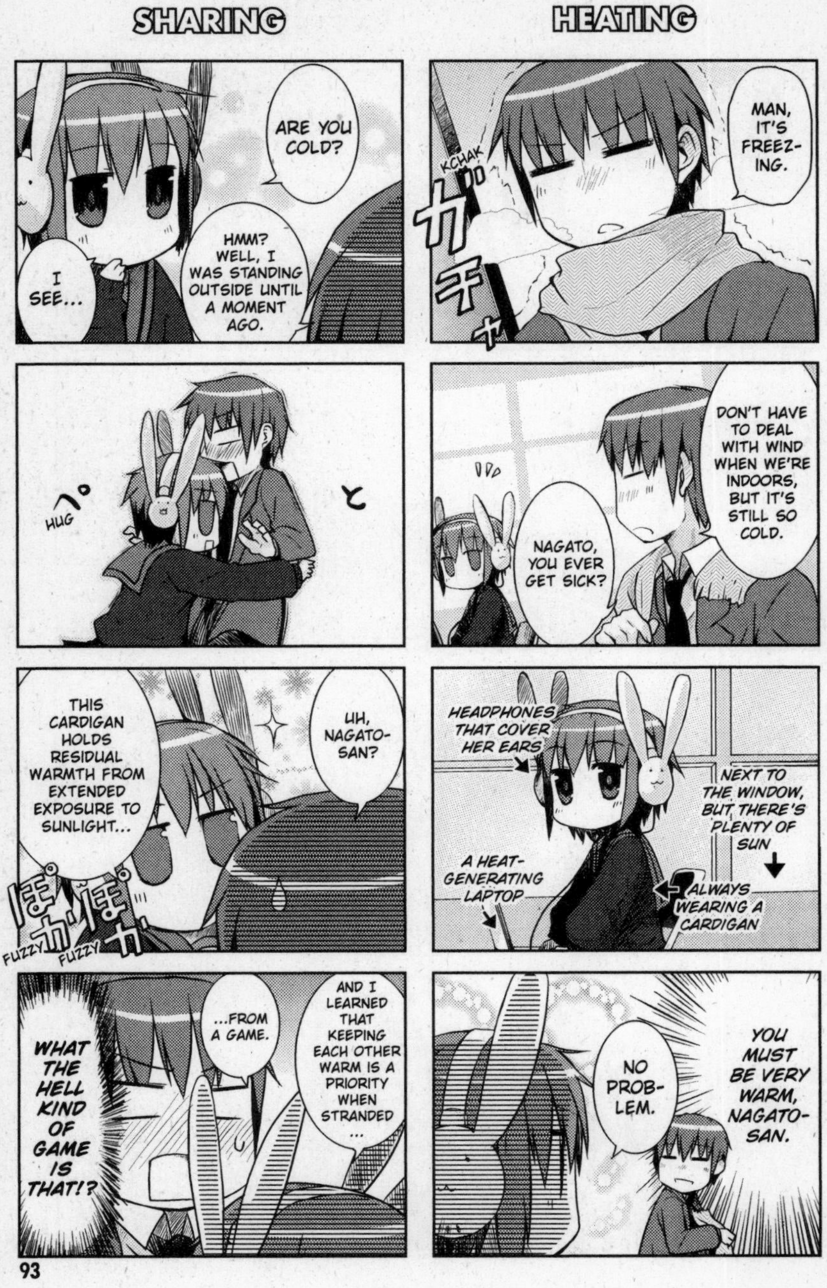
HEATING
KCHAK
カチャ
MAN, IT'S FREEZ-ING.
DON'T HAVE TO DEAL WITH WIND WHEN WE'RE INDOORS, BUT IT'S STILL SO COLD.
NAGATO, YOU EVER GET SICK?
HEADPHONES THAT COVER HER EARS
NEXT TO THE WINDOW, BUT THERE'S PLENTY OF SUN
A HEAT-GENERATING LAPTOP
ALWAYS WEARING A CARDIGAN
YOU MUST BE VERY WARM, NAGATO-SAN.
NO PROB-LEM.
SHARING
ARE YOU COLD?
HMM? WELL, I WAS STANDING OUTSIDE UNTIL A MOMENT AGO.
I SEE...
ぺと
HUG
UH, NAGATO-SAN?
THIS CARDIGAN HOLDS RESIDUAL WARMTH FROM EXTENDED EXPOSURE TO SUNLIGHT...
ぽかぽか
FUZZY FUZZY
AND I LEARNED THAT KEEPING EACH OTHER WARM IS A PRIORITY WHEN STRANDED...
...FROM A GAME.
WHAT THE HELL KIND OF GAME IS THAT!?

ONE APOLOGY AFTER ANOTHER

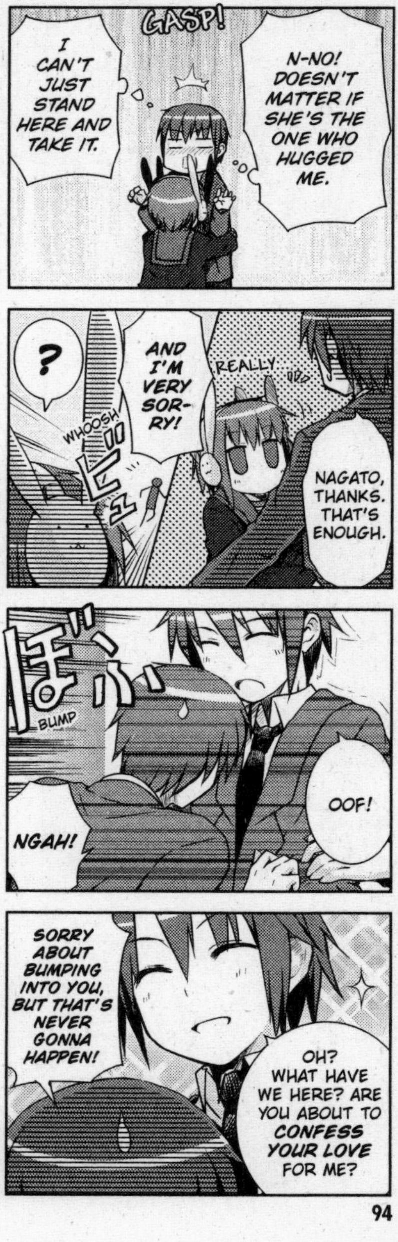
GASP!
N-NO! DOESN'T MATTER IF SHE'S THE ONE WHO HUGGED ME.
I CAN'T JUST STAND HERE AND TAKE IT.
NAGATO, THANKS. THAT'S ENOUGH.
REALLY
AND I'M VERY SORRY!
?
WHOOSH
OOF!
BUMP
NGAH!
OH? WHAT HAVE WE HERE? ARE YOU ABOUT TO CONFESS YOUR LOVE FOR ME?
SORRY ABOUT BUMPING INTO YOU, BUT THAT'S NEVER GONNA HAPPEN!

IN MODERATION

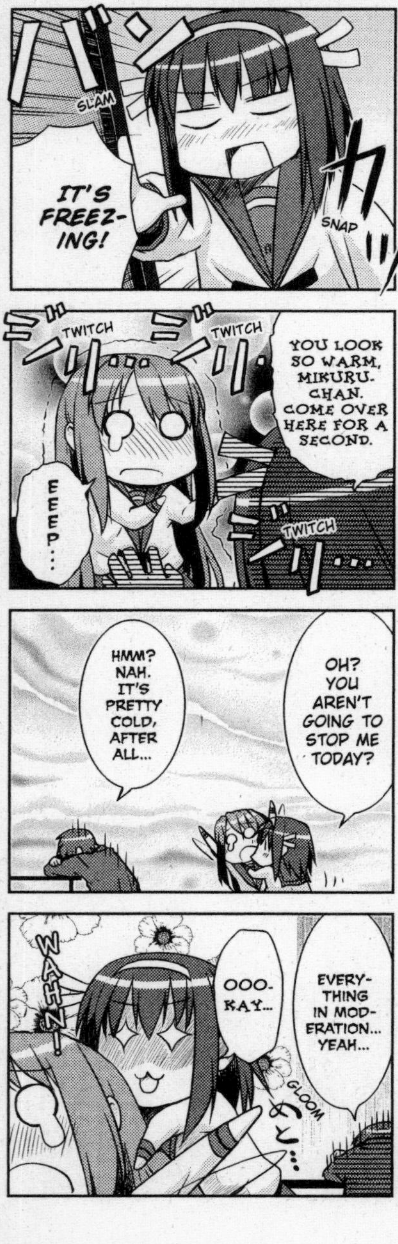
SLAM
SNAP
IT'S FREEZING!
YOU LOOK SO WARM, MIKURU-CHAN. COME OVER HERE FOR A SECOND.
TWITCH
TWITCH
EEEP...
TWITCH
OH? YOU AREN'T GOING TO STOP ME TODAY?
HMM? NAH. IT'S PRETTY COLD, AFTER ALL...
EVERYTHING IN MODERATION... YEAH...
OOO-KAY...
WAHN!
GLOOM

STAND

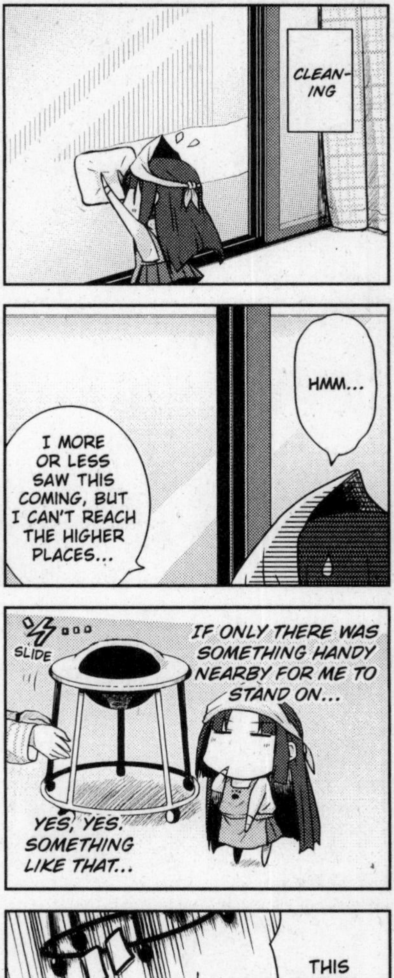
CLEAN-
ING
HMM...
I MORE OR LESS SAW THIS COMING, BUT I CAN'T REACH THE HIGHER PLACES...
IF ONLY THERE WAS SOMETHING HANDY NEARBY FOR ME TO STAND ON...
SLIDE
YES, YES. SOMETHING LIKE THAT...
THIS IS A BABY WALKER!
CRASH
OOH.

IN THE END

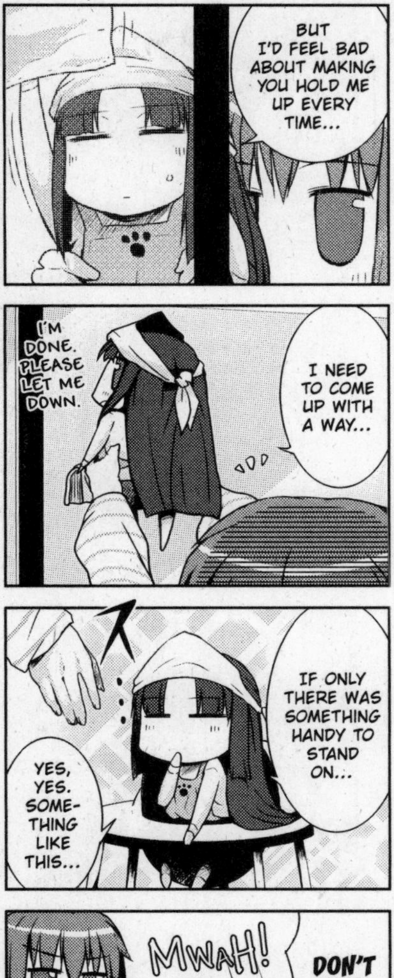
BUT I'D FEEL BAD ABOUT MAKING YOU HOLD ME UP EVERY TIME...
I NEED TO COME UP WITH A WAY...
I'M DONE. PLEASE LET ME DOWN.
IF ONLY THERE WAS SOMETHING HANDY TO STAND ON...
YES, YES. SOMETHING LIKE THIS...
DON'T PUT ME IN HERE—!
MWAH!
OOH.

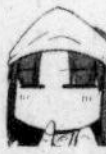

•Achakura-san •Back in miniature action after being destroyed in her battle with Nagato. Currently crashing at Nagato's place.

PRIDE

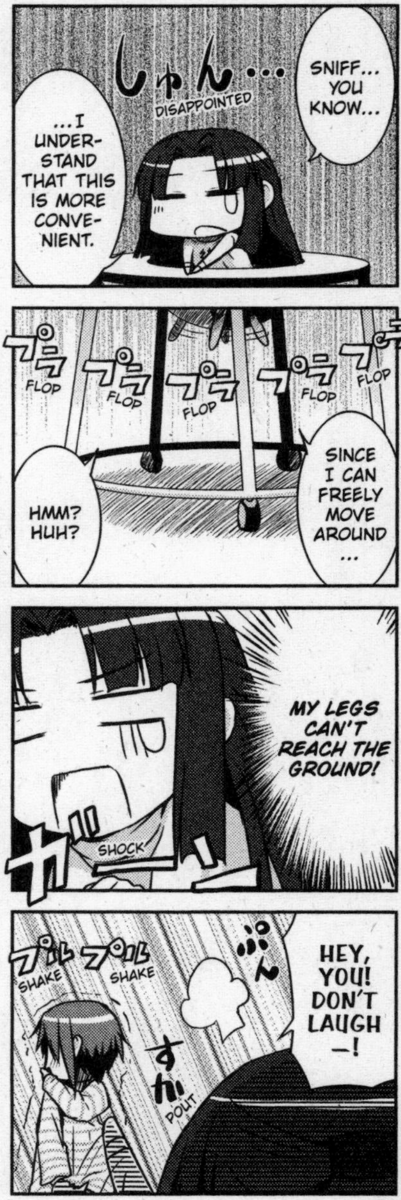
SNIFF... YOU KNOW...
しゅん…
DISAPPOINTED
...I UNDERSTAND THAT THIS IS MORE CONVENIENT.
FLOP
FLOP
FLOP
FLOP
FLOP
SINCE I CAN FREELY MOVE AROUND...
HMM? HUH?
MY LEGS CAN'T REACH THE GROUND!
SHOCK
HEY, YOU! DON'T LAUGH—!
SHAKE
SHAKE
POUT

CRISIS AVERTED

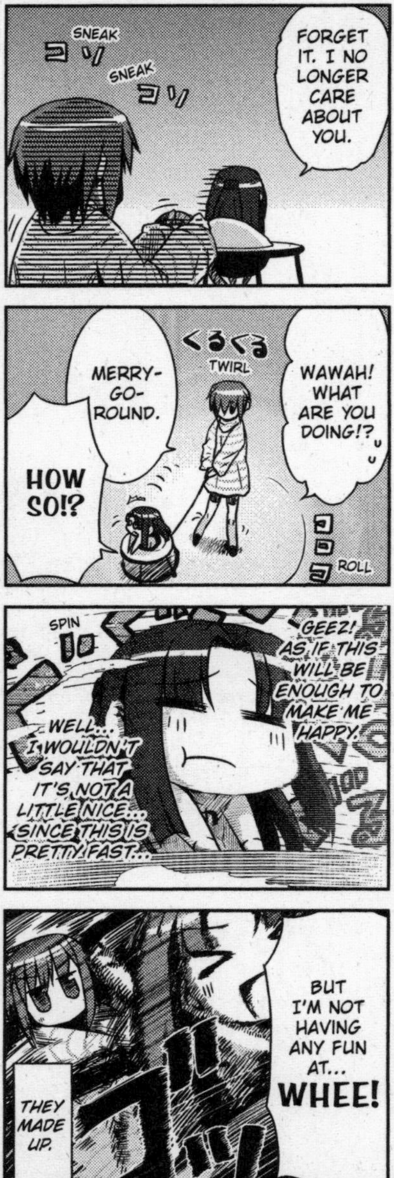
FORGET IT. I NO LONGER CARE ABOUT YOU.
SNEAK
SNEAK
WAWAH! WHAT ARE YOU DOING!?
ROLL
くるくる
TWIRL
MERRY-GO-ROUND.
HOW SO!?
GEEZ! AS IF THIS WILL BE ENOUGH TO MAKE ME HAPPY.
SPIN
WELL... I WOULDN'T SAY THAT IT'S NOT A LITTLE NICE... SINCE THIS IS PRETTY FAST...
BUT I'M NOT HAVING ANY FUN AT... WHEE!
THEY MADE UP.
FWOOM

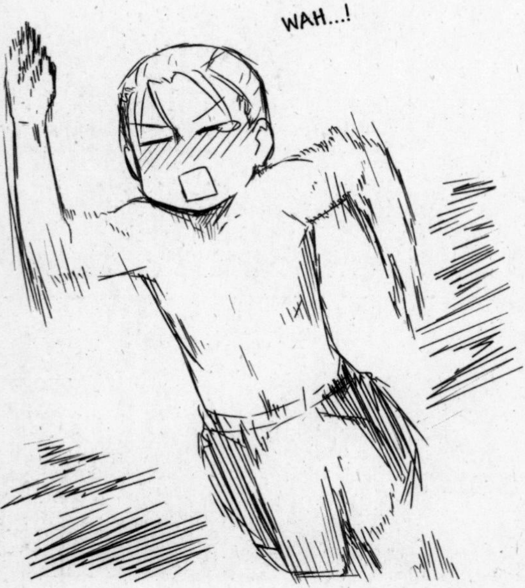
WAH...!

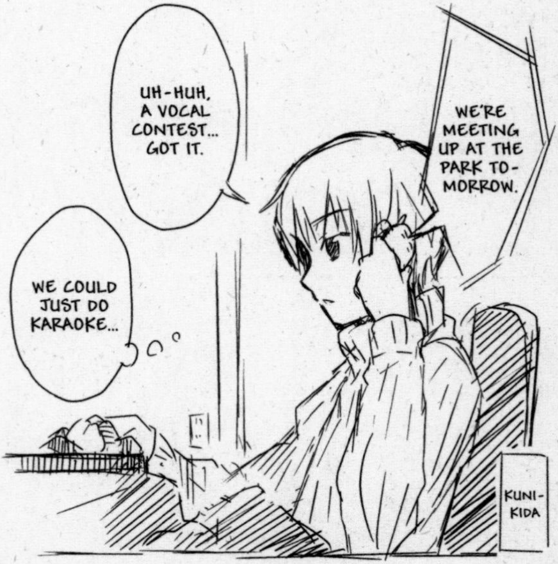
WE'RE MEETING UP AT THE PARK TO-MORROW.
UH-HUH, A VOCAL CONTEST... GOT IT.
WE COULD JUST DO KARAOKE...
KUNI-KIDA

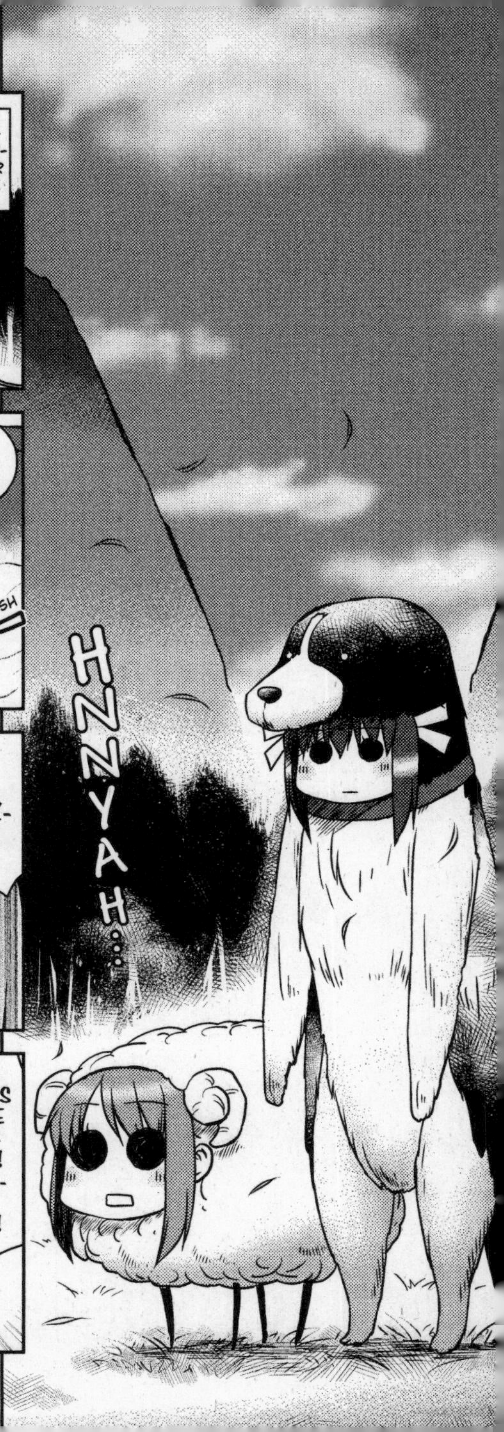
HNNYAH...

IN THE PARK

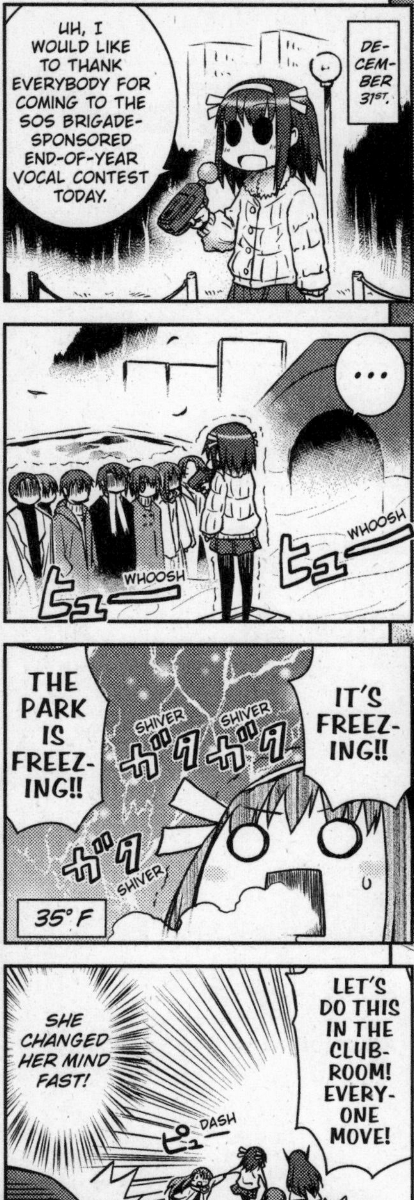
DECEMBER 31ST.
UH, I WOULD LIKE TO THANK EVERYBODY FOR COMING TO THE SOS BRIGADE-SPONSORED END-OF-YEAR VOCAL CONTEST TODAY.
...
ヒュー WHOOSH
ヒュー WHOOSH
IT'S FREEZING!!
THE PARK IS FREEZING!!
ガタガタ SHIVER SHIVER
ガタ SHIVER
35° F
LET'S DO THIS IN THE CLUBROOM! EVERYONE MOVE!
SHE CHANGED HER MIND FAST!
ピュ DASH

BEFORE THE SCHOOL GATE

ヒュー
WHOOSH
CLOSED UNTIL NEXT YEAR -NORTH HIGH
DON'T UNDERESTIMATE THE MODERN YOUTH'S DEPENDENCE ON CENTRAL HEATING!
A BAT THAT COULD EASILY SMASH A WINDOW
SHIVER ガタガタ
STOP IT! AND THAT ISN'T SOMETHING TO BRAG ABOUT!
KYON, DON'T TRY TO STOP ME!
YOU BET I'M GONNA STOP YOU!
...SAY.
HMM—?
ヒュー
WHOOSH
COULDN'T WE JUST GO TO A KARAOKE PLACE?
WHAT A COINCIDENCE. I'VE BEEN THINKING THE SAME THING. SINCE YESTER-DAY.

SNEEZE

WELP, THIS MIGHT TAKE A WHILE.
ACHOO!
GYAH!
GRR!
MIKURU, YOU LOOK LIKE YOU'RE ABOUT TO CATCH A COLD.
ID'Z COLD...
ズズズ SNIFF
HERE, MIKURU. YOUR NOSE IS RUNNING.
SNUFFLE ズペー
FANKS!
HMM. MIKURU, YOU'RE SO CUTE... MIND IF I FONDLE YOU A BIT?
FON... WHAT ARE YOU GOING TO DO!?
MEEP!

•Haruhi-chan •SOS Brigade brigade chief. Fired up about all of the New Year's activities.

•Kyon •Supposed to be the main character in this story. His ripostes will save the world.

•Mikuru-chan •Actually from the future. Seems to have trouble with cold weather as her nose won't stop running.

•Infinity Lion •Space creature that Mikuru-chan keeps as a pet. Also serves as a scarf.

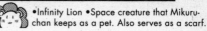

KARAOKE

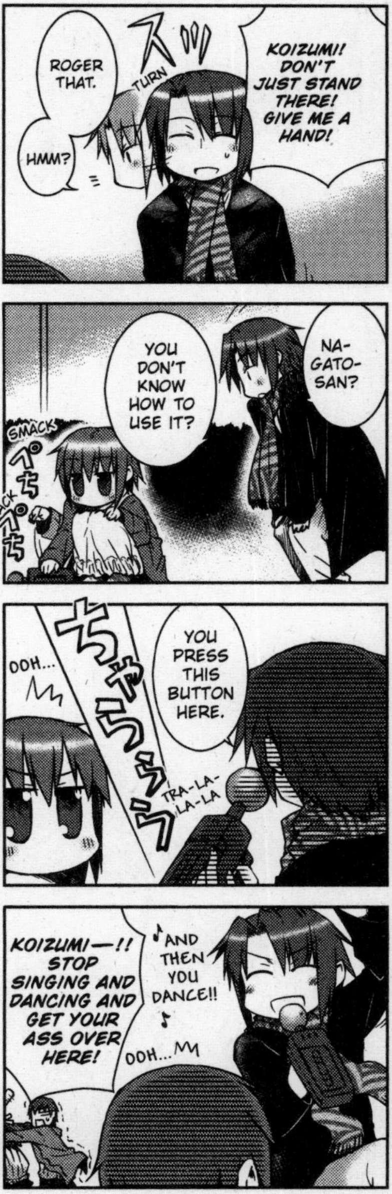
KOIZUMI! DON'T JUST STAND THERE! GIVE ME A HAND!
TURN
ROGER THAT.
HMM?
NA-GATO-SAN?
YOU DON'T KNOW HOW TO USE IT?
SMACK
SMACK
YOU PRESS THIS BUTTON HERE.
TRA-LA-LA-LA
OOH...
AND THEN YOU DANCE!!
KOIZUMI—!! STOP SINGING AND DANCING AND GET YOUR ASS OVER HERE!
OOH...

QUESTION

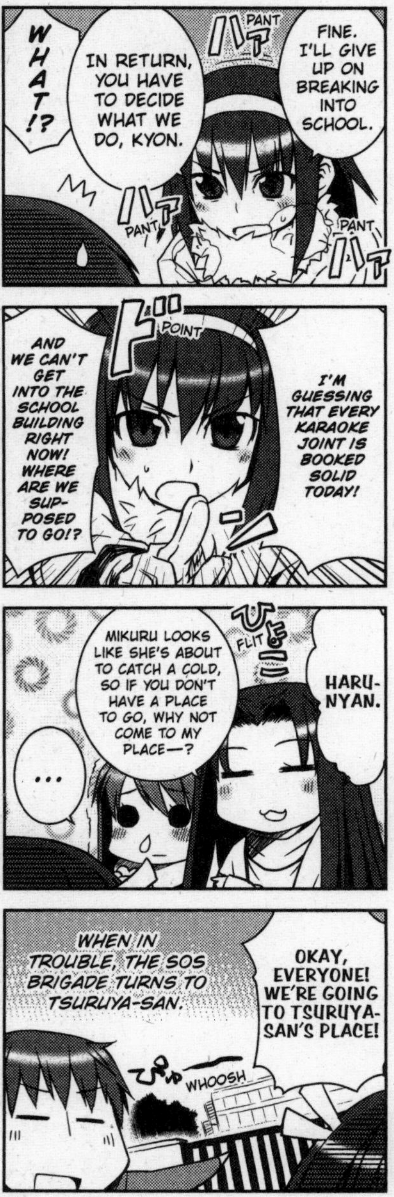
FINE. I'LL GIVE UP ON BREAKING INTO SCHOOL.
PANT
IN RETURN, YOU HAVE TO DECIDE WHAT WE DO, KYON.
WHAT!?
PANT
PANT
I'M GUESSING THAT EVERY KARAOKE JOINT IS BOOKED SOLID TODAY!
POINT
AND WE CAN'T GET INTO THE SCHOOL BUILDING RIGHT NOW! WHERE ARE WE SUPPOSED TO GO!?
HARU-NYAN.
FLIT
MIKURU LOOKS LIKE SHE'S ABOUT TO CATCH A COLD, SO IF YOU DON'T HAVE A PLACE TO GO, WHY NOT COME TO MY PLACE—?
...
OKAY, EVERYONE! WE'RE GOING TO TSURUYA-SAN'S PLACE!
WHEN IN TROUBLE, THE SOS BRIGADE TURNS TO TSURUYA-SAN.
WHOOSH

•Koizumi •An enigmatic transfer student who happens to be a singing and dancing esper. Can't stand his guts.

•Nagato •Actually an alien gamer. Fascinated by karaoke machines.

•Tsuruya-san •Mikuru-chan's buddy. She's rich and lives in a big house.

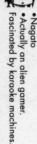

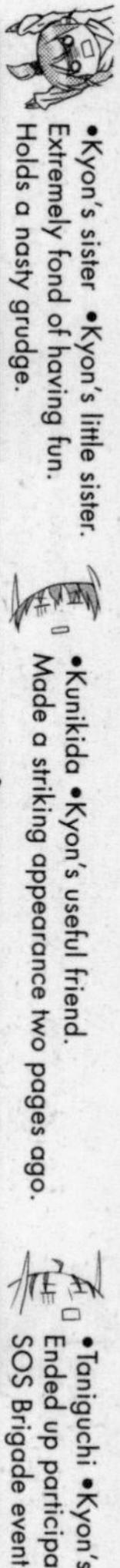
•Kyon's sister •Kyon's little sister. Extremely fond of having fun. Holds a nasty grudge.
•Kunikida •Kyon's useful friend. Made a striking appearance two pages ago.
•Taniguchi •Kyon's useless friend. Ended up participating in another SOS Brigade event.

GRUDGE

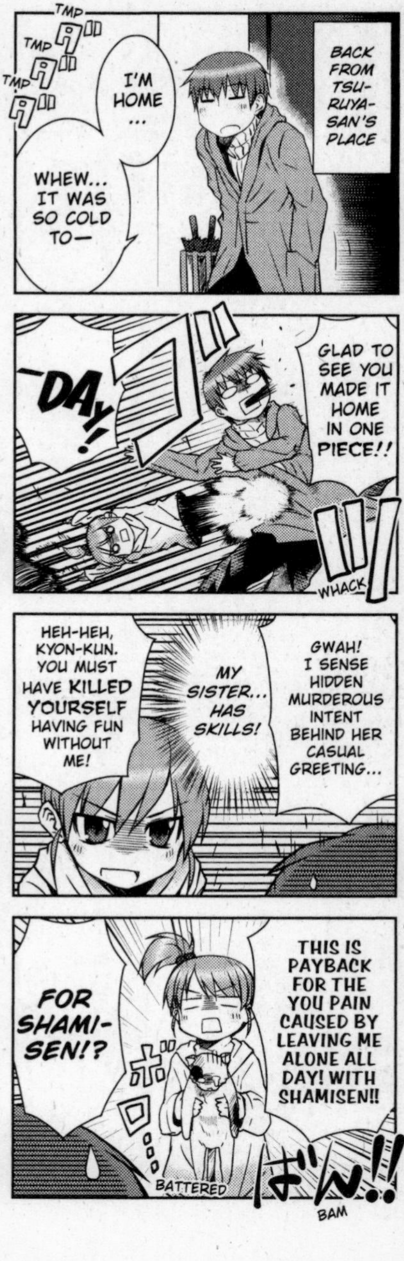
BACK FROM TSURUYA-SAN'S PLACE
TMP TMP TMP
I'M HOME...
WHEW... IT WAS SO COLD TO—
GLAD TO SEE YOU MADE IT HOME IN ONE PIECE!!
-DAY!
WHACK
GWAH! I SENSE HIDDEN MURDEROUS INTENT BEHIND HER CASUAL GREETING...
MY SISTER... HAS SKILLS!
HEH-HEH, KYON-KUN. YOU MUST HAVE KILLED YOURSELF HAVING FUN WITHOUT ME!
THIS IS PAYBACK FOR THE YOU PAIN CAUSED BY LEAVING ME ALONE ALL DAY! WITH SHAMISEN!!
FOR SHAMI-SEN!?
BATTERED
BAM

SHEEP

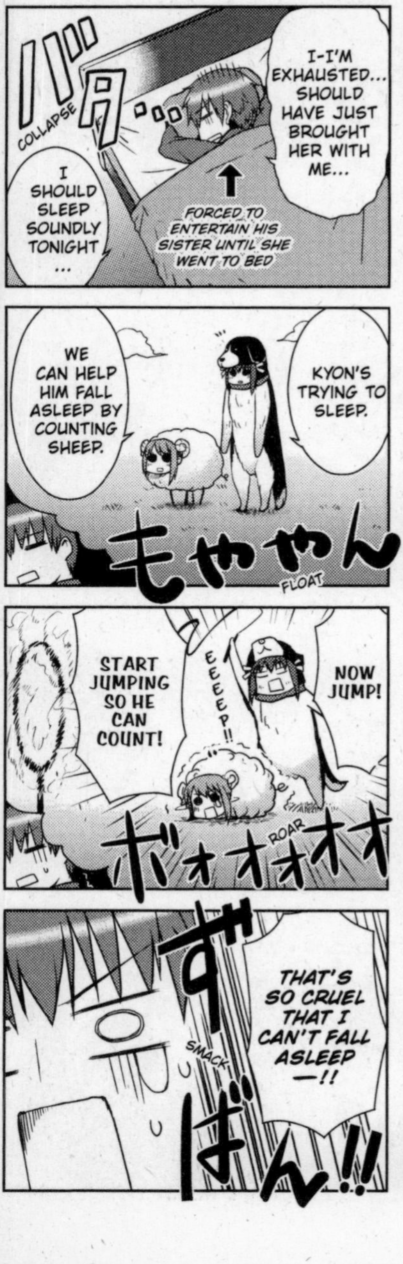
I-I'M EXHAUSTED... SHOULD HAVE JUST BROUGHT HER WITH ME...
COLLAPSE
FORCED TO ENTERTAIN HIS SISTER UNTIL SHE WENT TO BED
I SHOULD SLEEP SOUNDLY TONIGHT...
KYON'S TRYING TO SLEEP.
WE CAN HELP HIM FALL ASLEEP BY COUNTING SHEEP.
FLOAT
NOW JUMP!
EEEEP!!
START JUMPING SO HE CAN COUNT!
ROAR
THAT'S SO CRUEL THAT I CAN'T FALL ASLEEP—!!
SMACK

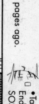

KYON'S FIRST DREAM OF THE YEAR

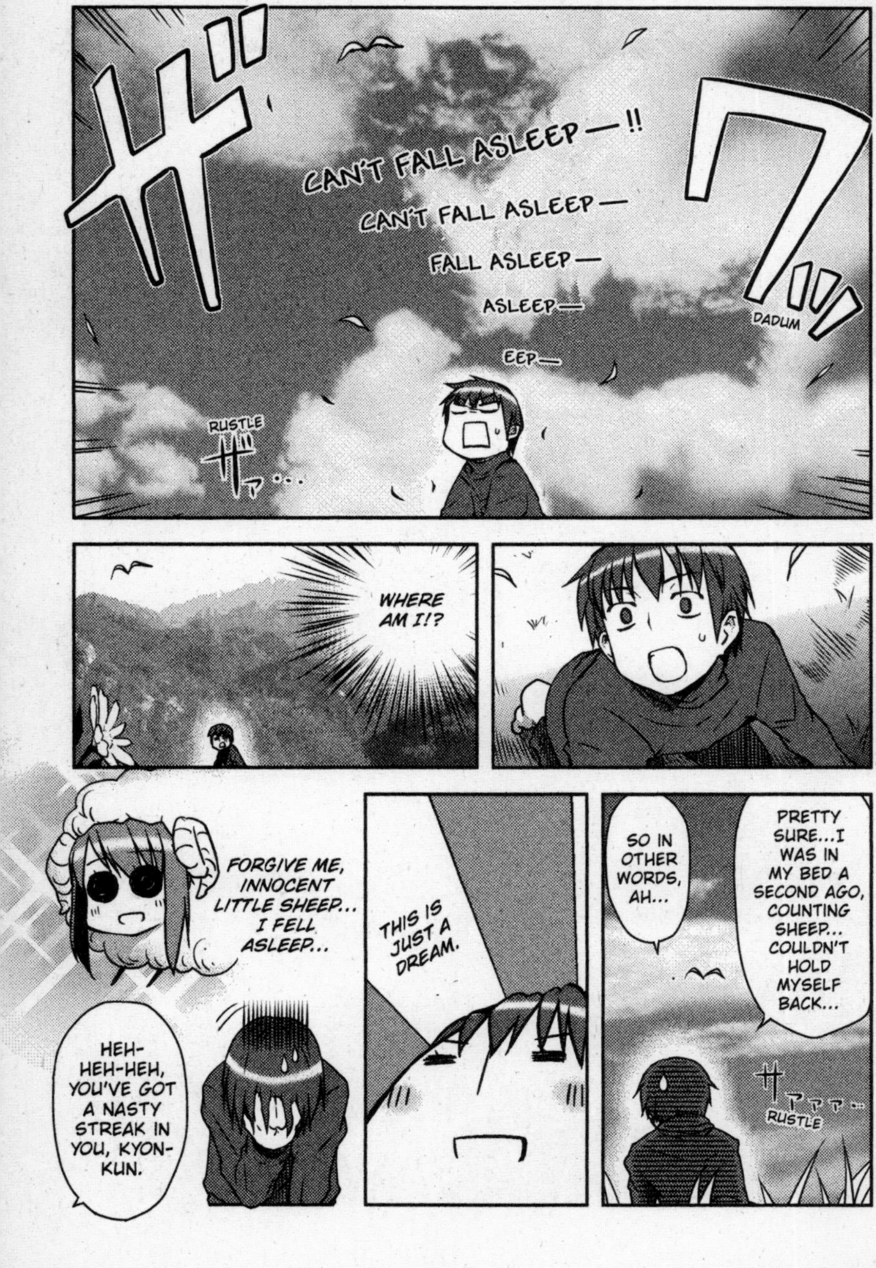
DADUM
CAN'T FALL ASLEEP—!!
CAN'T FALL ASLEEP—
FALL ASLEEP—
ASLEEP—
EEP—
RUSTLE
WHERE AM I!?
PRETTY SURE...I WAS IN MY BED A SECOND AGO, COUNTING SHEEP... COULDN'T HOLD MYSELF BACK...
SO IN OTHER WORDS, AH...
RUSTLE
THIS IS JUST A DREAM.
FORGIVE ME, INNOCENT LITTLE SHEEP... I FELL ASLEEP...
HEH-HEH-HEH, YOU'VE GOT A NASTY STREAK IN YOU, KYON-KUN.

•Fujiizumi •Lucky omen.
Able to move around by hovering.

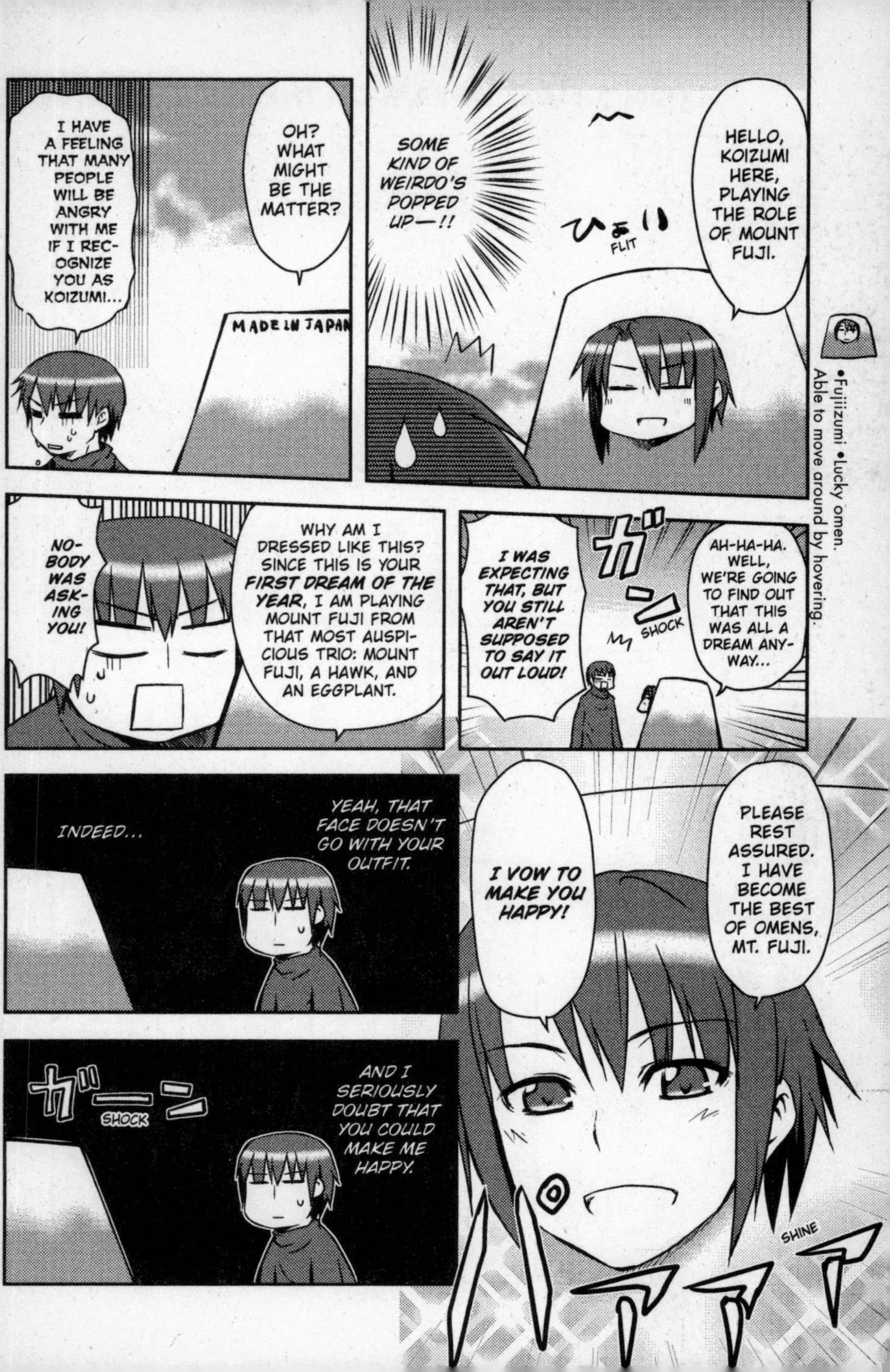
HELLO, KOIZUMI HERE, PLAYING THE ROLE OF MOUNT FUJI.
FLIT
SOME KIND OF WEIRDO'S POPPED UP—!!
MADE IN JAPAN
OH? WHAT MIGHT BE THE MATTER?
I HAVE A FEELING THAT MANY PEOPLE WILL BE ANGRY WITH ME IF I RECOGNIZE YOU AS KOIZUMI...
AH-HA-HA. WELL, WE'RE GOING TO FIND OUT THAT THIS WAS ALL A DREAM ANYWAY...
SHOCK
I WAS EXPECTING THAT, BUT YOU STILL AREN'T SUPPOSED TO SAY IT OUT LOUD!
WHY AM I DRESSED LIKE THIS? SINCE THIS IS YOUR FIRST DREAM OF THE YEAR, I AM PLAYING MOUNT FUJI FROM THAT MOST AUSPICIOUS TRIO: MOUNT FUJI, A HAWK, AND AN EGGPLANT.
NOBODY WAS ASKING YOU!
PLEASE REST ASSURED. I HAVE BECOME THE BEST OF OMENS, MT. FUJI.
I VOW TO MAKE YOU HAPPY!
SHINE
INDEED...
YEAH, THAT FACE DOESN'T GO WITH YOUR OUTFIT.
SHOCK
AND I SERIOUSLY DOUBT THAT YOU COULD MAKE ME HAPPY.

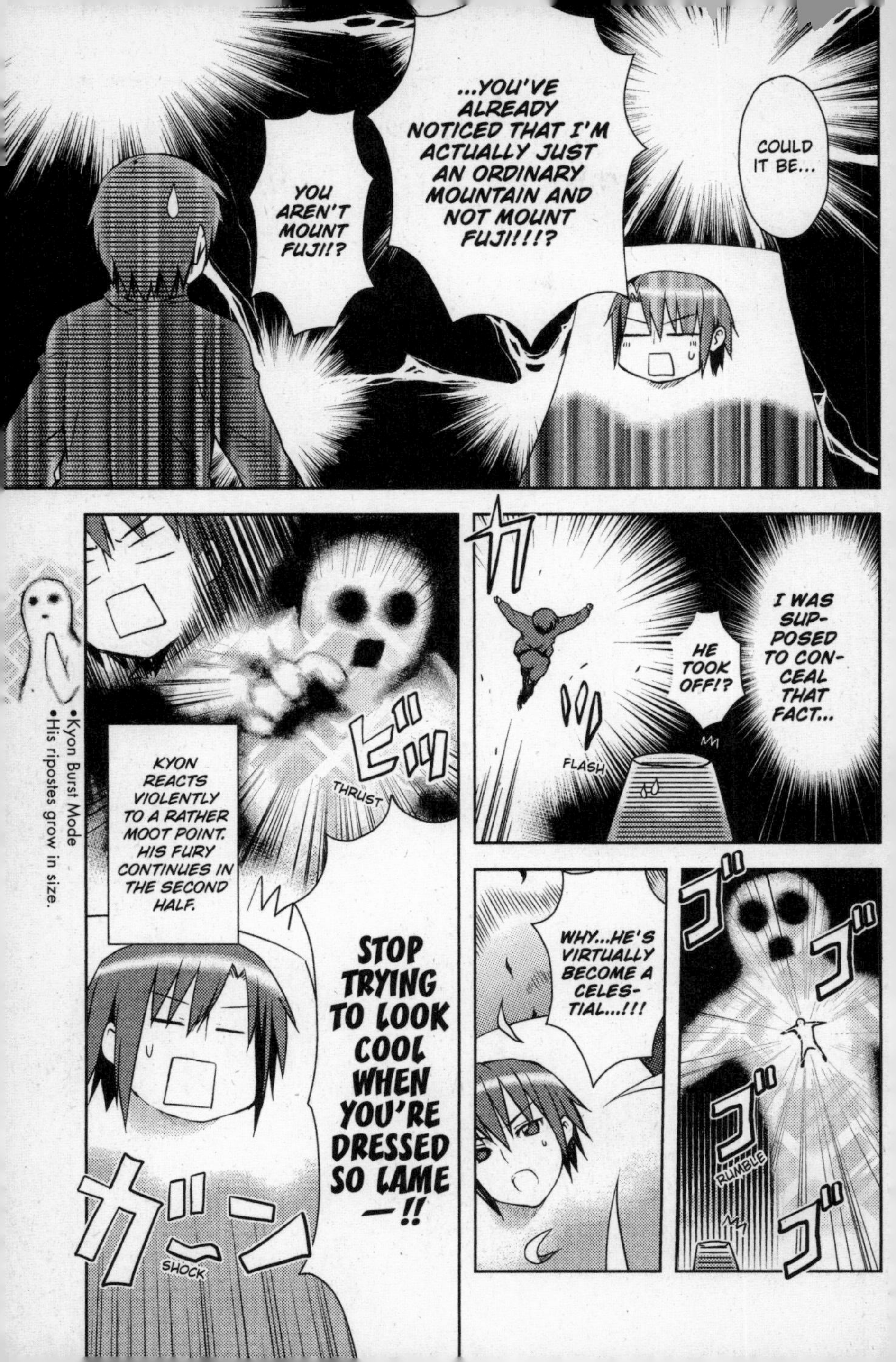
COULD IT BE...
...YOU'VE ALREADY NOTICED THAT I'M ACTUALLY JUST AN ORDINARY MOUNTAIN AND NOT MOUNT FUJI!!!?
YOU AREN'T MOUNT FUJI!?
I WAS SUP-POSED TO CON-CEAL THAT FACT...
HE TOOK OFF!?
FLASH
RUMBLE
WHY...HE'S VIRTUALLY BECOME A CELES-TIAL...!!!
THRUST
KYON REACTS VIOLENTLY TO A RATHER MOOT POINT. HIS FURY CONTINUES IN THE SECOND HALF.
STOP TRYING TO LOOK COOL WHEN YOU'RE DRESSED SO LAME—!!
SHOCK
•Kyon Burst Mode
•His ripostes grow in size.

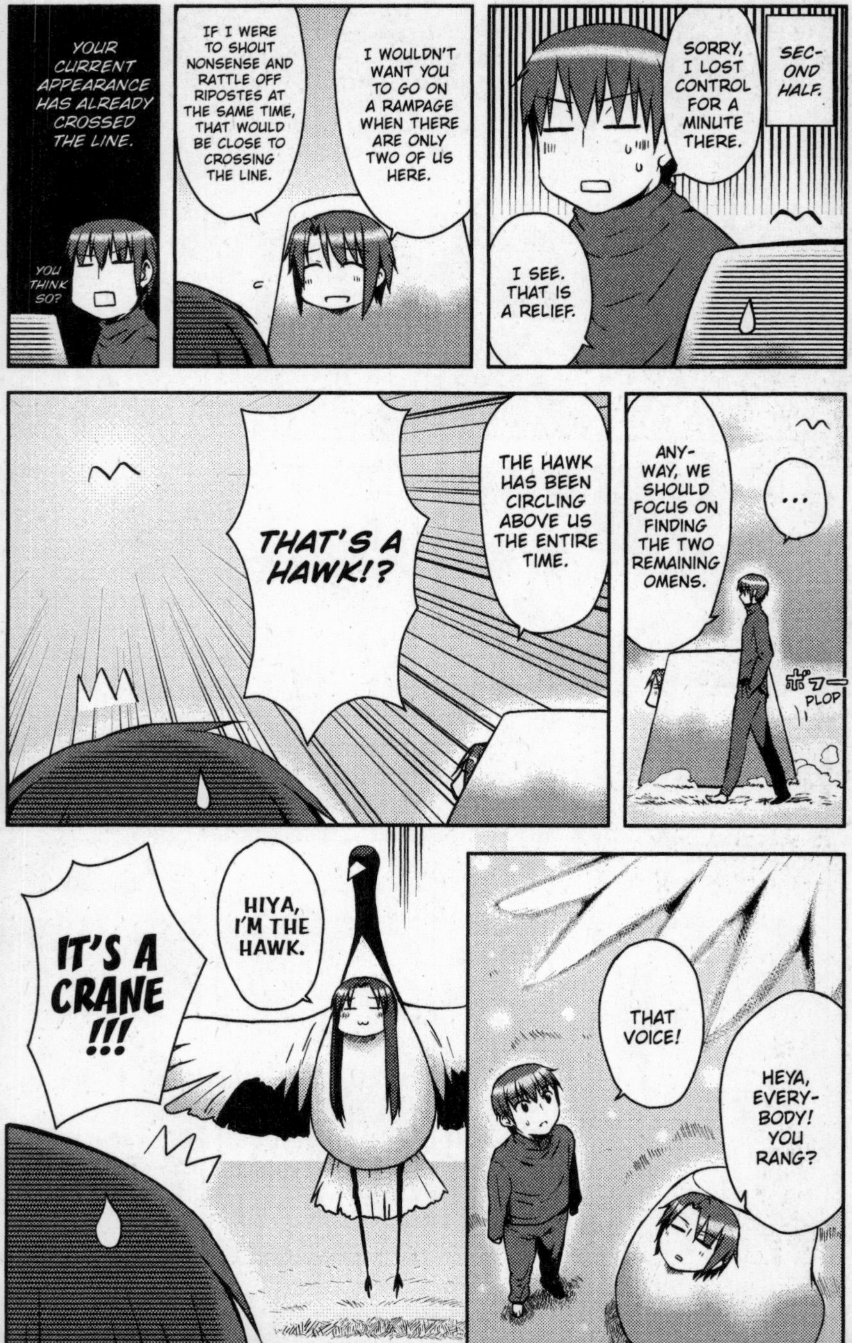
SEC-OND HALF.
SORRY, I LOST CONTROL FOR A MINUTE THERE.
I SEE. THAT IS A RELIEF.
I WOULDN'T WANT YOU TO GO ON A RAMPAGE WHEN THERE ARE ONLY TWO OF US HERE.
IF I WERE TO SHOUT NONSENSE AND RATTLE OFF RIPOSTES AT THE SAME TIME, THAT WOULD BE CLOSE TO CROSSING THE LINE.
YOUR CURRENT APPEARANCE HAS ALREADY CROSSED THE LINE.
YOU THINK SO?
ANY-WAY, WE SHOULD FOCUS ON FINDING THE TWO REMAINING OMENS.
...
ボフー
PLOP
THE HAWK HAS BEEN CIRCLING ABOVE US THE ENTIRE TIME.
THAT'S A HAWK!?
HEYA, EVERY-BODY! YOU RANG?
THAT VOICE!
HIYA, I'M THE HAWK.
IT'S A CRANE!!!

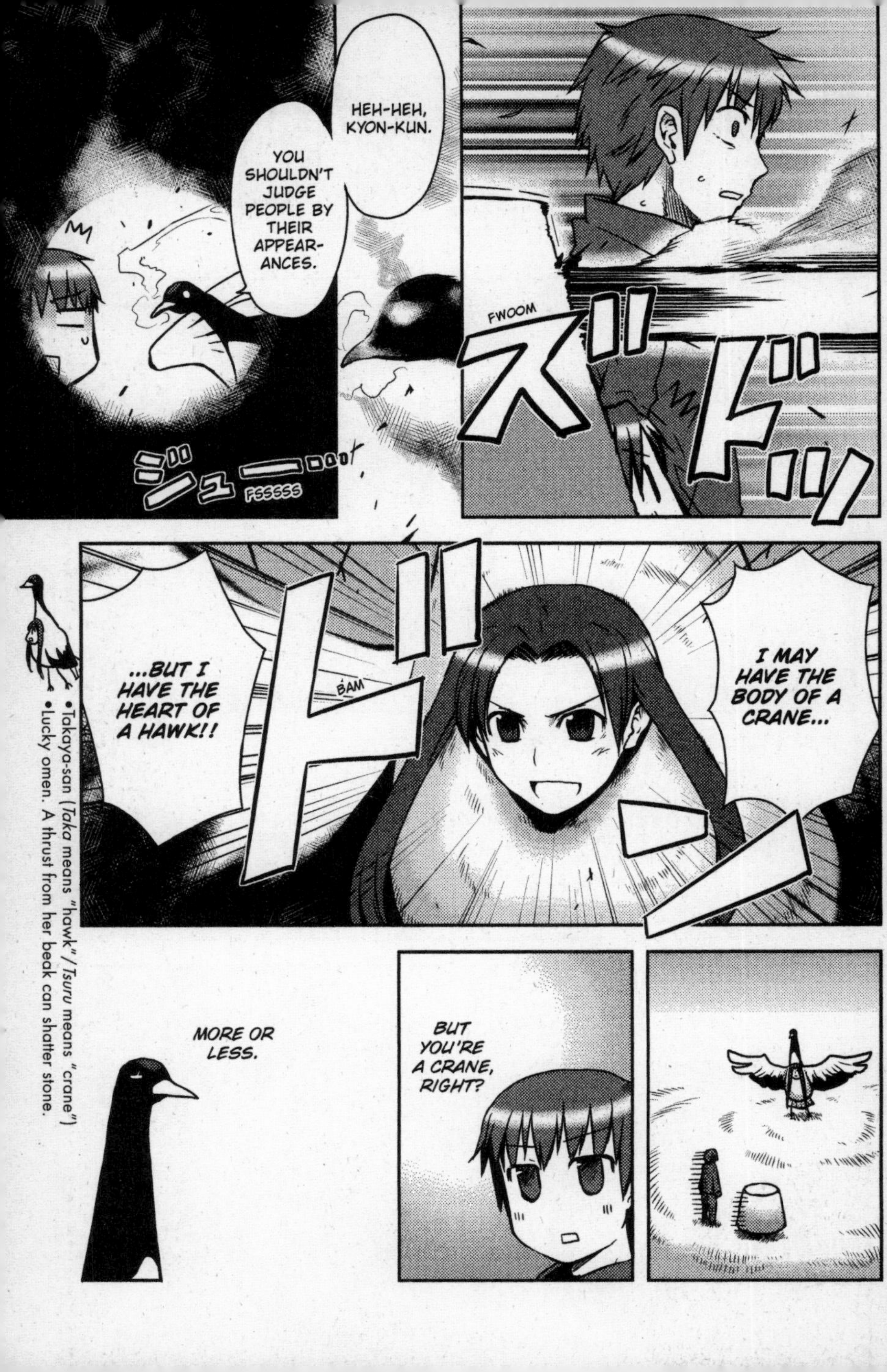
FWOOM
HEH-HEH, KYON-KUN.
YOU SHOULDN'T JUDGE PEOPLE BY THEIR APPEARANCES.
FSSSSS
I MAY HAVE THE BODY OF A CRANE...
BAM
...BUT I HAVE THE HEART OF A HAWK!!
BUT YOU'RE A CRANE, RIGHT?
MORE OR LESS.

•Takaya-san (*Taka* means "hawk"/*Tsuru* means "crane")
•Lucky omen. A thrust from her beak can shatter stone.

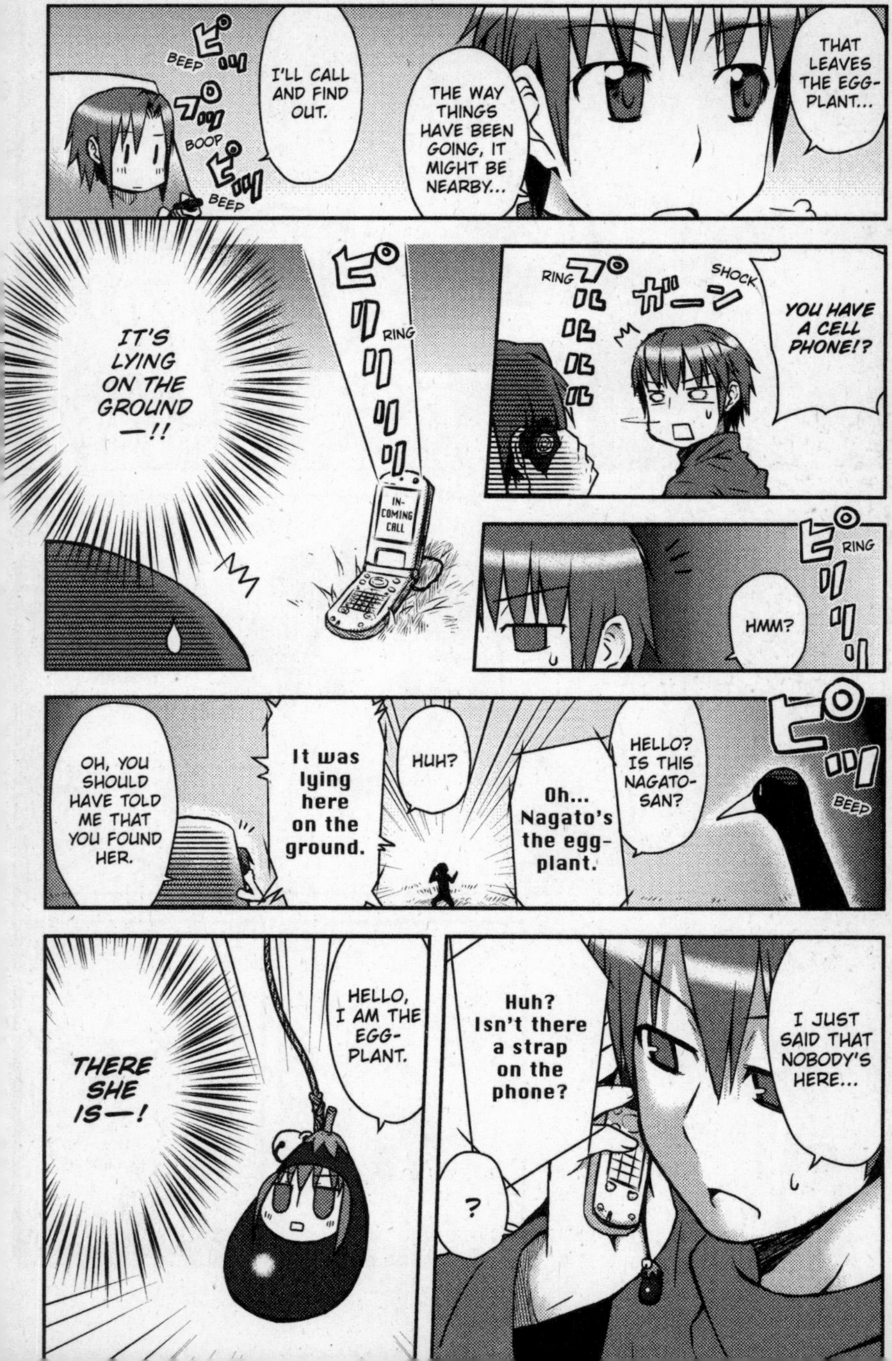
THAT LEAVES THE EGG-PLANT...
THE WAY THINGS HAVE BEEN GOING, IT MIGHT BE NEARBY...
I'LL CALL AND FIND OUT.
ピッ
BEEP
プッ
BOOP
ピッ
BEEP
YOU HAVE A CELL PHONE!?
SHOCK
ガーン
プルルルル
RING
ピッ
RING
HMM?
ピリリリ
RING
IN-COMING CALL
IT'S LYING ON THE GROUND—!!
ピッ
BEEP
HELLO? IS THIS NAGATO-SAN?
Oh... Nagato's the egg-plant.
HUH?
It was lying here on the ground.
OH, YOU SHOULD HAVE TOLD ME THAT YOU FOUND HER.
I JUST SAID THAT NOBODY'S HERE...
Huh? Isn't there a strap on the phone?
?
HELLO, I AM THE EGG-PLANT.
THERE SHE IS—!

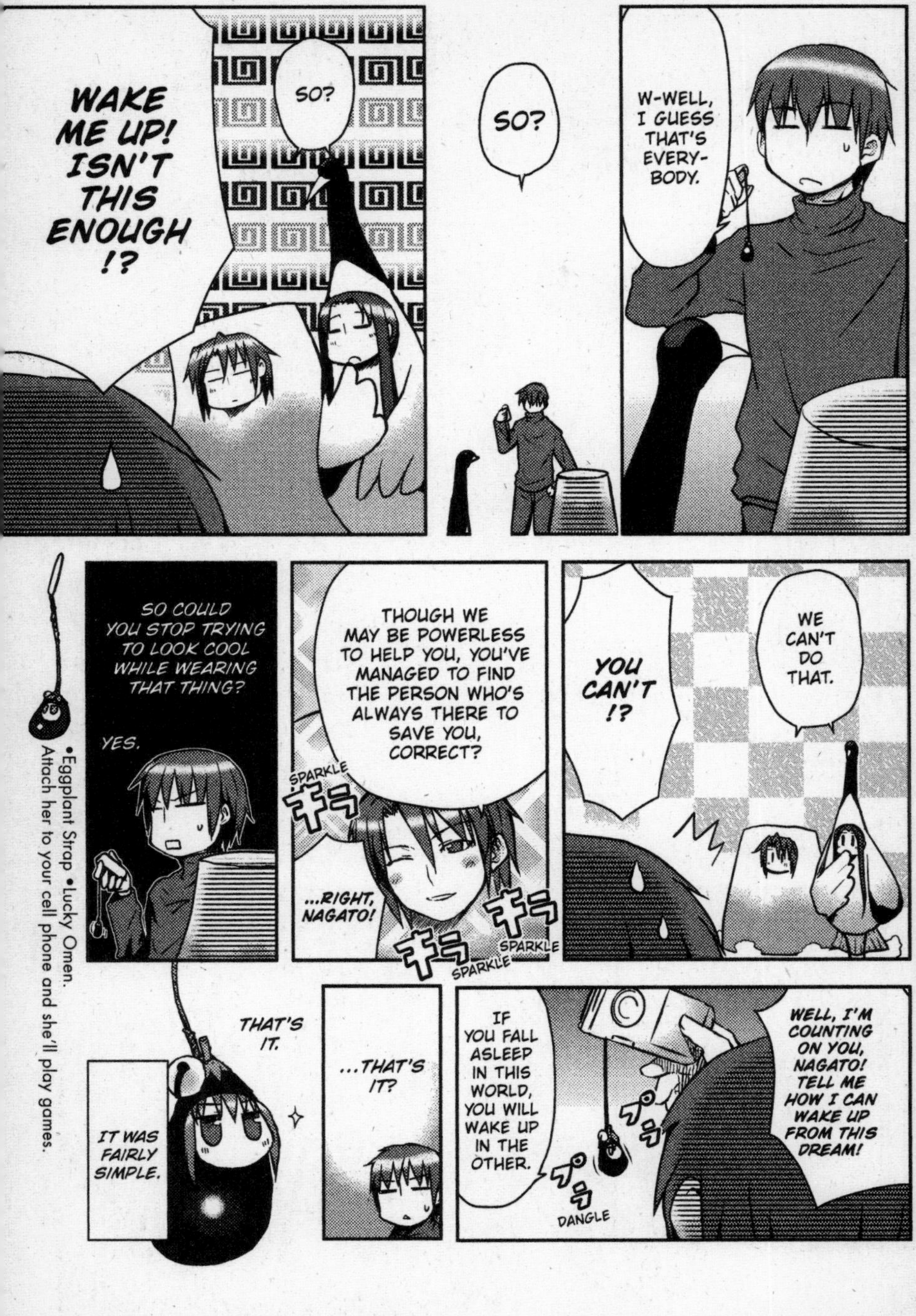
W-WELL, I GUESS THAT'S EVERY-BODY.
SO?
SO?
WAKE ME UP! ISN'T THIS ENOUGH!?
WE CAN'T DO THAT.
YOU CAN'T!?
THOUGH WE MAY BE POWERLESS TO HELP YOU, YOU'VE MANAGED TO FIND THE PERSON WHO'S ALWAYS THERE TO SAVE YOU, CORRECT?
キラ SPARKLE
...RIGHT, NAGATO!
キラ SPARKLE
キラ SPARKLE
SO COULD YOU STOP TRYING TO LOOK COOL WHILE WEARING THAT THING?
YES.
•Eggplant Strap •Lucky Omen. Attach her to your cell phone and she'll play games.
WELL, I'M COUNTING ON YOU, NAGATO! TELL ME HOW I CAN WAKE UP FROM THIS DREAM!
IF YOU FALL ASLEEP IN THIS WORLD, YOU WILL WAKE UP IN THE OTHER.
プラ プラ DANGLE
...THAT'S IT?
THAT'S IT.
IT WAS FAIRLY SIMPLE.

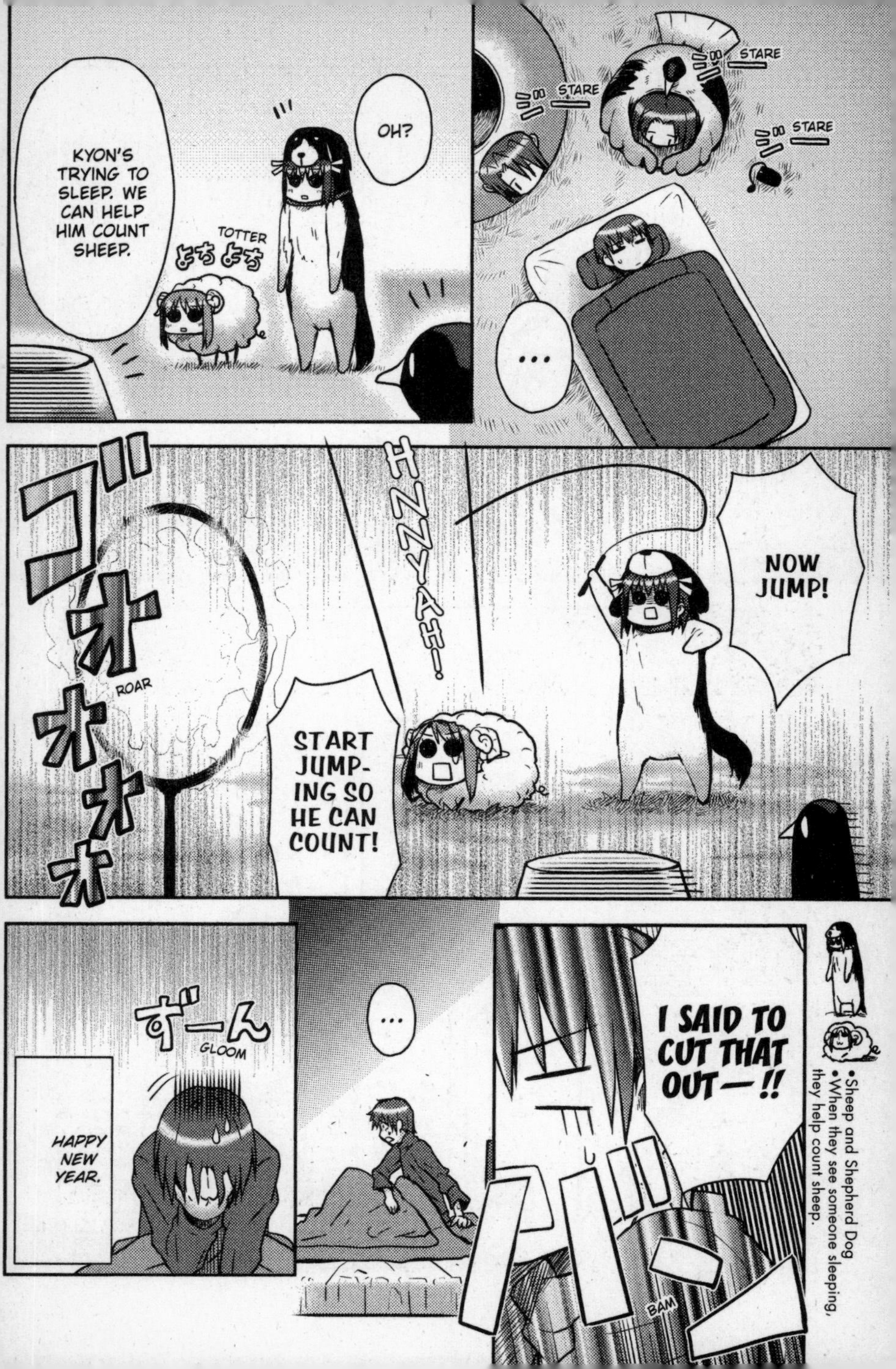
STARE
STARE
STARE
...
OH?
KYON'S TRYING TO SLEEP. WE CAN HELP HIM COUNT SHEEP.
よちよち
TOTTER
NOW JUMP!
HNNYAH!
START JUMPING SO HE CAN COUNT!
ゴオオオオ
ROAR
•Sheep and Shepherd Dog
•When they see someone sleeping, they help count sheep.
I SAID TO CUT THAT OUT—!!
BAM
...
ずーん
GLOOM
HAPPY NEW YEAR.

VISITING THE SHRINE ON NEW YEAR'S

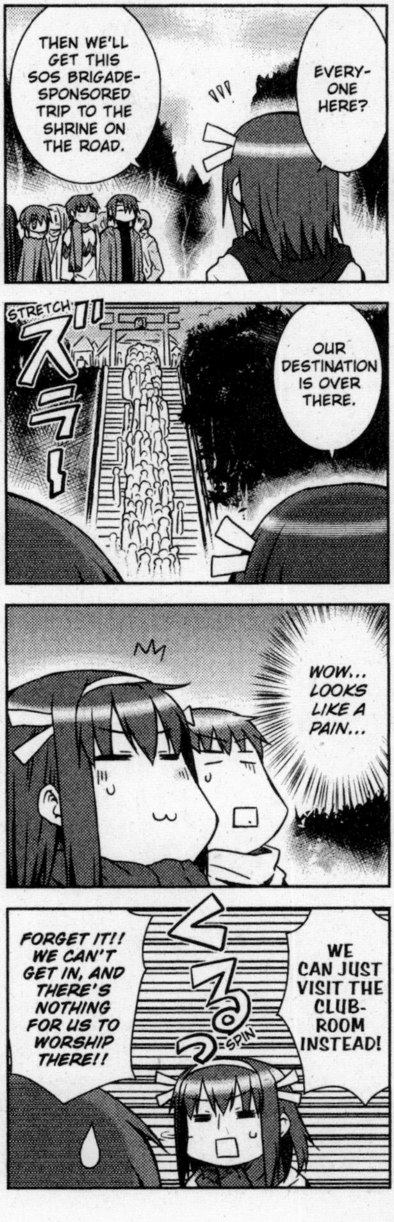
EVERY-ONE HERE?
THEN WE'LL GET THIS SOS BRIGADE-SPONSORED TRIP TO THE SHRINE ON THE ROAD.
OUR DESTINATION IS OVER THERE.
STRETCH
WOW... LOOKS LIKE A PAIN...
WE CAN JUST VISIT THE CLUB-ROOM INSTEAD!
SPIN
FORGET IT!! WE CAN'T GET IN, AND THERE'S NOTHING FOR US TO WORSHIP THERE!!

LOOK AWAY

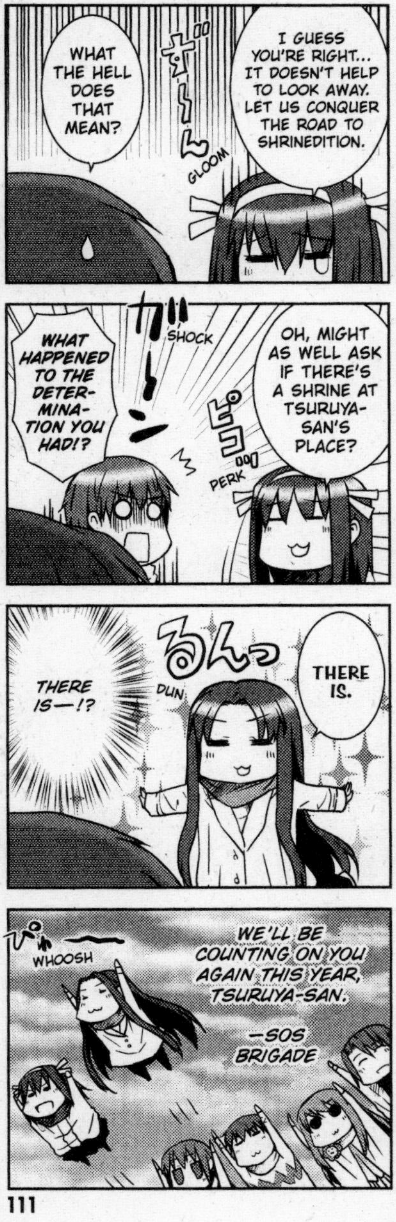
I GUESS YOU'RE RIGHT... IT DOESN'T HELP TO LOOK AWAY. LET US CONQUER THE ROAD TO SHRINEDITION.
GLOOM
WHAT THE HELL DOES THAT MEAN?
OH, MIGHT AS WELL ASK IF THERE'S A SHRINE AT TSURUYA-SAN'S PLACE?
PERK
SHOCK
WHAT HAPPENED TO THE DETERMINATION YOU HAD!?
THERE IS.
DUN
THERE IS—!?
WE'LL BE COUNTING ON YOU AGAIN THIS YEAR, TSURUYA-SAN.
—SOS BRIGADE
WHOOSH

FORTUNES

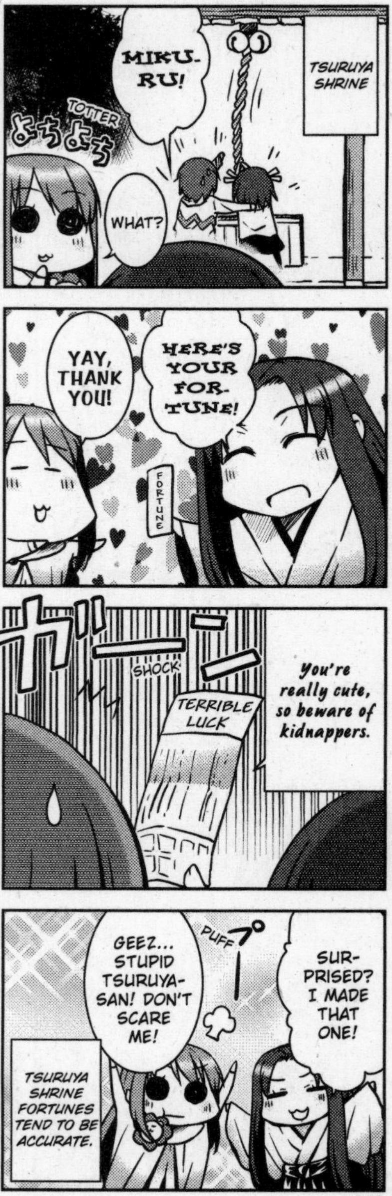
TSURUYA SHRINE
MIKU-RU!
TOTTER
WHAT?
HERE'S YOUR FOR-TUNE!
YAY, THANK YOU!
FORTUNE
You're really cute, so beware of kidnappers.
SHOCK
TERRIBLE LUCK
SUR-PRISED? I MADE THAT ONE!
PUFF
GEEZ... STUPID TSURUYA-SAN! DON'T SCARE ME!
TSURUYA SHRINE FORTUNES TEND TO BE ACCURATE.

FORTUNES 2

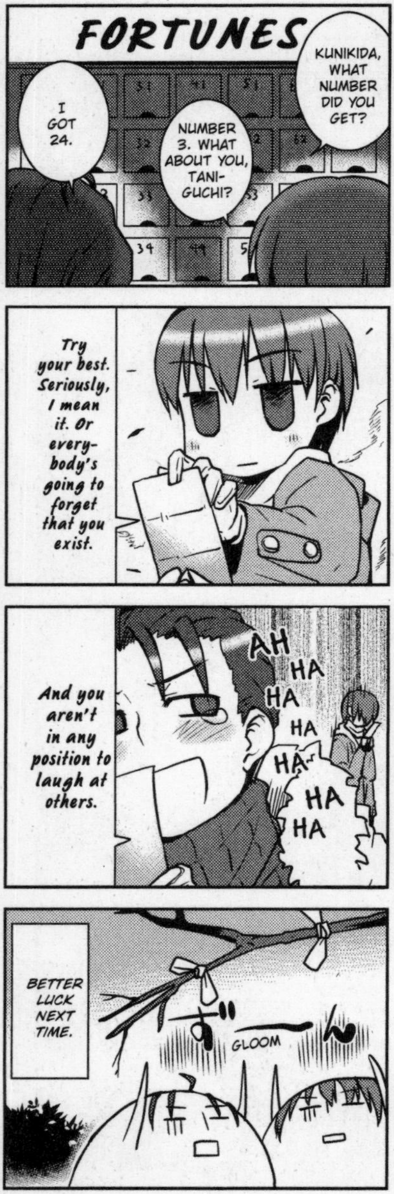
KUNIKIDA, WHAT NUMBER DID YOU GET?
FORTUNES
NUMBER 3. WHAT ABOUT YOU, TANI-GUCHI?
I GOT 24.
Try your best. Seriously, I mean it. Or every-body's going to forget that you exist.
AH HA HA HA HA HA HA
And you aren't in any position to laugh at others.
GLOOM
BETTER LUCK NEXT TIME.

FOOD

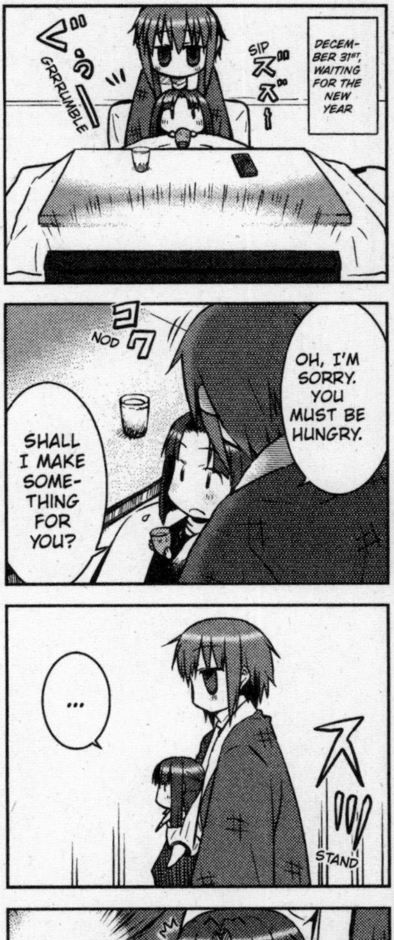
DECEMBER 31ST, WAITING FOR THE NEW YEAR
SIP
GRRRUMBLE
OH, I'M SORRY. YOU MUST BE HUNGRY.
SHALL I MAKE SOMETHING FOR YOU?
NOD
...
STAND
SHE PUT ME IN SOMETHING ELSE THAT'S FOR BABIES!
DANGLE

END-OF-YEAR SOBA

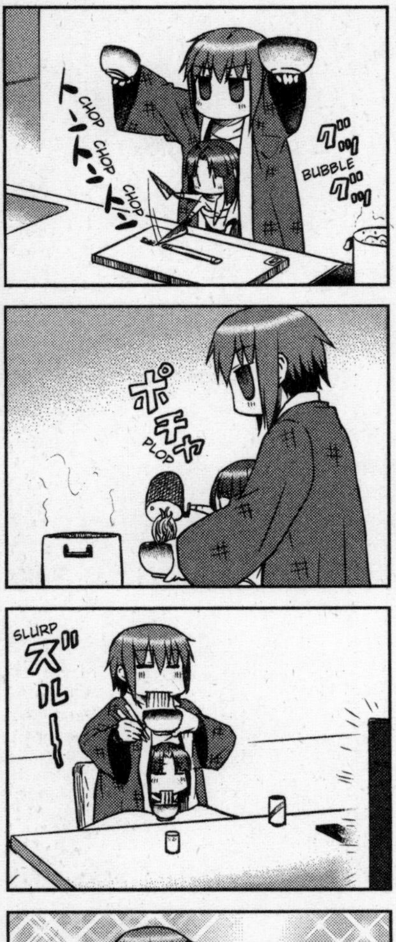
BUBBLE
CHOP
CHOP
CHOP
PLOP
SLURP
WHEW...

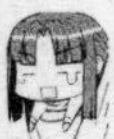

•Achakura-san •Back in miniature action after being destroyed in her battle with Nagato. Spending New Year's Eve with Nagato.

RICE CAKE

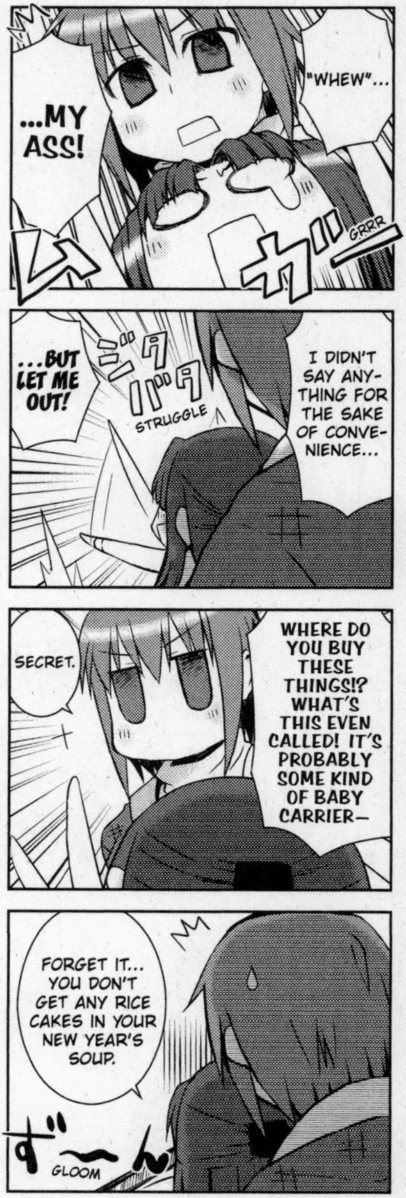

"WHEW"...
...MY ASS!
GRRR
I DIDN'T SAY ANYTHING FOR THE SAKE OF CONVENIENCE...
STRUGGLE
...BUT LET ME OUT!
WHERE DO YOU BUY THESE THINGS!? WHAT'S THIS EVEN CALLED! IT'S PROBABLY SOME KIND OF BABY CARRIER—
SECRET.
FORGET IT... YOU DON'T GET ANY RICE CAKES IN YOUR NEW YEAR'S SOUP.
GLOOM

POWER OF SONG

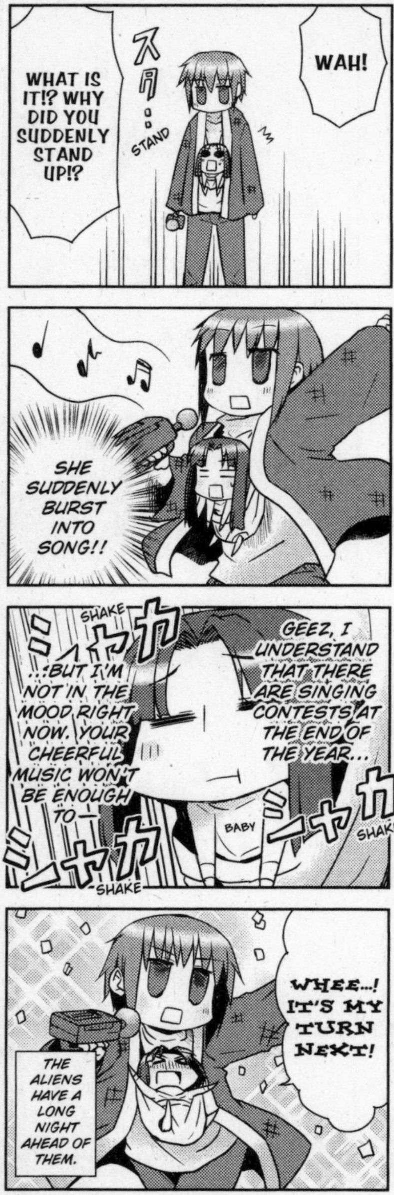

WAH!
STAND
WHAT IS IT!? WHY DID YOU SUDDENLY STAND UP!?
SHE SUDDENLY BURST INTO SONG!!
GEEZ, I UNDERSTAND THAT THERE ARE SINGING CONTESTS AT THE END OF THE YEAR...
SHAKE
...BUT I'M NOT IN THE MOOD RIGHT NOW. YOUR CHEERFUL MUSIC WON'T BE ENOUGH TO—
BABY
SHAKE
SHAKE
WHEE...! IT'S MY TURN NEXT!
THE ALIENS HAVE A LONG NIGHT AHEAD OF THEM.

SHAMISEN...

LET'S PLAY...

EEEP...

WELL, YUKI...

WE'LL SEE
YOU LATER...

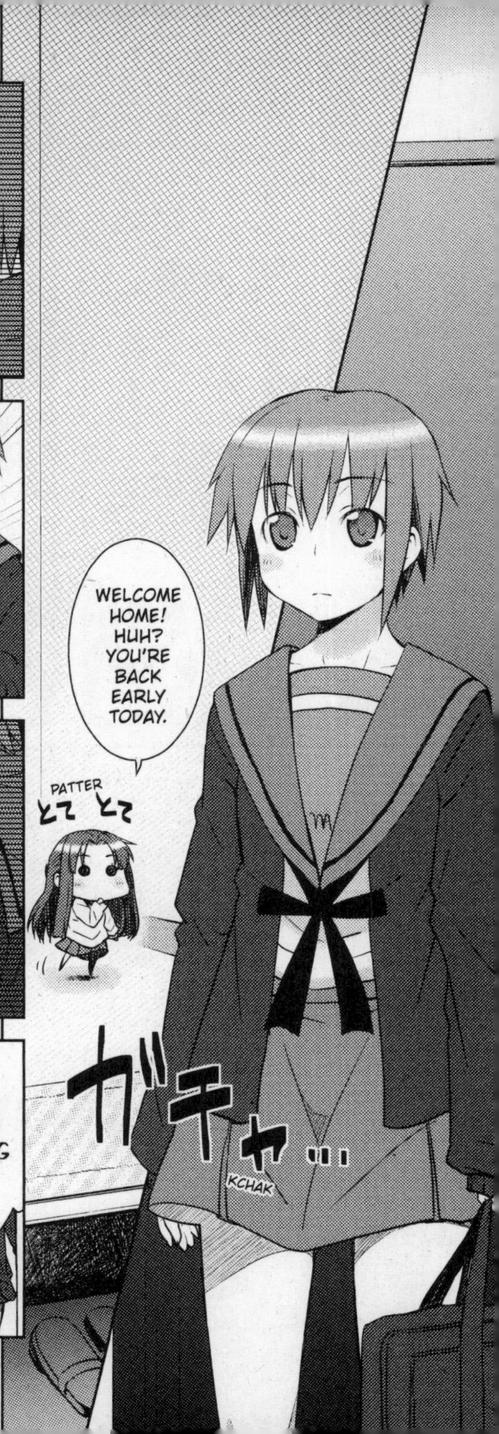
WELCOME HOME! HUH? YOU'RE BACK EARLY TODAY.
PATTER
とて とて
ガチャ
KCHAK

STASH

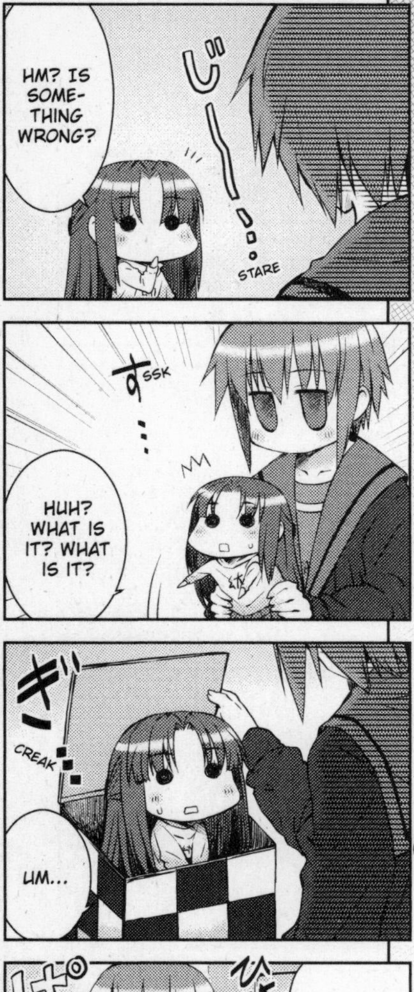
HM? IS SOME-THING WRONG?
じー
STARE
す
SSK
...
HUH? WHAT IS IT? WHAT IS IT?
ぎ
CREAK
UM...
YUKI! WE'RE COMING IN!
FLIT
ぱたんっ
SLAM

OPERATION VALENTINE

EVERY-THING'S READY.
SO LET'S GET THIS SOS BRIGADE-SPONSORED, NO BOYS ALLOWED, VALENTINE CHOCOLATE FEST ROLLING.
YAY—!
FIRST, WE'LL NEED YOU TO TAKE OFF YOUR CLOTHES, MIKURU-CHAN.
FWEH? TAKING A BATH?
WE'LL START BY MAKING A *LIFE-SIZE CHOCOLATE* MIKURU-CHAN...
HNNYAH!!
BAM
HUH—!?
I REFUSE—!!
NOW, NOW. THERE'S NOTHING TO WORRY ABOUT.
YOU TOO, TSURU-YA-SAN!?
SHOCK

•Haruhi-chan •SOS Brigade brigade chief. February is time for Valentine's.

•Nagato •Actually an alien gamer. Pays close attention to the story in a game.

•Achakura-san •Back in miniature action after being destroyed in her battle with Nagato. Crashing at Nagato's place.

FIXATED ON THE SHAPE

IT IS DIFFICULT TO MAINTAIN THE DESIRED SHAPE OF A HUMAN-SIZED CHOCOLATE SCULPTURE.
OH, REALLY...? GUESS IT'S NOT POSSIBLE.
HUH...? THEY WERE GOING TO TRY TO MAKE A HUMAN-SIZED CHOCOLATE!?
BUT THAT'S A PROBLEM. WE'RE GOING TO END UP WITH EXTRA CHOCOLATE LEFT OVER...
YEPPERS...
HMM...
WE CAN USE THE EXTRA CHOCOLATE TO MAKE OUR OWN INDIVIDUAL CREATIONS.
DING
I SEE. FAILURE IS PART OF THE PRO-CESS.
TIME FOR SCULPTING?

REPLICATION

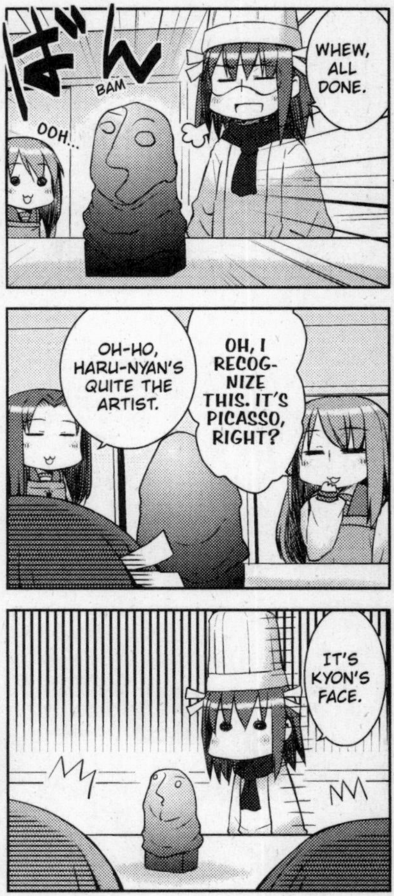
WHEW, ALL DONE.
BAM
OOH...
OH, I RECOGNIZE THIS. IT'S PICASSO, RIGHT?
OH-HO, HARU-NYAN'S QUITE THE ARTIST.
IT'S KYON'S FACE.
A 99.8% ACCURATE REPLICATION. HOWEVER, HUMAN BEINGS ARE STILL RELIANT ON THEIR SIGHT AND THUS INCAPABLE OF PERCEIVING THE RESEMBLANCE.
YUKI... I'M PRETTY SURE YOU AREN'T HELPING.
LIFT

RESTORATION

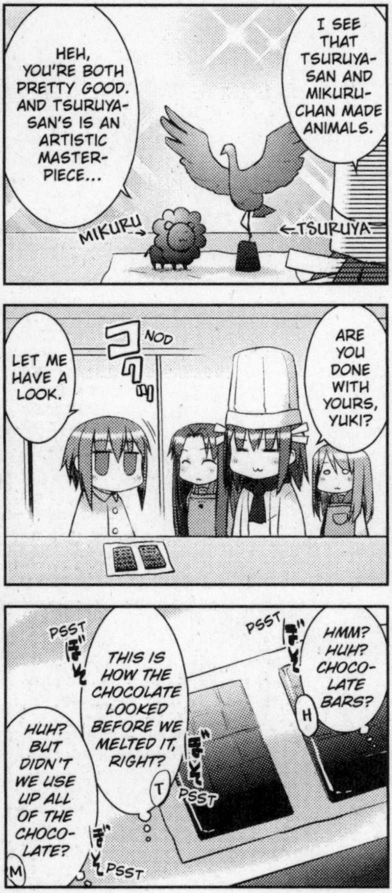
I SEE THAT TSURUYA-SAN AND MIKURU-CHAN MADE ANIMALS.
HEH, YOU'RE BOTH PRETTY GOOD. AND TSURUYA-SAN'S IS AN ARTISTIC MASTERPIECE...
←TSURUYA
MIKURU→
ARE YOU DONE WITH YOURS, YUKI?
NOD
LET ME HAVE A LOOK.
HMM? HUH? CHOCOLATE BARS?
H
PSST
THIS IS HOW THE CHOCOLATE LOOKED BEFORE WE MELTED IT, RIGHT?
T
PSST
HUH? BUT DIDN'T WE USE UP ALL OF THE CHOCOLATE?
M
PSST
PSST
HUH? THEN SHE MADE THESE FROM SCRATCH?
THAT'S AMAZING.
AMAZING, BUT INCREDIBLY POINTLESS.
PFFT...

•Mikuru-chan •Actually from the future. Always being toyed with by Haruhi and Tsuruya-san.

•Tsuruya-san •Mikuru-chan's buddy. A martial arts master who's a real grappler.

•Kyon •Supposed to be the main character in this story. Will he be receiving chocolate this time?

TRUFFLE

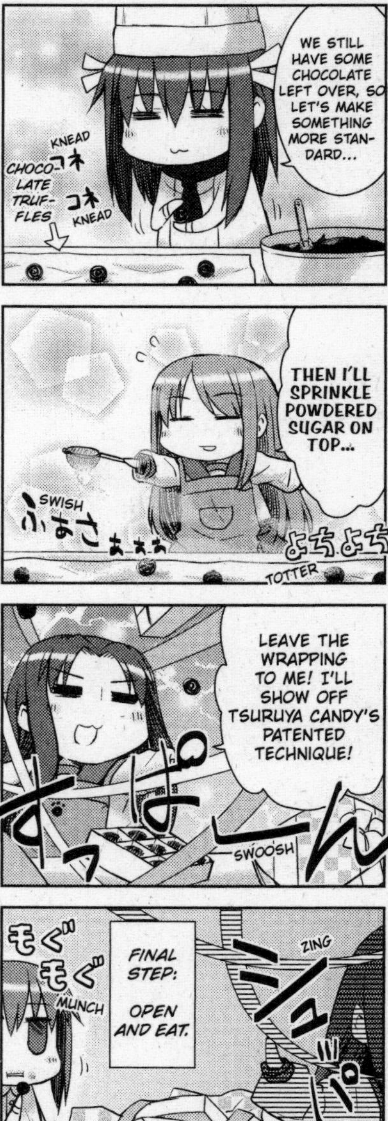
WE STILL HAVE SOME CHOCOLATE LEFT OVER, SO LET'S MAKE SOMETHING MORE STAN-DARD...
KNEAD コネ
コネ KNEAD
CHOCO-LATE TRUF-FLES
THEN I'LL SPRINKLE POWDERED SUGAR ON TOP...
よちよち
TOTTER
SWISH
LEAVE THE WRAPPING TO ME! I'LL SHOW OFF TSURUYA CANDY'S PATENTED TECHNIQUE!
SWOOSH
ZING
FINAL STEP: OPEN AND EAT.
もぐもぐ
MUNCH

PRACTICAL APPLICATION

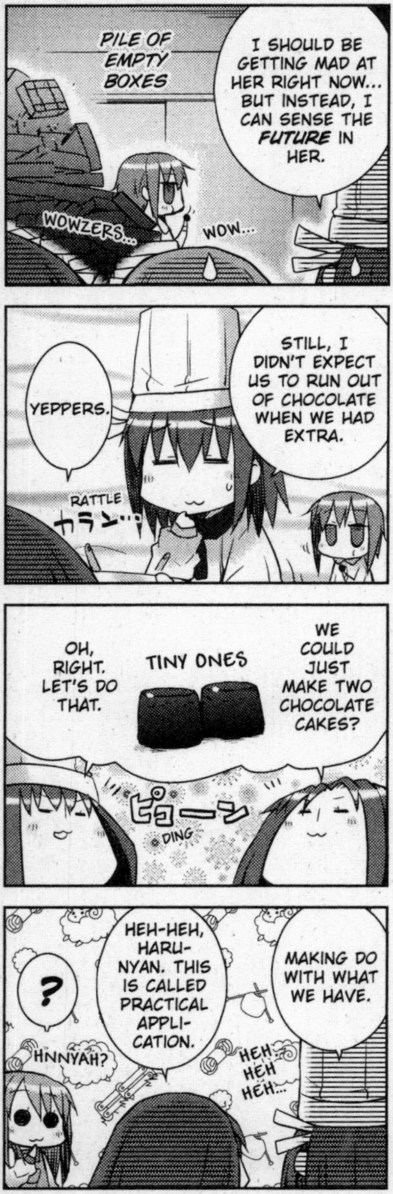
I SHOULD BE GETTING MAD AT HER RIGHT NOW... BUT INSTEAD, I CAN SENSE THE *FUTURE* IN HER.
PILE OF EMPTY BOXES
WOW...
WOWZERS...
STILL, I DIDN'T EXPECT US TO RUN OUT OF CHOCOLATE WHEN WE HAD EXTRA.
YEPPERS.
RATTLE
WE COULD JUST MAKE TWO CHOCOLATE CAKES?
TINY ONES
OH, RIGHT. LET'S DO THAT.
DING
MAKING DO WITH WHAT WE HAVE.
HEH-HEH, HARU-NYAN. THIS IS CALLED PRACTICAL APPLI-CATION.
?
HNNYAH?
HEH HEH HEH...

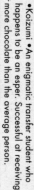

•Koizumi •An enigmatic transfer student who happens to be an esper. Successful at receiving more chocolate than the average person.

THE MEN'S VALENTINE'S DAY

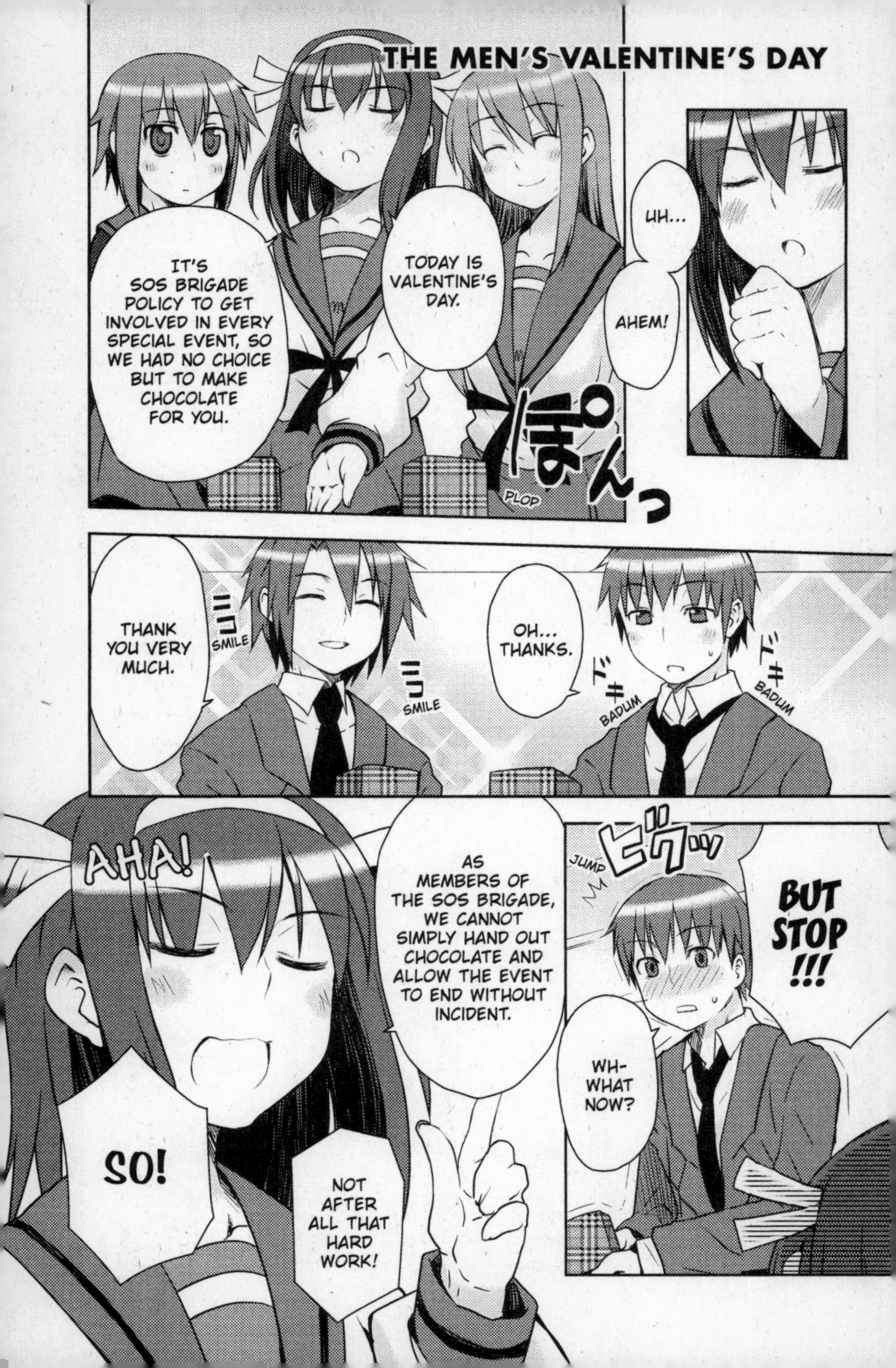

UH...
AHEM!
TODAY IS VALENTINE'S DAY.
IT'S SOS BRIGADE POLICY TO GET INVOLVED IN EVERY SPECIAL EVENT, SO WE HAD NO CHOICE BUT TO MAKE CHOCOLATE FOR YOU.
ぽんっ
PLOP
ドキ
BADUM
ドキ
BADUM
OH... THANKS.
ニコ
SMILE
ニコ
SMILE
THANK YOU VERY MUCH.
BUT STOP!!!
ビクッ
JUMP
WH-WHAT NOW?
AS MEMBERS OF THE SOS BRIGADE, WE CANNOT SIMPLY HAND OUT CHOCOLATE AND ALLOW THE EVENT TO END WITHOUT INCIDENT.
AHA!
NOT AFTER ALL THAT HARD WORK!
SO!

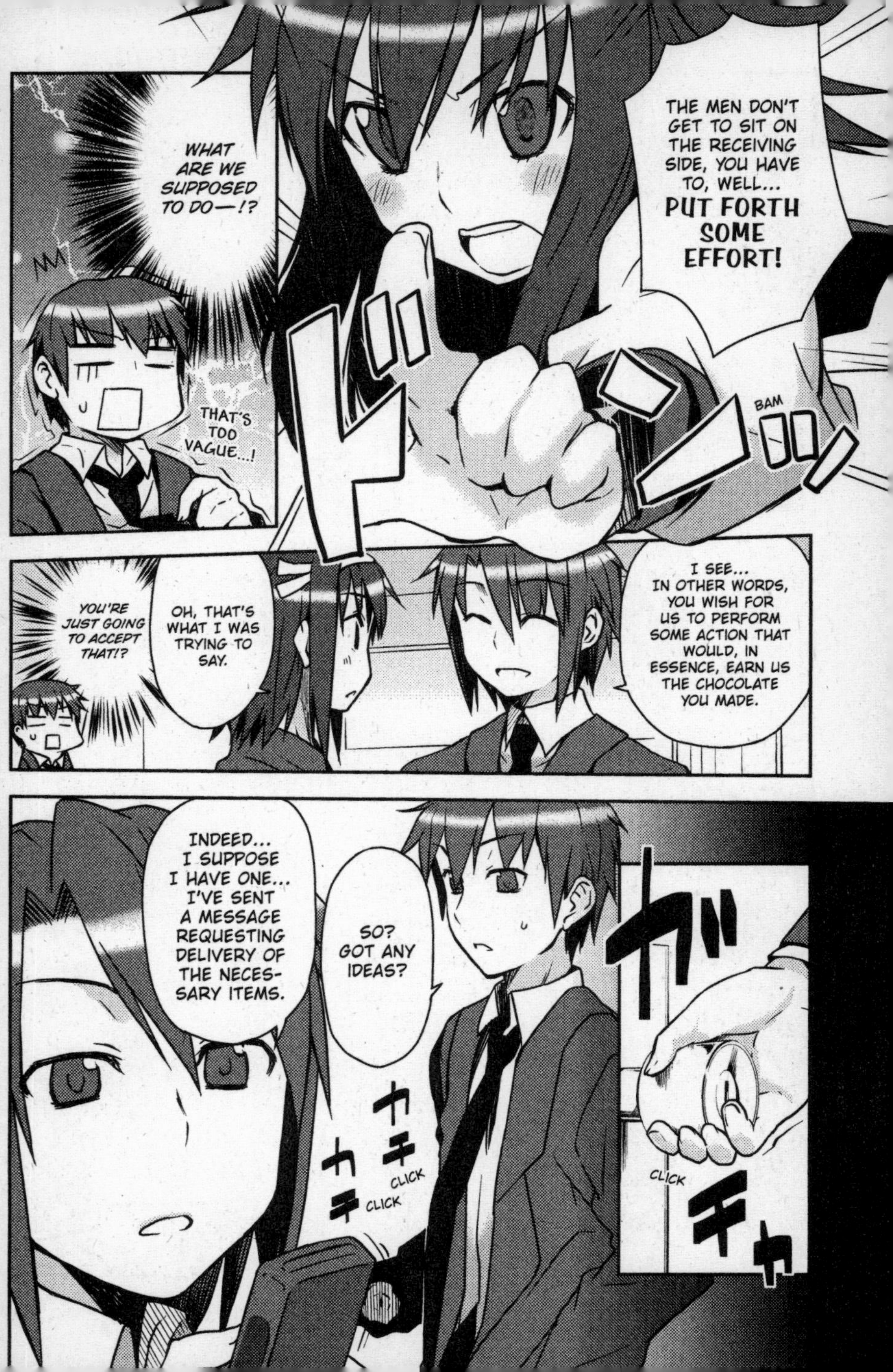
THE MEN DON'T GET TO SIT ON THE RECEIVING SIDE, YOU HAVE TO, WELL... **PUT FORTH SOME EFFORT!**
BAM
WHAT ARE WE SUPPOSED TO DO—!?
THAT'S TOO VAGUE...!
I SEE... IN OTHER WORDS, YOU WISH FOR US TO PERFORM SOME ACTION THAT WOULD, IN ESSENCE, EARN US THE CHOCOLATE YOU MADE.
OH, THAT'S WHAT I WAS TRYING TO SAY.
YOU'RE JUST GOING TO ACCEPT THAT!?
CLICK
SO? GOT ANY IDEAS?
INDEED... I SUPPOSE I HAVE ONE... I'VE SENT A MESSAGE REQUESTING DELIVERY OF THE NECES-SARY ITEMS.
CLICK
CLICK

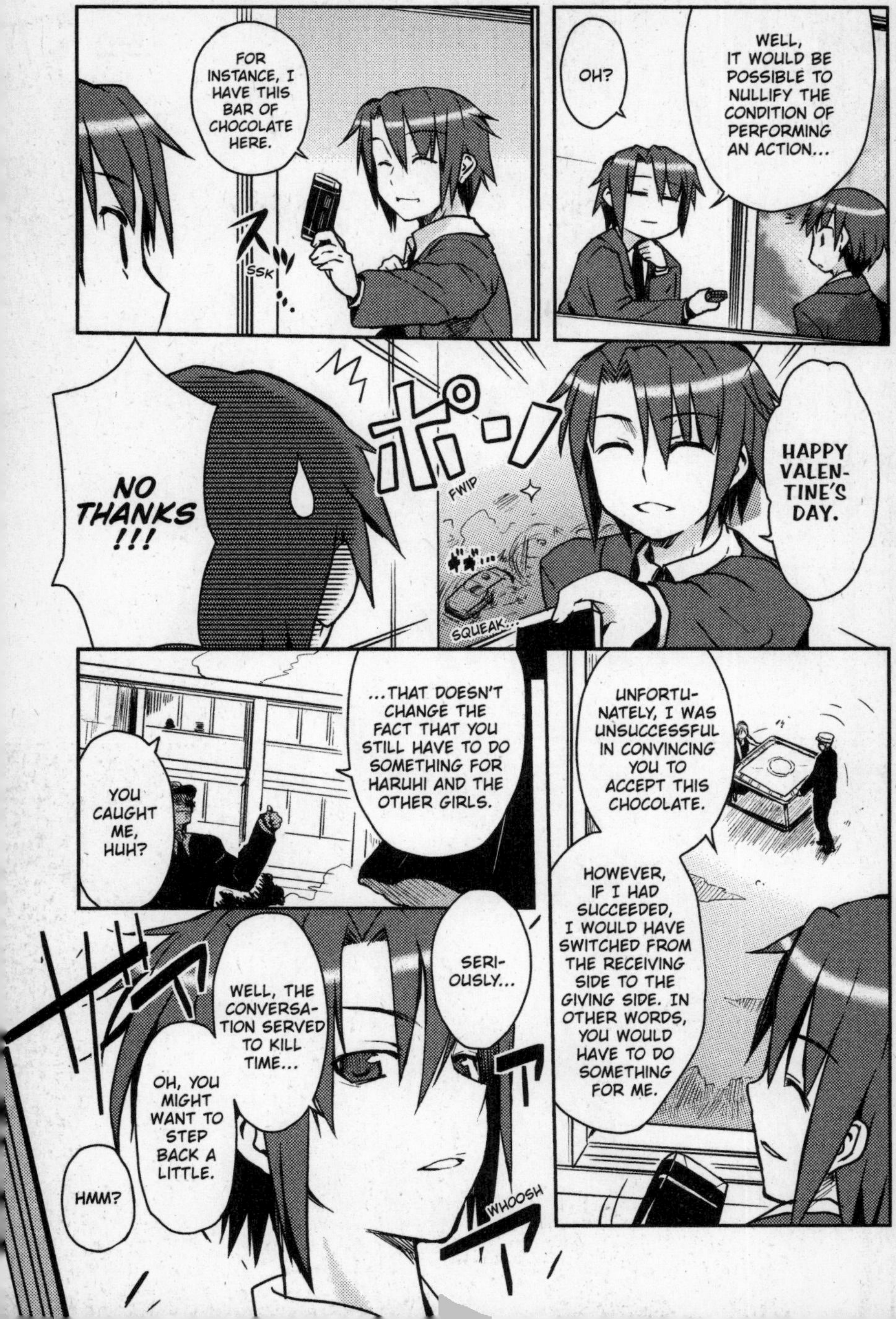
WELL, IT WOULD BE POSSIBLE TO NULLIFY THE CONDITION OF PERFORMING AN ACTION...
OH?
FOR INSTANCE, I HAVE THIS BAR OF CHOCOLATE HERE.
SSK
HAPPY VALEN-TINE'S DAY.
FWIP
SQUEAK...
NO THANKS!!!
UNFORTU-NATELY, I WAS UNSUCCESSFUL IN CONVINCING YOU TO ACCEPT THIS CHOCOLATE.
HOWEVER, IF I HAD SUCCEEDED, I WOULD HAVE SWITCHED FROM THE RECEIVING SIDE TO THE GIVING SIDE. IN OTHER WORDS, YOU WOULD HAVE TO DO SOMETHING FOR ME.
...THAT DOESN'T CHANGE THE FACT THAT YOU STILL HAVE TO DO SOMETHING FOR HARUHI AND THE OTHER GIRLS.
YOU CAUGHT ME, HUH?
SERI-OUSLY...
WELL, THE CONVERSA-TION SERVED TO KILL TIME...
OH, YOU MIGHT WANT TO STEP BACK A LITTLE.
HMM?
WHOOSH

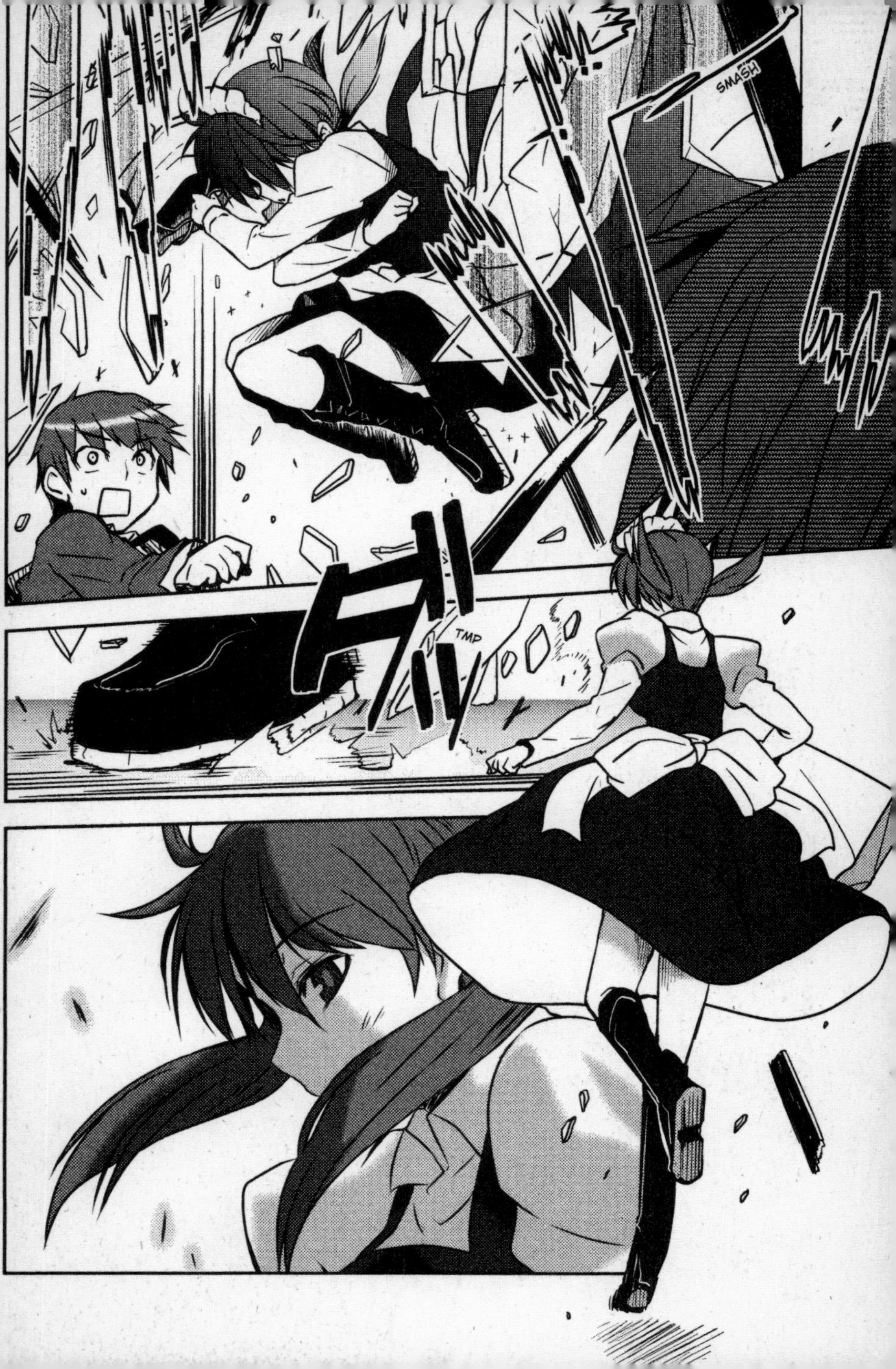
SMASH
TMP

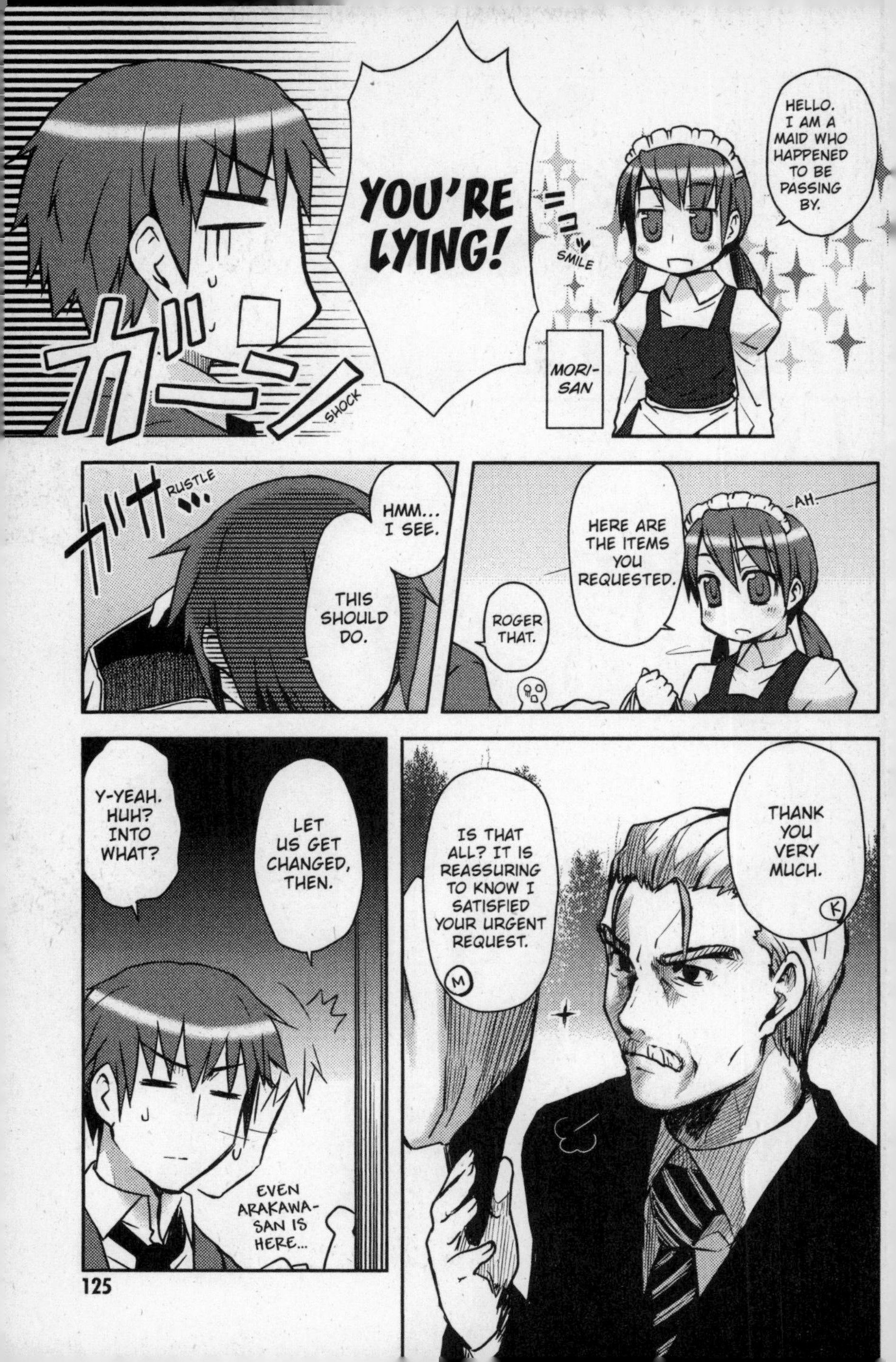
HELLO. I AM A MAID WHO HAPPENED TO BE PASSING BY.
SMILE
MORI-SAN
YOU'RE LYING!
SHOCK
AH
HERE ARE THE ITEMS YOU REQUESTED.
ROGER THAT.
HMM... I SEE.
THIS SHOULD DO.
RUSTLE
THANK YOU VERY MUCH.
K
IS THAT ALL? IT IS REASSURING TO KNOW I SATISFIED YOUR URGENT REQUEST.
M
LET US GET CHANGED, THEN.
Y-YEAH. HUH? INTO WHAT?
EVEN ARAKAWA-SAN IS HERE...

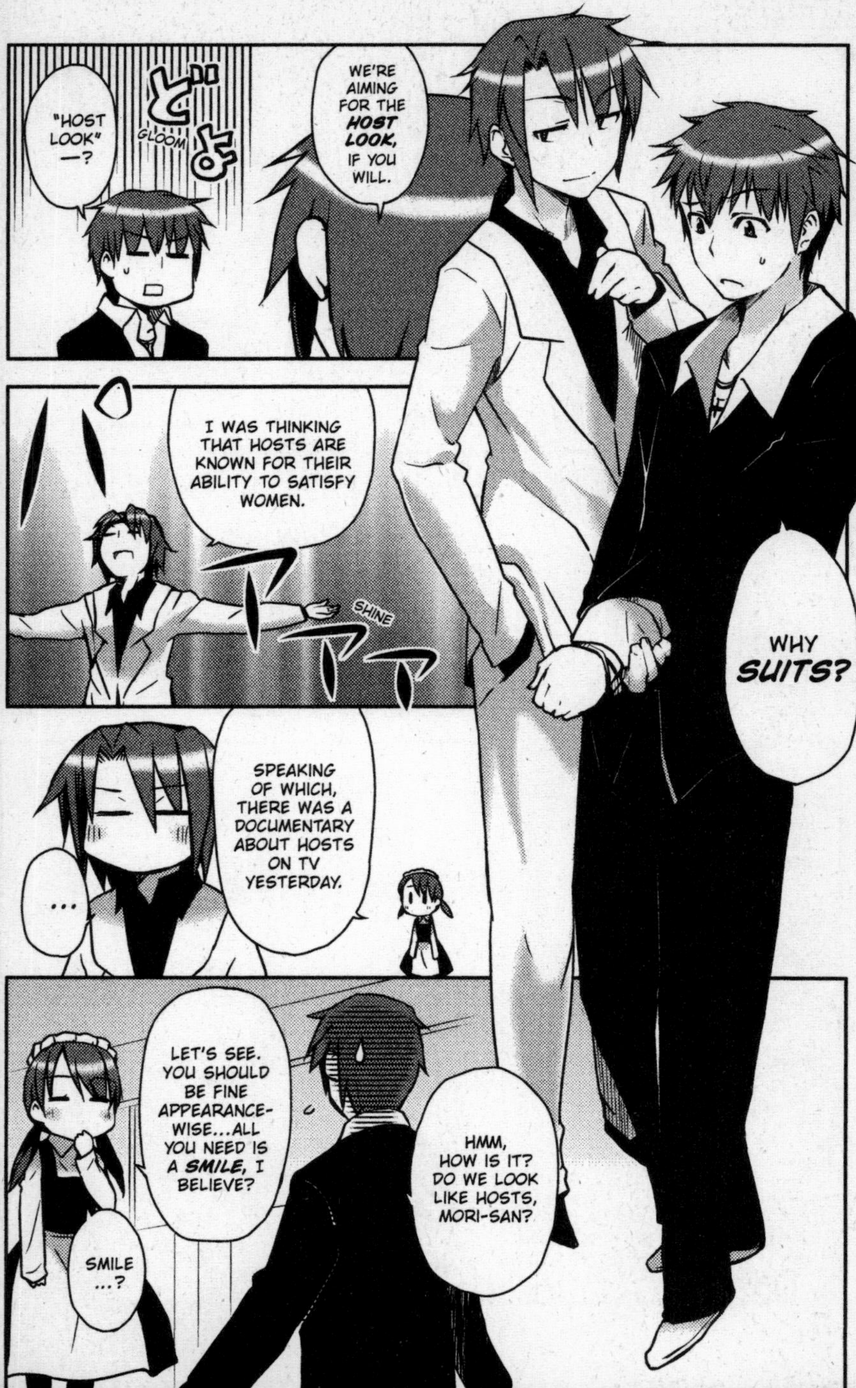
WHY SUITS?
WE'RE AIMING FOR THE HOST LOOK, IF YOU WILL.
どよ
GLOOM
"HOST LOOK" —?
I WAS THINKING THAT HOSTS ARE KNOWN FOR THEIR ABILITY TO SATISFY WOMEN.
SHINE
SPEAKING OF WHICH, THERE WAS A DOCUMENTARY ABOUT HOSTS ON TV YESTERDAY.
...
HMM, HOW IS IT? DO WE LOOK LIKE HOSTS, MORI-SAN?
LET'S SEE. YOU SHOULD BE FINE APPEARANCE-WISE...ALL YOU NEED IS A SMILE, I BELIEVE?
SMILE ...?

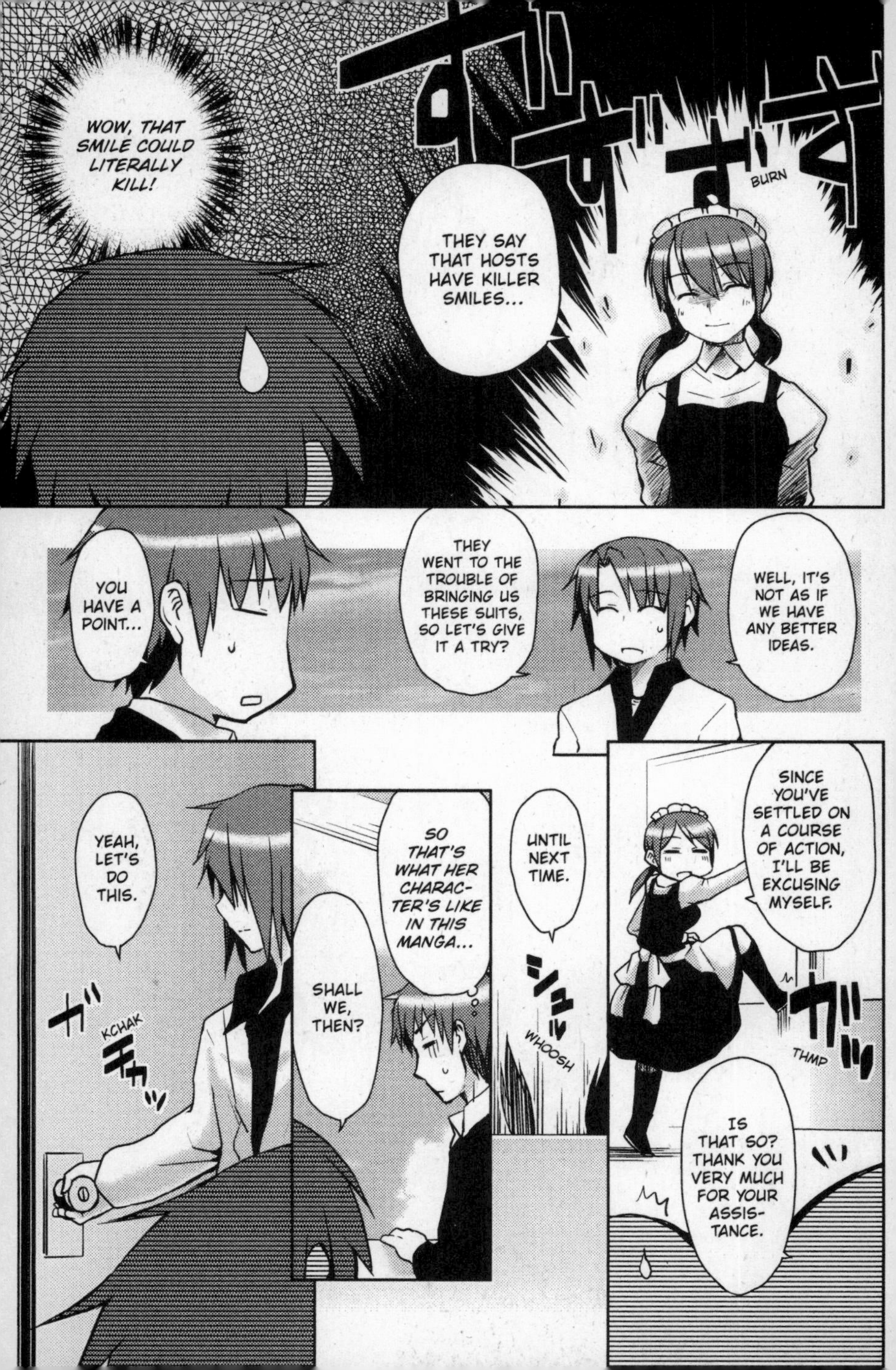
BURN
THEY SAY THAT HOSTS HAVE KILLER SMILES...
WOW, THAT SMILE COULD LITERALLY KILL!
WELL, IT'S NOT AS IF WE HAVE ANY BETTER IDEAS.
THEY WENT TO THE TROUBLE OF BRINGING US THESE SUITS, SO LET'S GIVE IT A TRY?
YOU HAVE A POINT...
SINCE YOU'VE SETTLED ON A COURSE OF ACTION, I'LL BE EXCUSING MYSELF.
THMP
IS THAT SO? THANK YOU VERY MUCH FOR YOUR ASSISTANCE.
UNTIL NEXT TIME.
WHOOSH
SO THAT'S WHAT HER CHARACTER'S LIKE IN THIS MANGA...
SHALL WE, THEN?
YEAH, LET'S DO THIS.
KCHAK

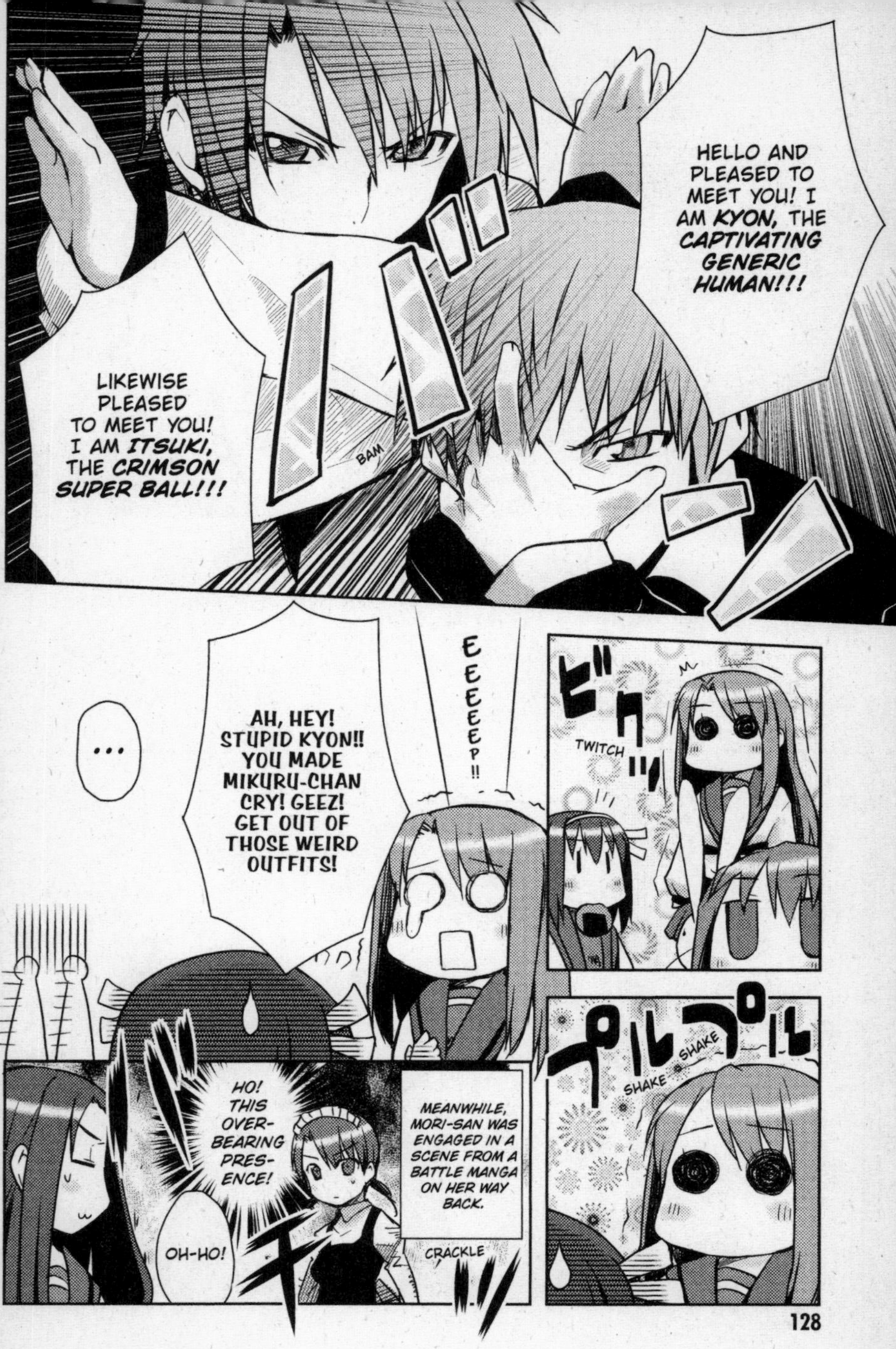
HELLO AND PLEASED TO MEET YOU! I AM KYON, THE CAPTIVATING GENERIC HUMAN!!!
LIKEWISE PLEASED TO MEET YOU! I AM ITSUKI, THE CRIMSON SUPER BALL!!!
BAM
ビク
TWITCH
プルプル
SHAKE SHAKE
SHAKE
EEEEEEP!!
AH, HEY! STUPID KYON!! YOU MADE MIKURU-CHAN CRY! GEEZ! GET OUT OF THOSE WEIRD OUTFITS!
...
MEANWHILE, MORI-SAN WAS ENGAGED IN A SCENE FROM A BATTLE MANGA ON HER WAY BACK.
HO! THIS OVER-BEARING PRES-ENCE!
OH-HO!
CRACKLE

START OF SPRING

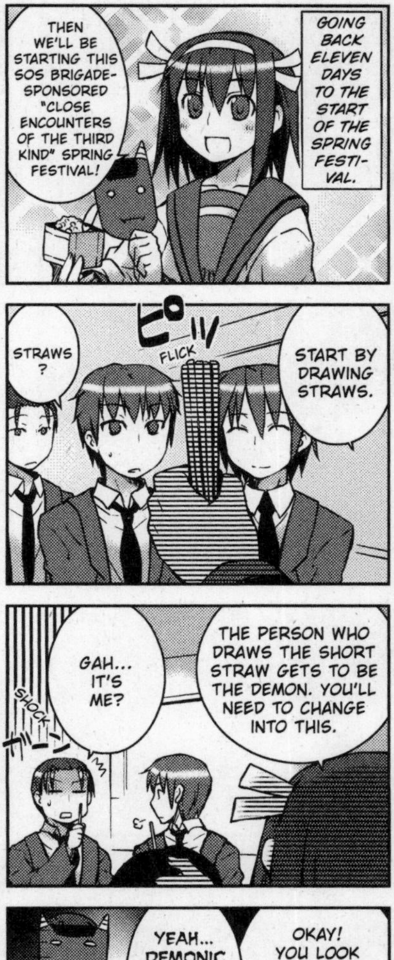
GOING BACK ELEVEN DAYS TO THE START OF THE SPRING FESTI-VAL.
THEN WE'LL BE STARTING THIS SOS BRIGADE-SPONSORED "CLOSE ENCOUNTERS OF THE THIRD KIND" SPRING FESTIVAL!
START BY DRAWING STRAWS.
ピッ
FLICK
STRAWS ?
THE PERSON WHO DRAWS THE SHORT STRAW GETS TO BE THE DEMON. YOU'LL NEED TO CHANGE INTO THIS.
GAH... IT'S ME?
ガーン
SHOCK
OKAY! YOU LOOK DEMONIC ENOUGH TO BRING EVERY COP RUNNING OVER TO QUESTION YOU.
YEAH... DEMONIC ENOUGH TO MAKE ANY KID CRY.
ずーん
GLOOM

WELCOME

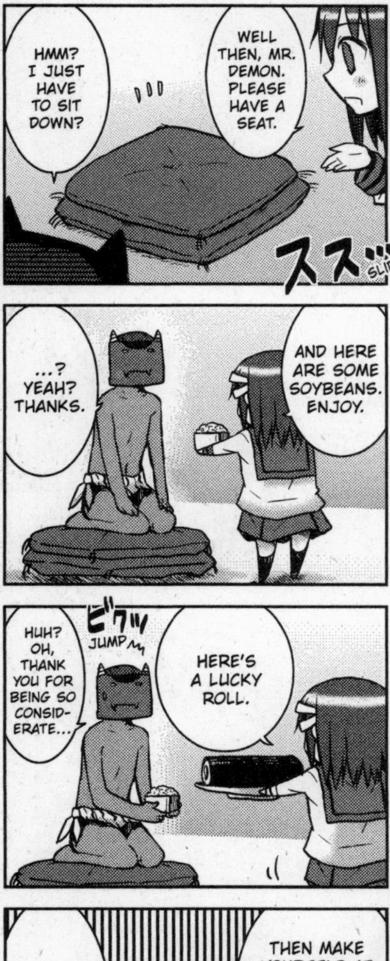
WELL THEN, MR. DEMON. PLEASE HAVE A SEAT.
HMM? I JUST HAVE TO SIT DOWN?
スス
SLIDE
AND HERE ARE SOME SOYBEANS. ENJOY.
...? YEAH? THANKS.
HERE'S A LUCKY ROLL.
ビクッ
JUMP
HUH? OH, THANK YOU FOR BEING SO CONSID-ERATE...
THEN MAKE YOURSELF AT HOME WHILE WE GET OUT OF YOUR WAY TO GO THROW BEANS.
OH, YOU'RE LEAVING? HAVE FUN...

*HAVING A FAMILY MEMBER DRESS UP LIKE A DEMON, THROWING BEANS, EATING AN UNCUT SUSHI ROLL, AND CHANTING "DEMONS OUT, LUCK IN!" ARE TRADITIONS OFTEN OBSERVED DURING THE SETSUBUN FESTIVAL CELEBRATED IN JAPAN JUST BEFORE SPRING BEGINS.

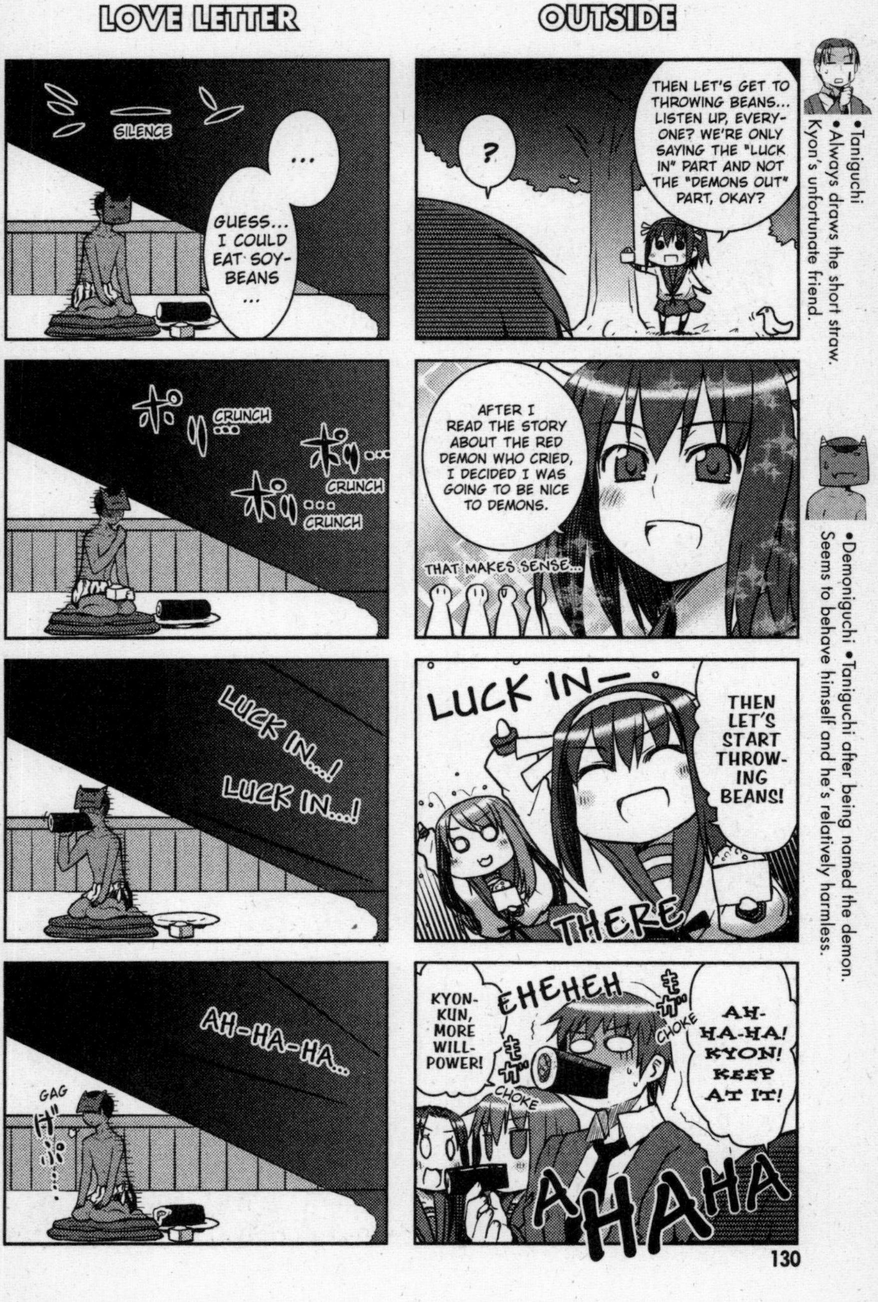
•Taniguchi
•Always draws the short straw. Kyon's unfortunate friend.
•Demoniguchi •Taniguchi after being named the demon. Seems to behave himself and he's relatively harmless.
OUTSIDE
THEN LET'S GET TO THROWING BEANS... LISTEN UP, EVERYONE? WE'RE ONLY SAYING THE "LUCK IN" PART AND NOT THE "DEMONS OUT" PART, OKAY?
?
AFTER I READ THE STORY ABOUT THE RED DEMON WHO CRIED, I DECIDED I WAS GOING TO BE NICE TO DEMONS.
THAT MAKES SENSE...
THEN LET'S START THROWING BEANS!
LUCK IN—
THERE
AH-HA-HA! KYON! KEEP AT IT!
CHOKE
EHEHEH
KYON-KUN, MORE WILLPOWER!
CHOKE
AHAHAHA
LOVE LETTER
SILENCE
...
GUESS... I COULD EAT SOYBEANS ...
CRUNCH...
CRUNCH
CRUNCH
LUCK IN...!
LUCK IN...!
AH-HA-HA...
GAG

STEALTH

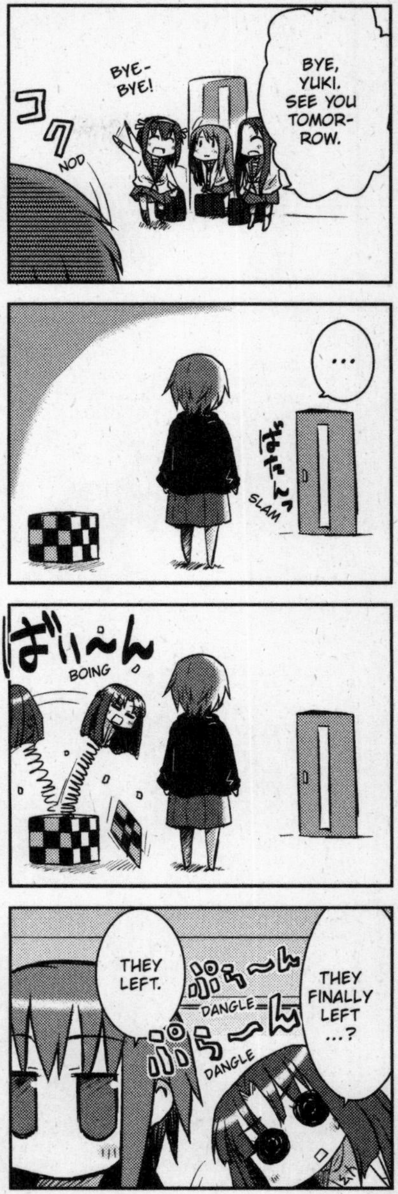
BYE, YUKI. SEE YOU TOMORROW.
BYE-BYE!
コク
NOD
...
ばたん
SLAM
ばぃ〜ん
BOING
THEY FINALLY LEFT ...?
ぶら〜ん
DANGLE
ぶら〜ん
DANGLE
THEY LEFT.

STASH AWAY 2

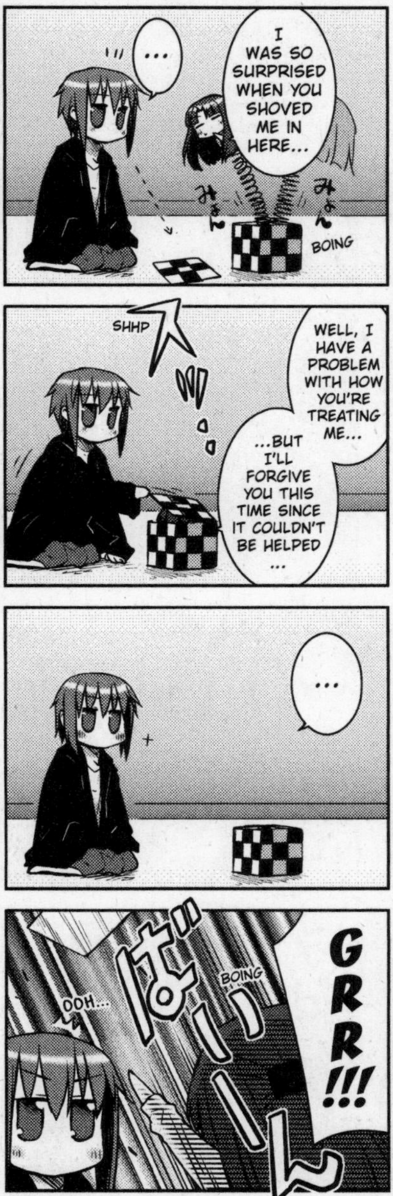
I WAS SO SURPRISED WHEN YOU SHOVED ME IN HERE...
みょん
みょん
BOING
...
WELL, I HAVE A PROBLEM WITH HOW YOU'RE TREATING ME...
...BUT I'LL FORGIVE YOU THIS TIME SINCE IT COULDN'T BE HELPED ...
ス
SHHP
...
GRR!!!
ばぃ〜ん
BOING
OOH...

•Achakura-in-the-box
•Achakura-san stashed away in a jack-in-the-box. Capable of jumping.

TOY

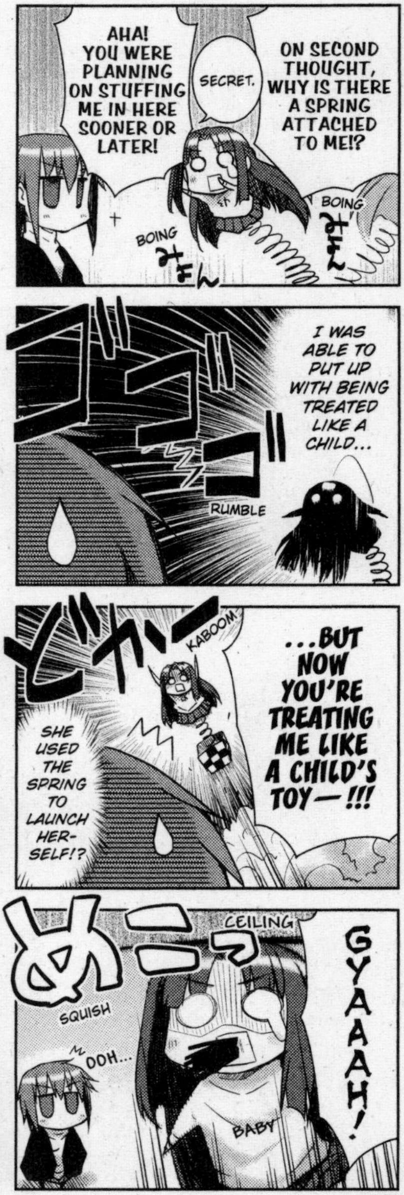
ON SECOND THOUGHT, WHY IS THERE A SPRING ATTACHED TO ME!?
SECRET.
AHA! YOU WERE PLANNING ON STUFFING ME IN HERE SOONER OR LATER!
BOING
BOING
I WAS ABLE TO PUT UP WITH BEING TREATED LIKE A CHILD...
RUMBLE
...BUT NOW YOU'RE TREATING ME LIKE A CHILD'S TOY—!!!
KABOOM
SHE USED THE SPRING TO LAUNCH HER-SELF!?
GYAAAH!
CEILING
SQUISH
OOH...
BABY

CAKE

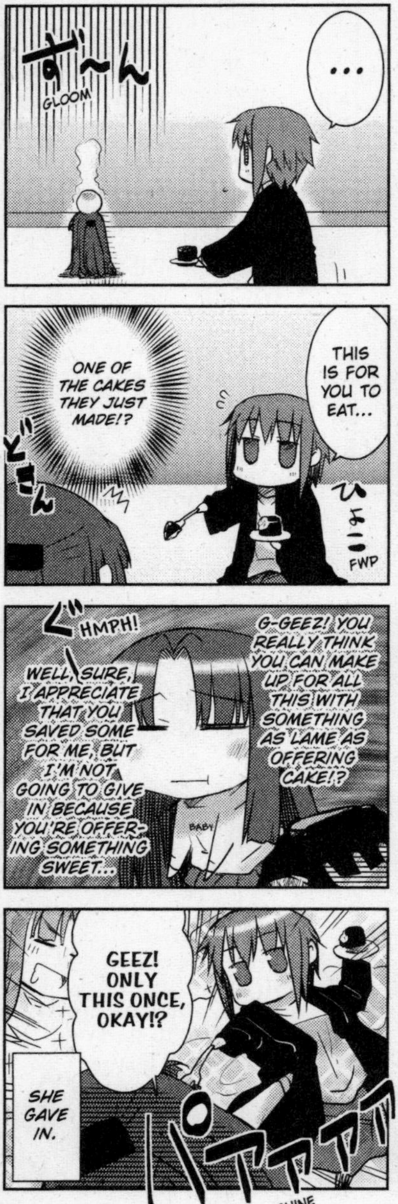
...
GLOOM
THIS IS FOR YOU TO EAT...
FWP
ONE OF THE CAKES THEY JUST MADE!?
G-GEEZ! YOU REALLY THINK YOU CAN MAKE UP FOR ALL THIS WITH SOMETHING AS LAME AS OFFERING CAKE!?
HMPH!
WELL, SURE, I APPRECIATE THAT YOU SAVED SOME FOR ME, BUT I'M NOT GOING TO GIVE IN BECAUSE YOU'RE OFFER-ING SOMETHING SWEET...
BABY
GEEZ! ONLY THIS ONCE, OKAY!?
SHE GAVE IN.
SHINE

I WON'T GET
A CHANCE
DURING
THE ACTUAL
STORY...

...SO HERE'S
MORI-SAN
WITH HER
HAIR DOWN.

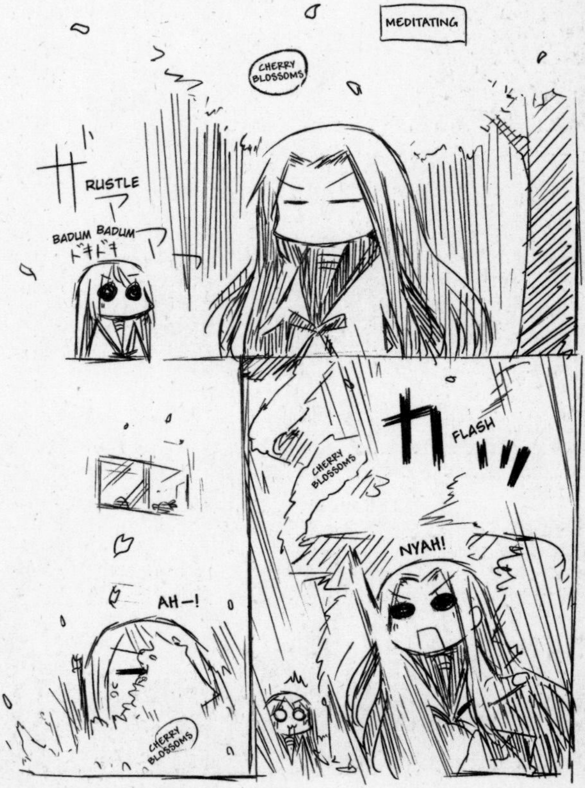
MEDITATING
CHERRY BLOSSOMS
RUSTLE
BADUM BADUM
ドキドキ
カッ
FLASH
CHERRY BLOSSOMS
NYAH!
AH—!
CHERRY BLOSSOMS

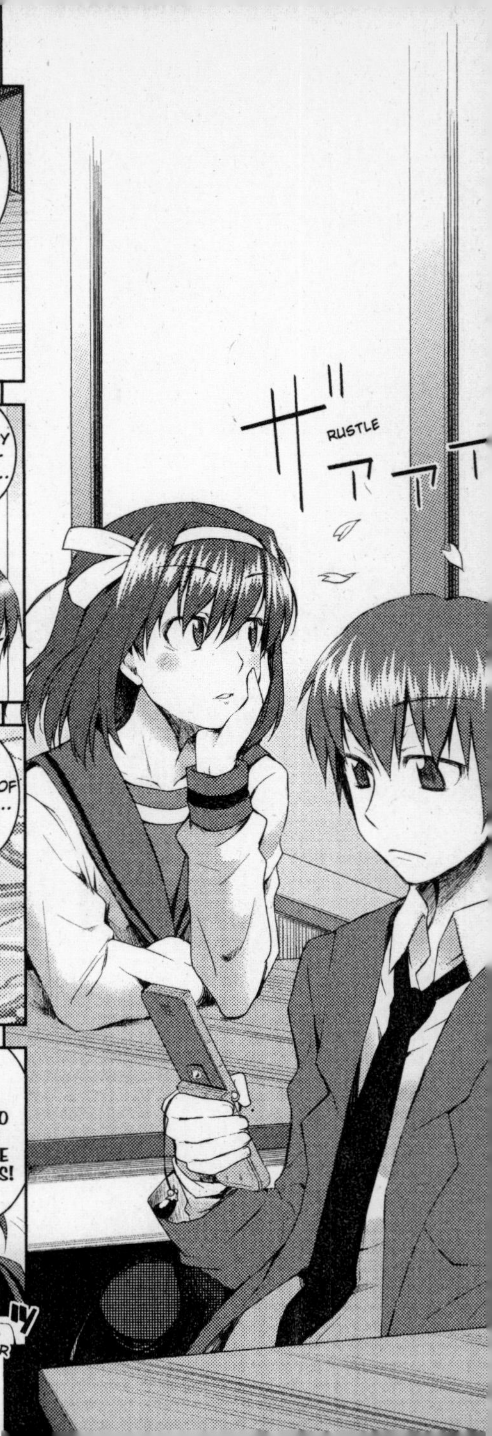
RUSTLE

FLOWER WATCHING

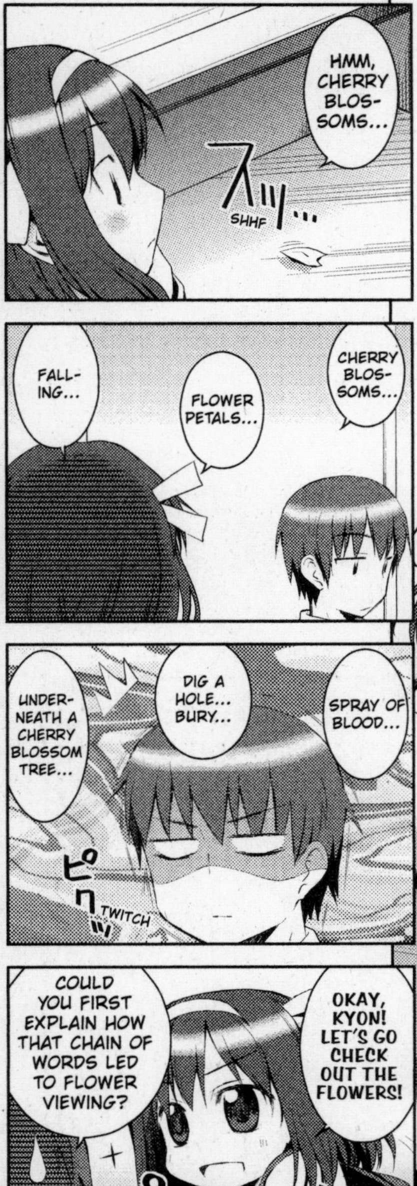
HMM, CHERRY BLOSSOMS...
SHHF
CHERRY BLOSSOMS...
FLOWER PETALS...
FALLING...
SPRAY OF BLOOD...
DIG A HOLE... BURY...
UNDERNEATH A CHERRY BLOSSOM TREE...
TWITCH
OKAY, KYON! LET'S GO CHECK OUT THE FLOWERS!
COULD YOU FIRST EXPLAIN HOW THAT CHAIN OF WORDS LED TO FLOWER VIEWING?
CLATTER
PAT

•Haruhi-chan •SOS Brigade brigade chief. She appears to be interested in some dangerous flower watching...

•Kyon •Supposed to be the main character in this story. Scared of being driven into some dangerous flower watching.

•Koizumi •An enigmatic transfer student who happens to be an esper. His previous performance as a host received rave reviews.

UNDERSTAND

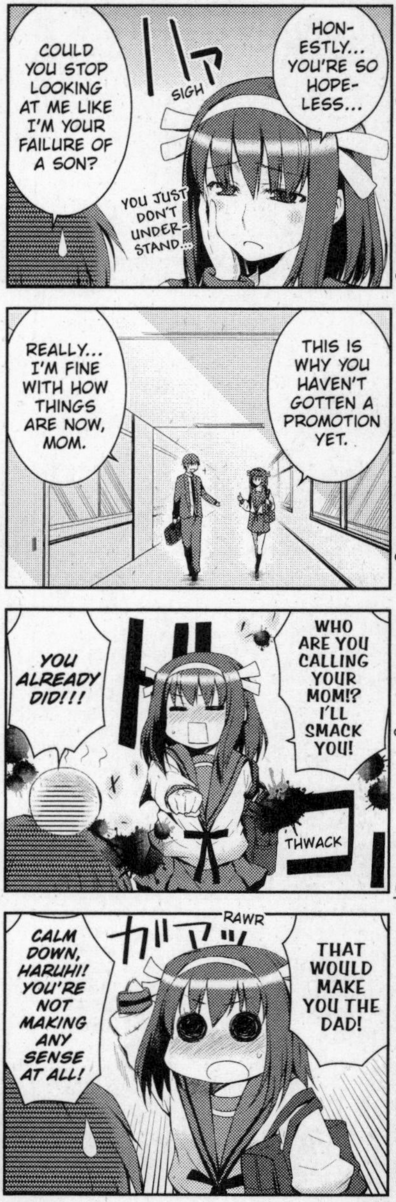
HON-ESTLY... YOU'RE SO HOPE-LESS...
SIGH
COULD YOU STOP LOOKING AT ME LIKE I'M YOUR FAILURE OF A SON?
YOU JUST DON'T UNDER-STAND...
THIS IS WHY YOU HAVEN'T GOTTEN A PROMOTION YET.
REALLY... I'M FINE WITH HOW THINGS ARE NOW, MOM.
WHO ARE YOU CALLING YOUR MOM!? I'LL SMACK YOU!
YOU ALREADY DID!!!
THWACK
RAWR
THAT WOULD MAKE YOU THE DAD!
CALM DOWN, HARUHI! YOU'RE NOT MAKING ANY SENSE AT ALL!

THE DEPUTY BRIGADE CHIEF'S TRUE ABILITY

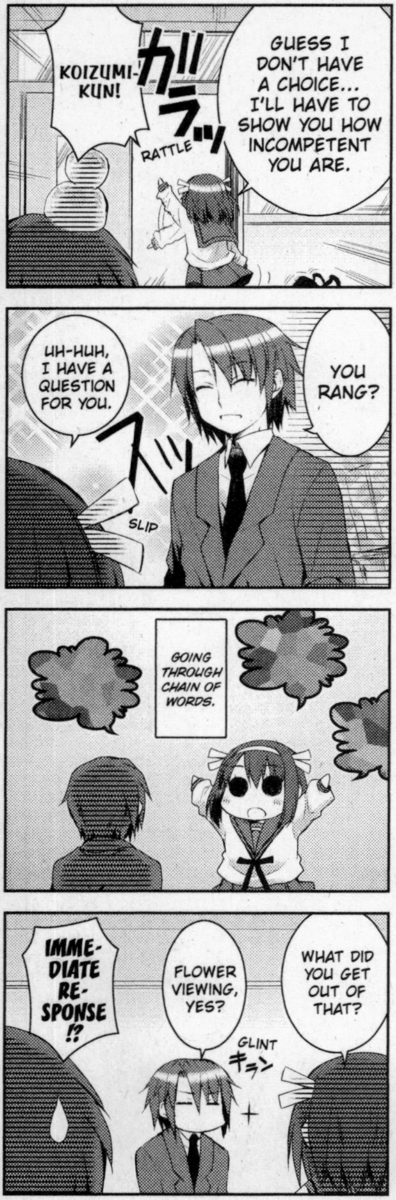
GUESS I DON'T HAVE A CHOICE... I'LL HAVE TO SHOW YOU HOW INCOMPETENT YOU ARE.
RATTLE
KOIZUMI-KUN!
YOU RANG?
UH-HUH, I HAVE A QUESTION FOR YOU.
SLIP
GOING THROUGH CHAIN OF WORDS.
WHAT DID YOU GET OUT OF THAT?
GLINT
FLOWER VIEWING, YES?
IMME-DIATE RE-SPONSE!?

SIMPLE EXPLANATION

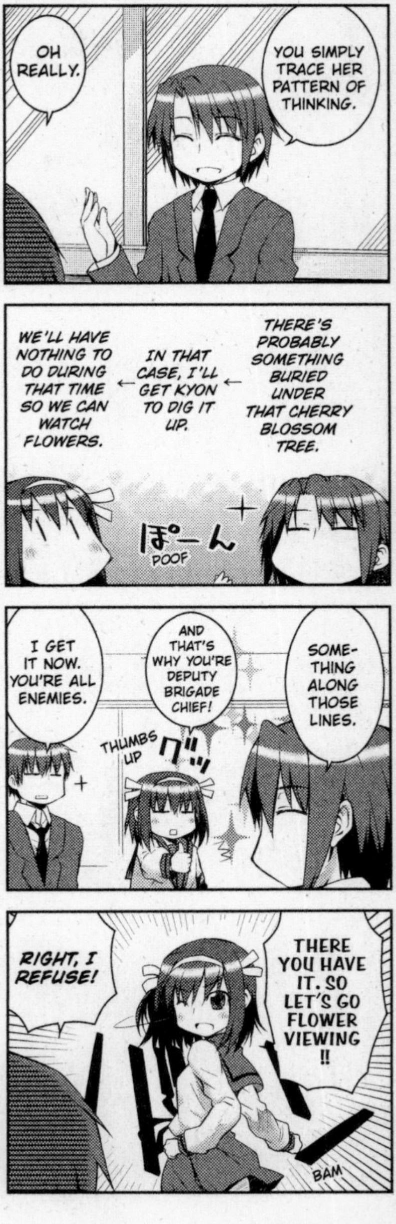
YOU SIMPLY TRACE HER PATTERN OF THINKING.
OH REALLY.
THERE'S PROBABLY SOMETHING BURIED UNDER THAT CHERRY BLOSSOM TREE.
IN THAT CASE, I'LL GET KYON TO DIG IT UP.
WE'LL HAVE NOTHING TO DO DURING THAT TIME SO WE CAN WATCH FLOWERS.
ぽーん
POOF
SOMETHING ALONG THOSE LINES.
AND THAT'S WHY YOU'RE DEPUTY BRIGADE CHIEF!
グッ
THUMBS UP
I GET IT NOW. YOU'RE ALL ENEMIES.
THERE YOU HAVE IT. SO LET'S GO FLOWER VIEWING !!
RIGHT, I REFUSE!
BAM

INITIAL T

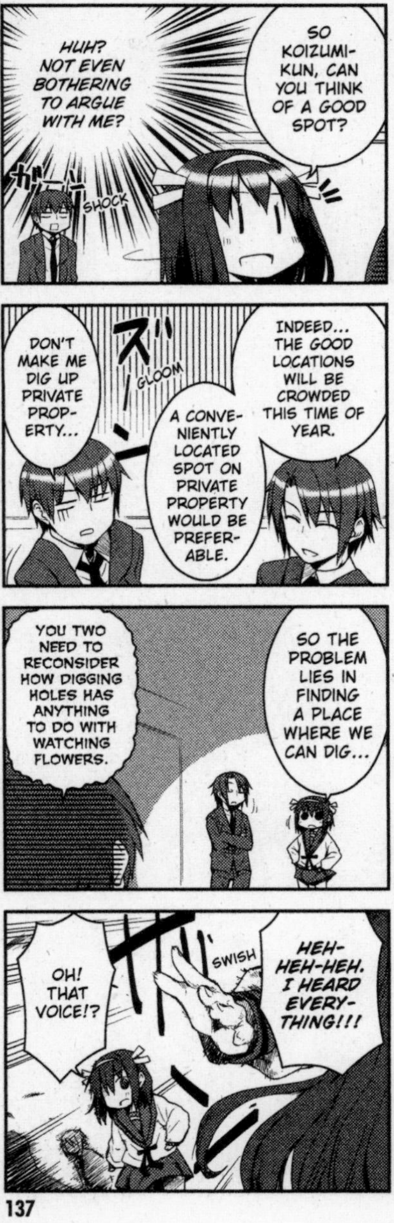
SO KOIZUMI-KUN, CAN YOU THINK OF A GOOD SPOT?
HUH? NOT EVEN BOTHERING TO ARGUE WITH ME?
SHOCK
INDEED... THE GOOD LOCATIONS WILL BE CROWDED THIS TIME OF YEAR.
A CONVENIENTLY LOCATED SPOT ON PRIVATE PROPERTY WOULD BE PREFERABLE.
GLOOM
DON'T MAKE ME DIG UP PRIVATE PROPERTY...
SO THE PROBLEM LIES IN FINDING A PLACE WHERE WE CAN DIG...
YOU TWO NEED TO RECONSIDER HOW DIGGING HOLES HAS ANYTHING TO DO WITH WATCHING FLOWERS.
HEH-HEH-HEH. I HEARD EVERYTHING!!!
SWISH
OH! THAT VOICE!?

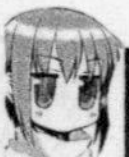

•Nagato •Actually an alien gamer. Recently picked up a new hobby of toying with Achakura-san.

TSURUYA-SAN

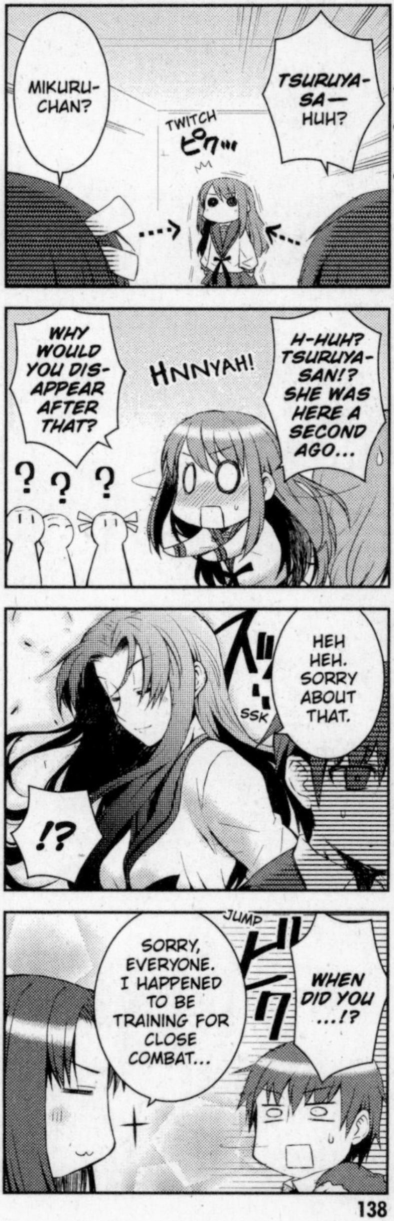
TSURUYA-SA— HUH?
TWITCH
MIKURU-CHAN?
H-HUH? TSURUYA-SAN!? SHE WAS HERE A SECOND AGO...
HNNYAH!
WHY WOULD YOU DIS-APPEAR AFTER THAT?
? ? ?
HEH HEH. SORRY ABOUT THAT.
SSK
!?
WHEN DID YOU ...!?
JUMP
SORRY, EVERYONE. I HAPPENED TO BE TRAINING FOR CLOSE COMBAT...

•Mikuru-chan •Actually from the future. Fooled by Tsuruya-san from the very beginning.

•Tsuruya-san •Mikuru-chan's buddy. Apparently a master of the Tsuruya School of Martial Arts.

HISTORY

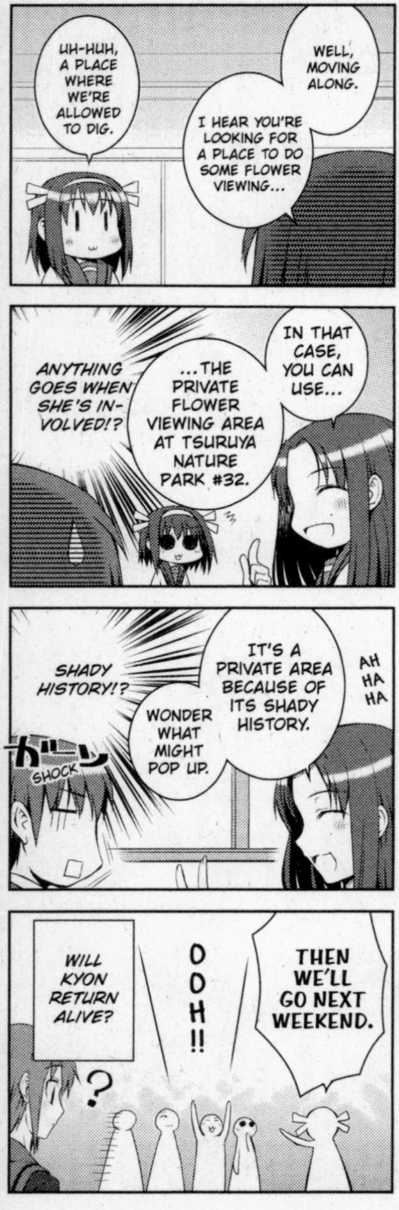
WELL, MOVING ALONG.
I HEAR YOU'RE LOOKING FOR A PLACE TO DO SOME FLOWER VIEWING...
UH-HUH, A PLACE WHERE WE'RE ALLOWED TO DIG.
IN THAT CASE, YOU CAN USE...
...THE PRIVATE FLOWER VIEWING AREA AT TSURUYA NATURE PARK #32.
ANYTHING GOES WHEN SHE'S IN-VOLVED!?
AH HA HA
IT'S A PRIVATE AREA BECAUSE OF ITS SHADY HISTORY.
WONDER WHAT MIGHT POP UP.
SHADY HISTORY!?
SHOCK
THEN WE'LL GO NEXT WEEKEND.
OOH!!
WILL KYON RETURN ALIVE?
?

DIG A HOLE BUT DON'T FALL IN

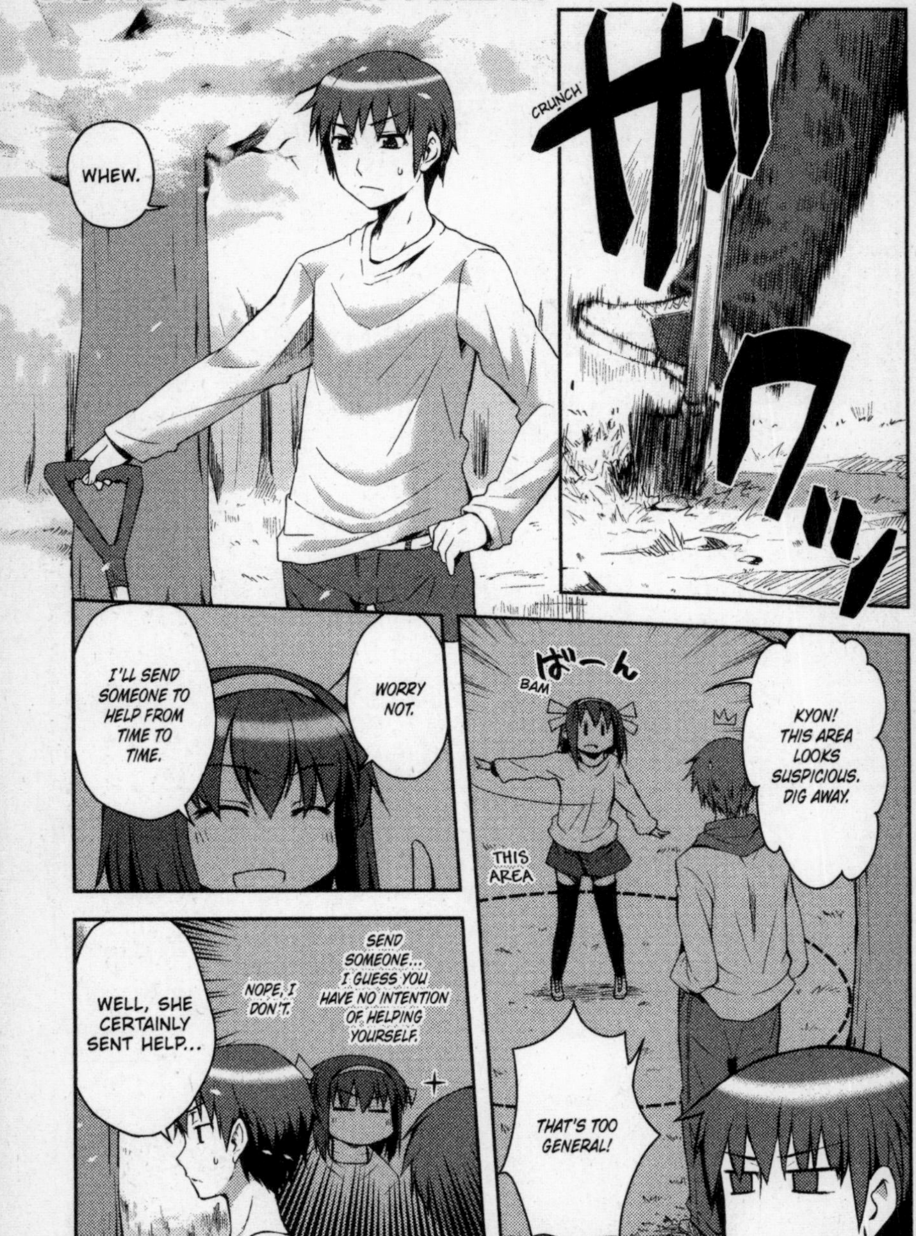
CRUNCH
ザクッ
WHEW.
ばーん
BAM
KYON! THIS AREA LOOKS SUSPICIOUS. DIG AWAY.
THIS AREA
THAT'S TOO GENERAL!
WORRY NOT.
I'LL SEND SOMEONE TO HELP FROM TIME TO TIME.
SEND SOMEONE... I GUESS YOU HAVE NO INTENTION OF HELPING YOURSELF.
NOPE, I DON'T.
WELL, SHE CERTAINLY SENT HELP...

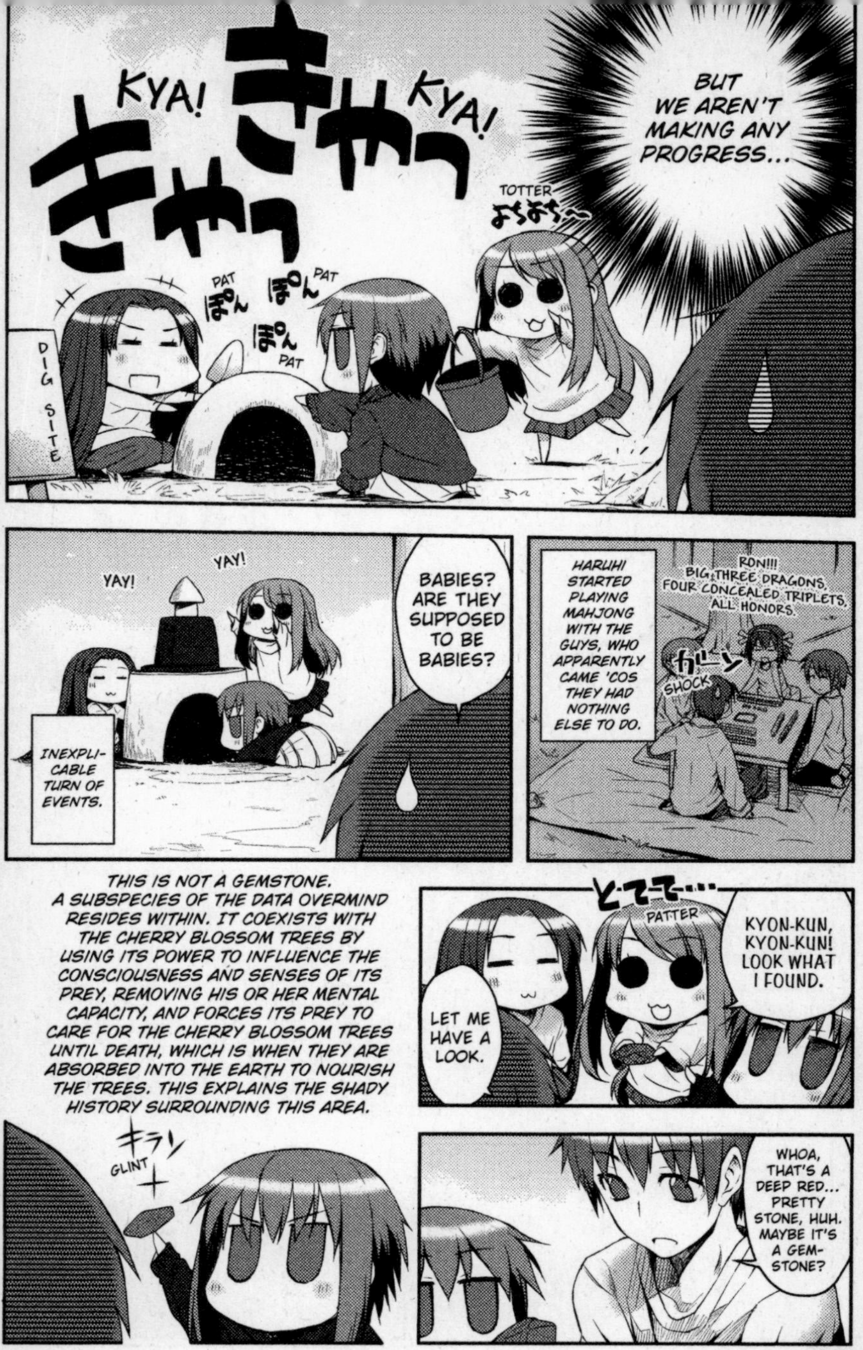
BUT WE AREN'T MAKING ANY PROGRESS...
KYA! KYA!
きゃっきゃっ
TOTTER
よちよち〜
PAT PAT PAT
ぽん ぽん ぽん
DIG SITE
HARUHI STARTED PLAYING MAHJONG WITH THE GUYS, WHO APPARENTLY CAME 'COS THEY HAD NOTHING ELSE TO DO.
RON!!! BIG THREE DRAGONS, FOUR CONCEALED TRIPLETS, ALL HONORS.
ガーン
SHOCK
BABIES? ARE THEY SUPPOSED TO BE BABIES?
YAY!
YAY!
INEXPLICABLE TURN OF EVENTS.
KYON-KUN, KYON-KUN! LOOK WHAT I FOUND.
とててて…
PATTER
LET ME HAVE A LOOK.
THIS IS NOT A GEMSTONE. A SUBSPECIES OF THE DATA OVERMIND RESIDES WITHIN. IT COEXISTS WITH THE CHERRY BLOSSOM TREES BY USING ITS POWER TO INFLUENCE THE CONSCIOUSNESS AND SENSES OF ITS PREY, REMOVING HIS OR HER MENTAL CAPACITY, AND FORCES ITS PREY TO CARE FOR THE CHERRY BLOSSOM TREES UNTIL DEATH, WHICH IS WHEN THEY ARE ABSORBED INTO THE EARTH TO NOURISH THE TREES. THIS EXPLAINS THE SHADY HISTORY SURROUNDING THIS AREA.
WHOA, THAT'S A DEEP RED... PRETTY STONE, HUH. MAYBE IT'S A GEMSTONE?
キラン
GLINT

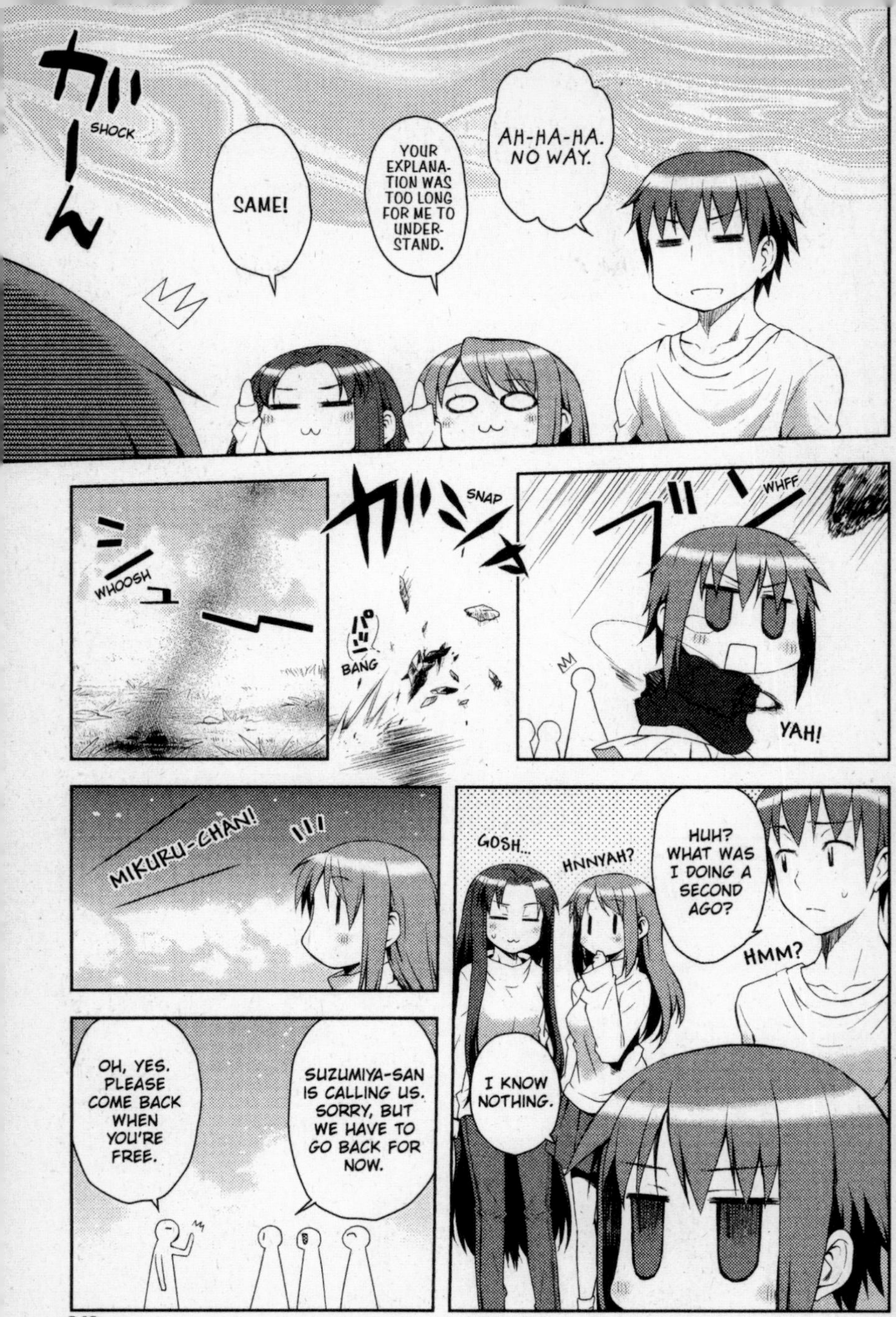
AH-HA-HA. NO WAY.
YOUR EXPLANATION WAS TOO LONG FOR ME TO UNDERSTAND.
SAME!
SHOCK
WHFF
YAH!
SNAP
BANG
WHOOSH
HUH? WHAT WAS I DOING A SECOND AGO?
HMM?
HNNYAH?
GOSH...
I KNOW NOTHING.
MIKURU-CHAN!
SUZUMIYA-SAN IS CALLING US. SORRY, BUT WE HAVE TO GO BACK FOR NOW.
OH, YES. PLEASE COME BACK WHEN YOU'RE FREE.

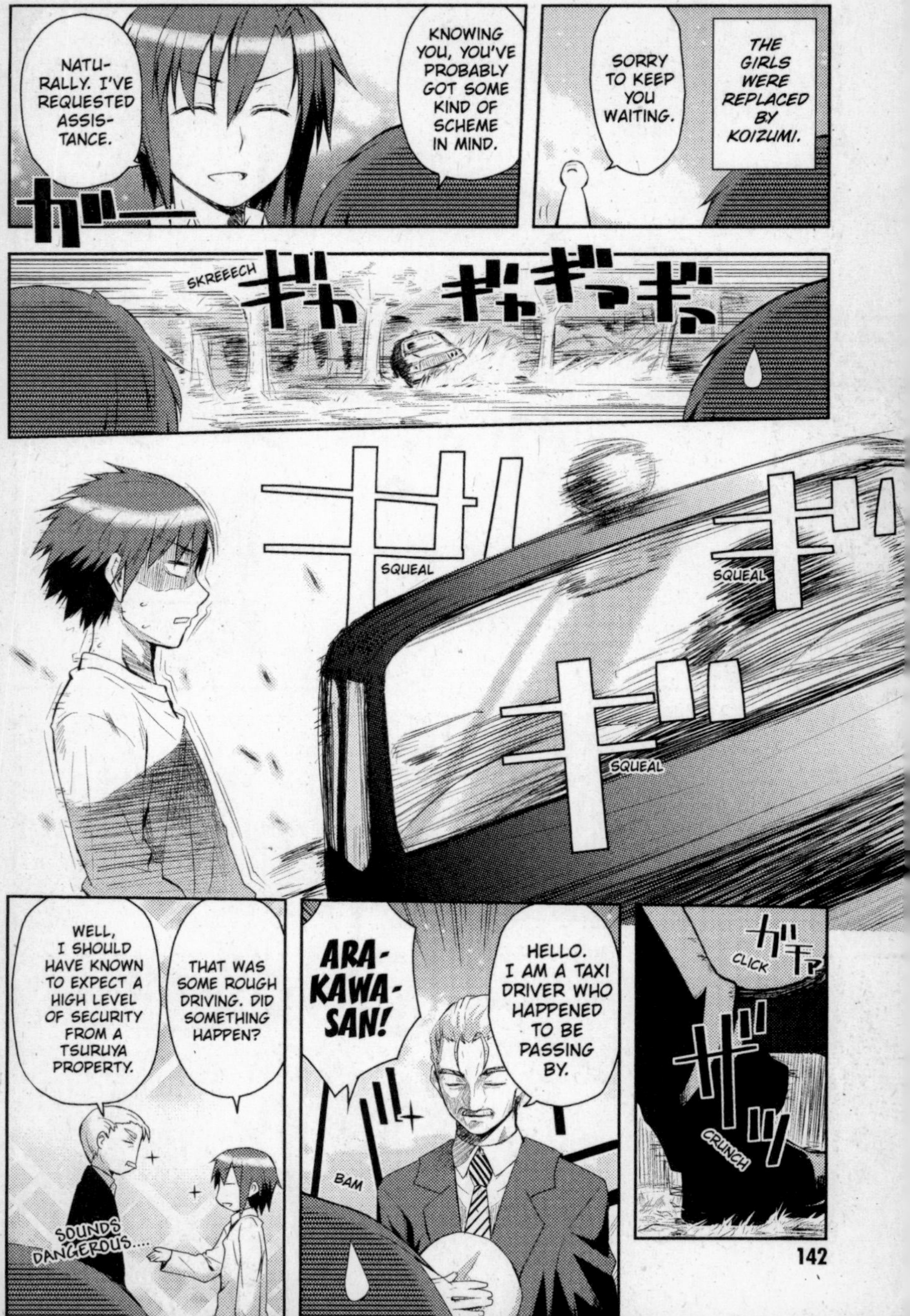
THE GIRLS WERE REPLACED BY KOIZUMI.
SORRY TO KEEP YOU WAITING.
KNOWING YOU, YOU'VE PROBABLY GOT SOME KIND OF SCHEME IN MIND.
NATU-RALLY. I'VE REQUESTED ASSIS-TANCE.
SKREEECH
SQUEAL
SQUEAL
SQUEAL
CLICK
CRUNCH
HELLO. I AM A TAXI DRIVER WHO HAPPENED TO BE PASSING BY.
ARA-KAWA-SAN!
BAM
THAT WAS SOME ROUGH DRIVING. DID SOMETHING HAPPEN?
WELL, I SHOULD HAVE KNOWN TO EXPECT A HIGH LEVEL OF SECURITY FROM A TSURUYA PROPERTY.
SOUNDS DANGEROUS....

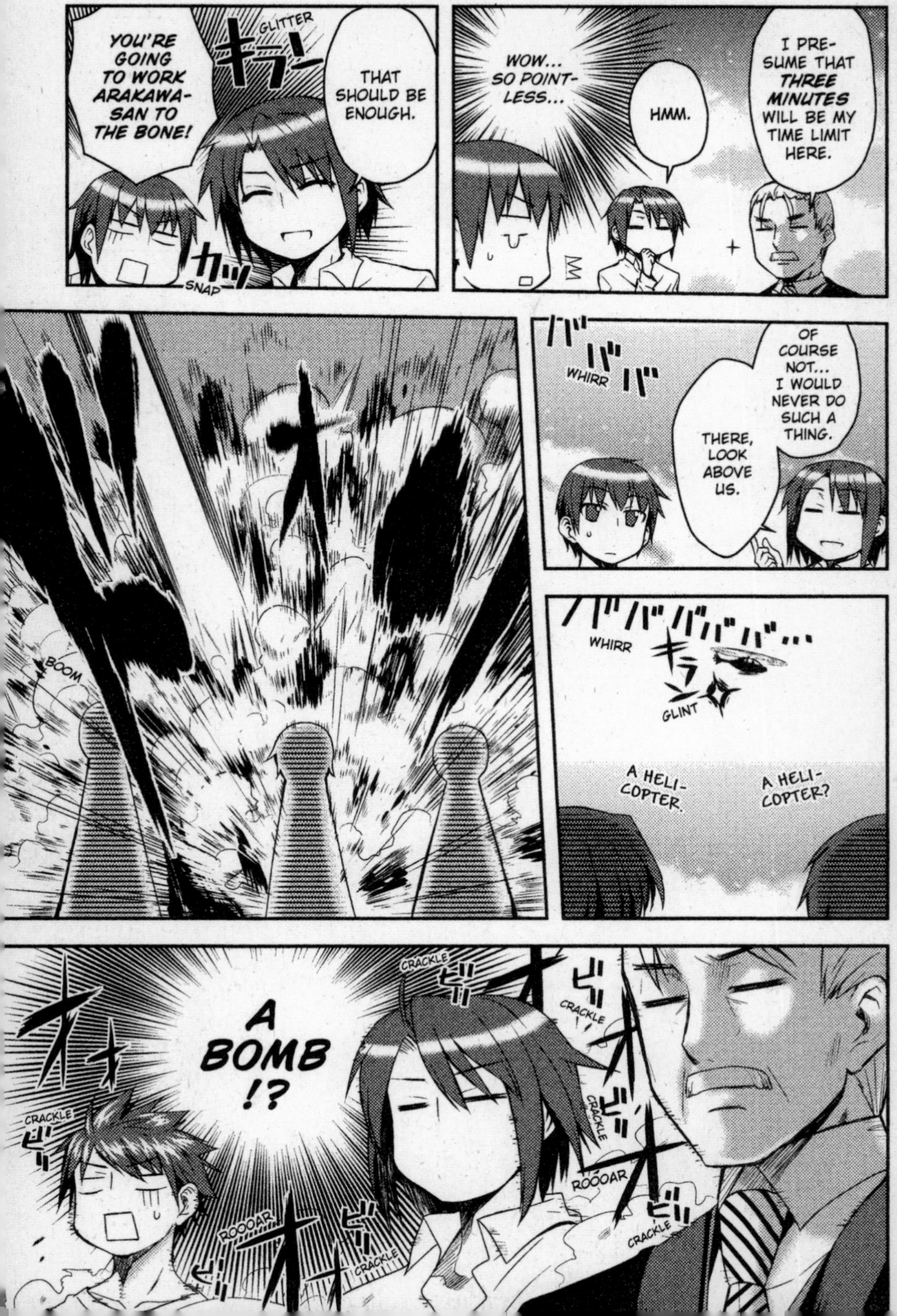
I PRESUME THAT **THREE MINUTES** WILL BE MY TIME LIMIT HERE.
HMM.
WOW... SO POINTLESS...
THAT SHOULD BE ENOUGH.
GLITTER
YOU'RE GOING TO WORK ARAKAWA-SAN TO THE BONE!
SNAP
WHIRR
OF COURSE NOT... I WOULD NEVER DO SUCH A THING.
THERE, LOOK ABOVE US.
WHIRR
GLINT
A HELICOPTER?
A HELICOPTER.
BOOM
CRACKLE
CRACKLE
A BOMB!?
CRACKLE
CRACKLE
ROOOAR
CRACKLE
ROOOAR
CRACKLE

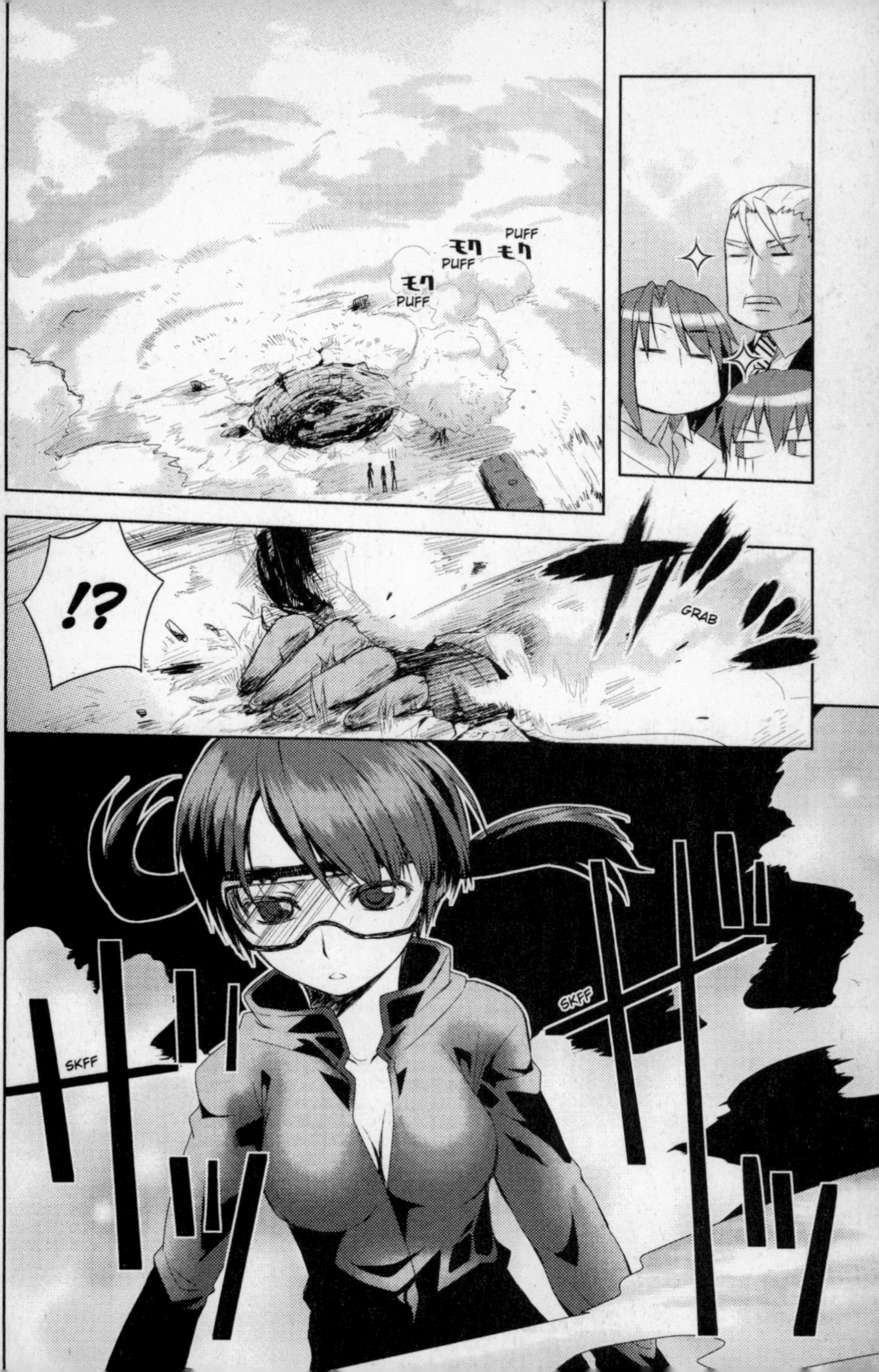
PUFF
モク
モク
PUFF
モク
PUFF
GRAB
!?
SKFF
SKFF

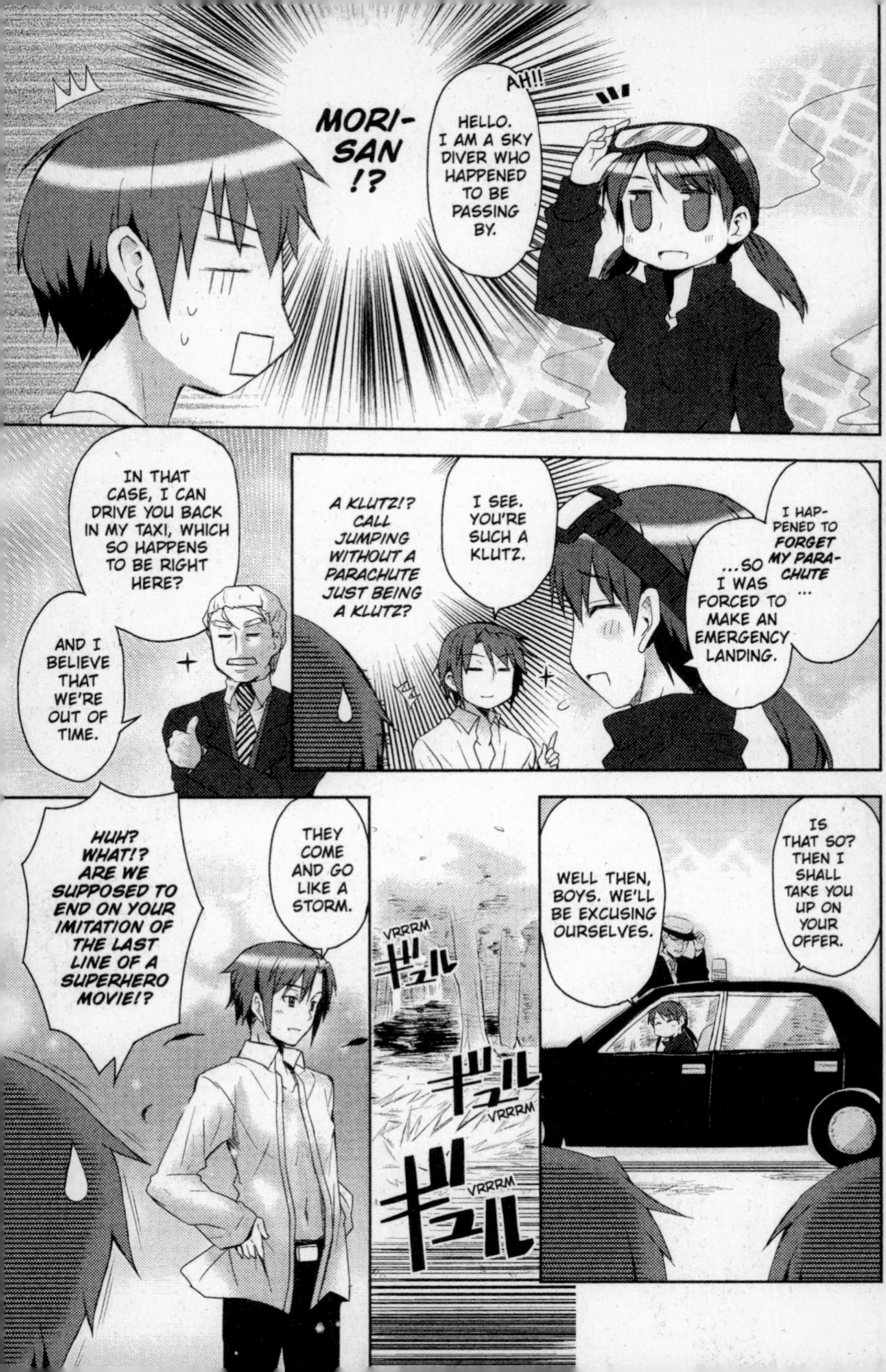
AH!!
HELLO. I AM A SKY DIVER WHO HAPPENED TO BE PASSING BY.
MORI-SAN!?
I HAPPENED TO FORGET MY PARACHUTE ...
...SO I WAS FORCED TO MAKE AN EMERGENCY LANDING.
I SEE. YOU'RE SUCH A KLUTZ.
A KLUTZ!? CALL JUMPING WITHOUT A PARACHUTE JUST BEING A KLUTZ?
IN THAT CASE, I CAN DRIVE YOU BACK IN MY TAXI, WHICH SO HAPPENS TO BE RIGHT HERE?
AND I BELIEVE THAT WE'RE OUT OF TIME.
IS THAT SO? THEN I SHALL TAKE YOU UP ON YOUR OFFER.
WELL THEN, BOYS. WE'LL BE EXCUSING OURSELVES.
ギュル
VRRRM
ギュル
VRRRM
ギュル
VRRRM
THEY COME AND GO LIKE A STORM.
HUH? WHAT!? ARE WE SUPPOSED TO END ON YOUR IMITATION OF THE LAST LINE OF A SUPERHERO MOVIE!?

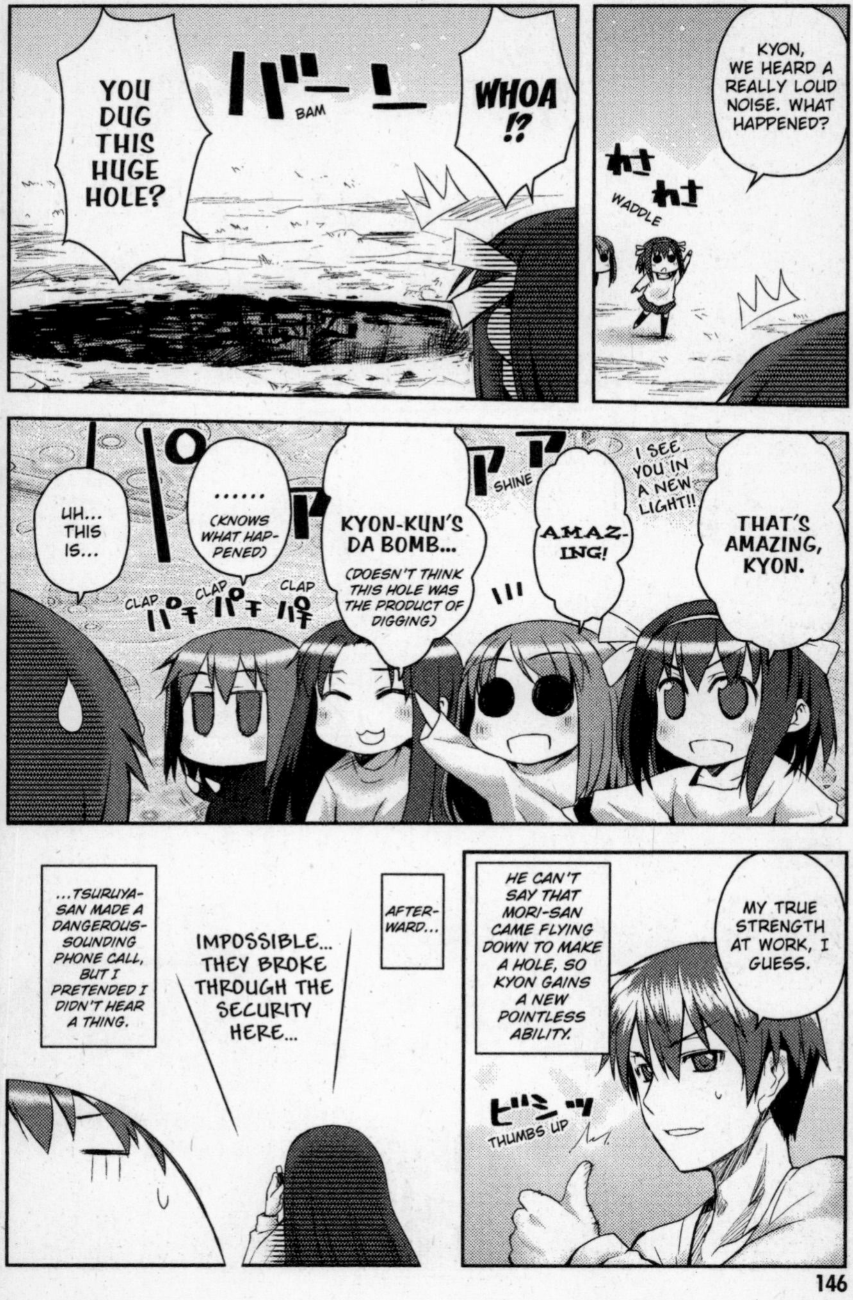
KYON, WE HEARD A REALLY LOUD NOISE. WHAT HAPPENED?
WADDLE
WHOA!?
BAM
YOU DUG THIS HUGE HOLE?
THAT'S AMAZING, KYON.
I SEE YOU IN A NEW LIGHT!!
AMAZ-ING!
SHINE
KYON-KUN'S DA BOMB...
(DOESN'T THINK THIS HOLE WAS THE PRODUCT OF DIGGING)
......
(KNOWS WHAT HAPPENED)
UH... THIS IS...
CLAP CLAP CLAP
MY TRUE STRENGTH AT WORK, I GUESS.
HE CAN'T SAY THAT MORI-SAN CAME FLYING DOWN TO MAKE A HOLE, SO KYON GAINS A NEW POINTLESS ABILITY.
THUMBS UP
AFTER-WARD...
IMPOSSIBLE... THEY BROKE THROUGH THE SECURITY HERE...
...TSURUYA-SAN MADE A DANGEROUS-SOUNDING PHONE CALL, BUT I PRETENDED I DIDN'T HEAR A THING.

COMPUTER SOCIETY

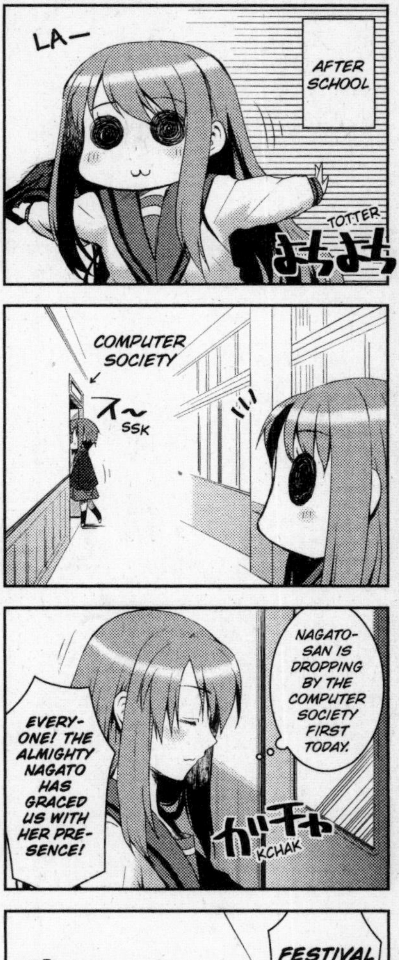
AFTER SCHOOL
LA—
よちよち
TOTTER
COMPUTER SOCIETY
ス〜
SSK
NAGATO-SAN IS DROPPING BY THE COMPUTER SOCIETY FIRST TODAY.
EVERYONE! THE ALMIGHTY NAGATO HAS GRACED US WITH HER PRESENCE!
ガチャ
KCHAK
FESTIVAL TIME! LET'S CELEBRATE!
ワッ
CHEER
ビクッ
JUMP

EAVESDROPPING

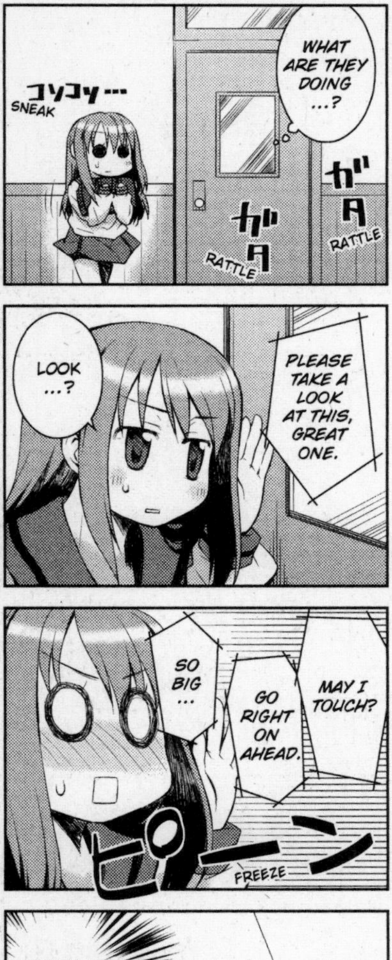
WHAT ARE THEY DOING ...?
ガタ
RATTLE
ガタ
RATTLE
コソコソ...
SNEAK
PLEASE TAKE A LOOK AT THIS, GREAT ONE.
LOOK ...?
MAY I TOUCH?
GO RIGHT ON AHEAD.
SO BIG ...
ピーン
FREEZE
WHAT'S GOING ON!?
ドキ
BADUM
ドキ
BADUM
MIKURU-CHAN?

ORGANIZE THOUGHTS

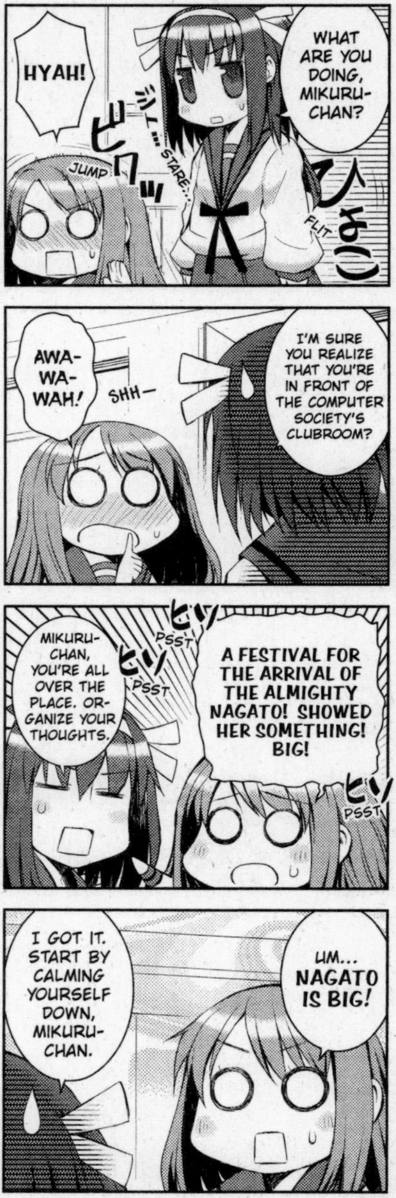
WHAT ARE YOU DOING, MIKURU-CHAN?
FLIT
STARE...
HYAH!
JUMP
I'M SURE YOU REALIZE THAT YOU'RE IN FRONT OF THE COMPUTER SOCIETY'S CLUBROOM?
SHH—
AWA-WA-WAH!
PSST
A FESTIVAL FOR THE ARRIVAL OF THE ALMIGHTY NAGATO! SHOWED HER SOMETHING! BIG!
PSST
MIKURU-CHAN, YOU'RE ALL OVER THE PLACE. ORGANIZE YOUR THOUGHTS.
PSST
UM... NAGATO IS BIG!
I GOT IT. START BY CALMING YOURSELF DOWN, MIKURU-CHAN.

TRUTH

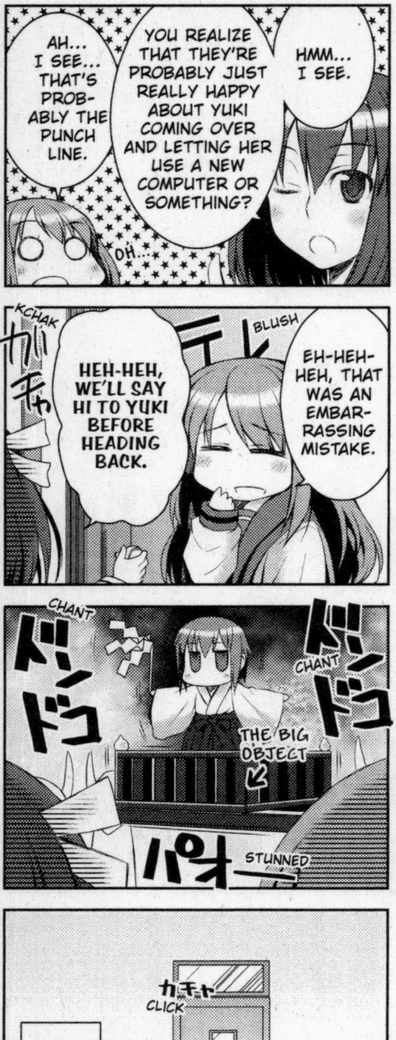
HMM... I SEE.
YOU REALIZE THAT THEY'RE PROBABLY JUST REALLY HAPPY ABOUT YUKI COMING OVER AND LETTING HER USE A NEW COMPUTER OR SOMETHING?
AH... I SEE... THAT'S PROBABLY THE PUNCH LINE.
OH...
EH-HEH-HEH, THAT WAS AN EMBARRASSING MISTAKE.
BLUSH
HEH-HEH, WE'LL SAY HI TO YUKI BEFORE HEADING BACK.
KCHAK
CHANT
CHANT
THE BIG OBJECT
STUNNED
CLICK
THEY'RE LITERALLY HOLDING A FESTIVAL.

TRAP

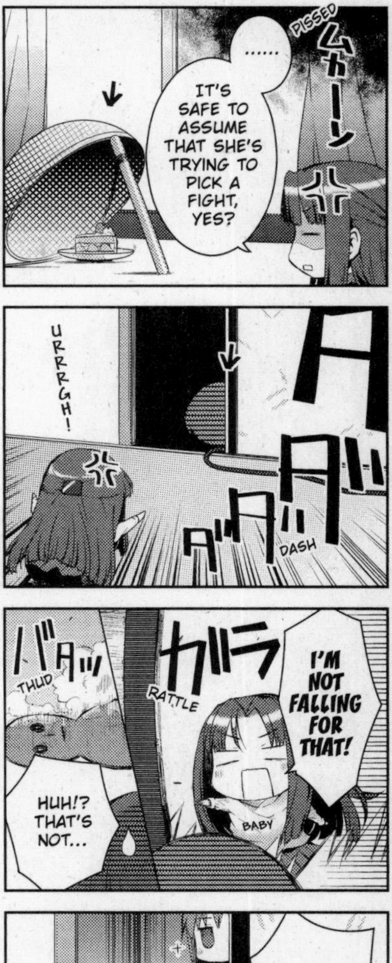

ムカーン
PISSED
......
IT'S SAFE TO ASSUME THAT SHE'S TRYING TO PICK A FIGHT, YES?
ダッ ダッ ダッ
DASH
URRRGH!
I'M NOT FALLING FOR THAT!
カラ
RATTLE
バタッ
THUD
BABY
HUH!? THAT'S NOT...
CURSES—!!!
ガシャン
CRASH

NAGATO'S DEALMAKING TECHNIQUE

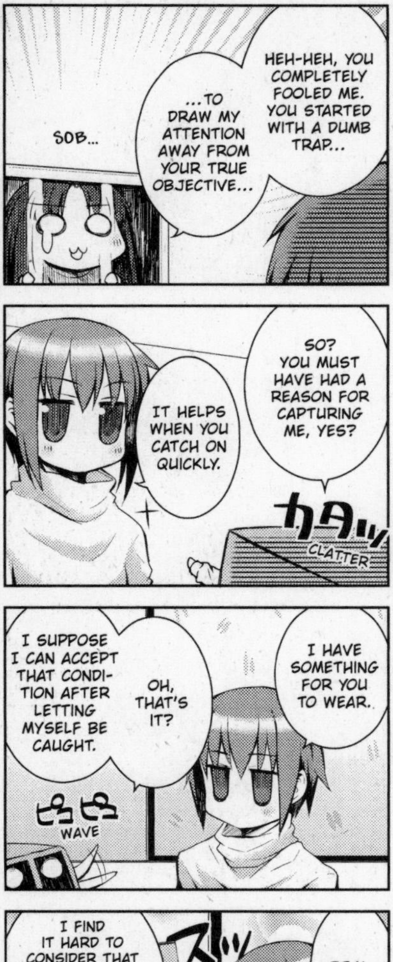

HEH-HEH, YOU COMPLETELY FOOLED ME. YOU STARTED WITH A DUMB TRAP...
...TO DRAW MY ATTENTION AWAY FROM YOUR TRUE OBJECTIVE...
SOB...
SO? YOU MUST HAVE HAD A REASON FOR CAPTURING ME, YES?
IT HELPS WHEN YOU CATCH ON QUICKLY.
カタッ
CLATTER
I HAVE SOMETHING FOR YOU TO WEAR.
OH, THAT'S IT?
I SUPPOSE I CAN ACCEPT THAT CONDI-TION AFTER LETTING MYSELF BE CAUGHT.
WAVE
DEAL.
スッ
LIFT
I FIND IT HARD TO CONSIDER THAT MAKING A DEAL... BUT AS LONG AS IT'S SOME-THING CUTE.
FLIT

•Achakura-san •Back in miniature action after being destroyed in her battle with Nagato. Reduced to being treated like a small animal.

RESTING PLACE

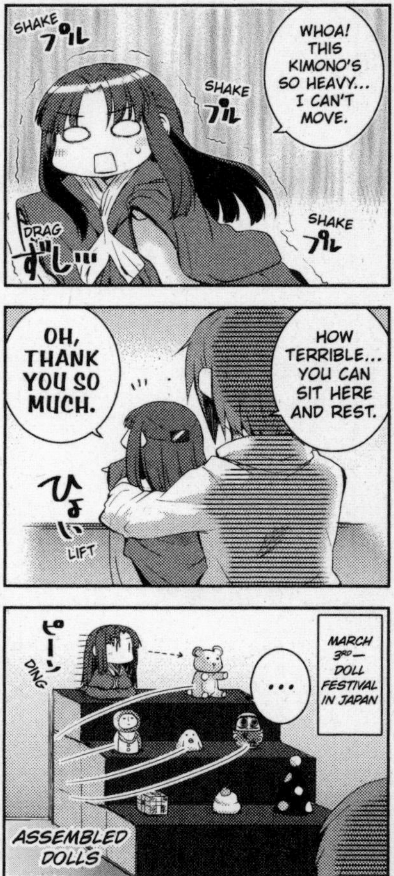
WHOA! THIS KIMONO'S SO HEAVY... I CAN'T MOVE.
SHAKE プル
SHAKE プル
SHAKE プル
DRAG ずしッ
HOW TERRIBLE... YOU CAN SIT HERE AND REST.
OH, THANK YOU SO MUCH.
ひょい LIFT
MARCH 3RD— DOLL FESTIVAL IN JAPAN
...
ピーン DING
ASSEMBLED DOLLS
SO THAT'S WHAT THIS IS ABOUT —!!!
GRR!!
FWAP

CUSTOM

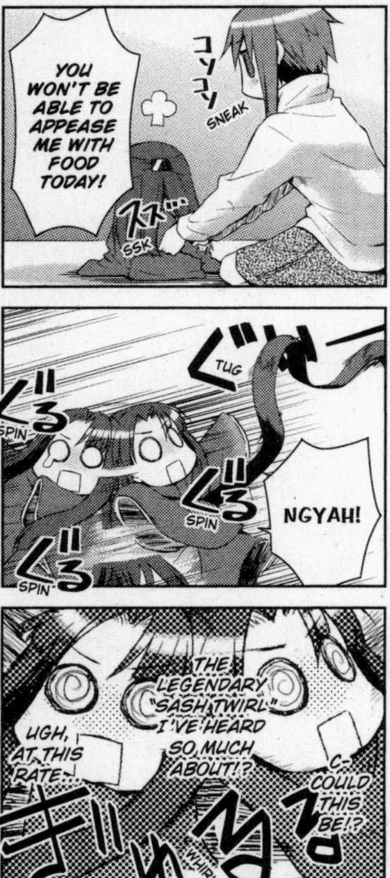
コソコソ SNEAK
YOU WON'T BE ABLE TO APPEASE ME WITH FOOD TODAY!
スズッ SSK
ぐいー TUG
NGYAH!
ぐる SPIN
ぐる SPIN
ぐる SPIN
C-COULD THIS BE!?
THE LEGENDARY "SASH TWIRL" I'VE HEARD SO MUCH ABOUT!?
UGH, AT THIS RATE...
ぎゅるる WHIRL
YOU KNOW YOU WANT THIS.
YOU KNOW YOU WANT THIS.
YOU'RE OKAY WITH IT...
OH WELL —!
ゴツッ THUD

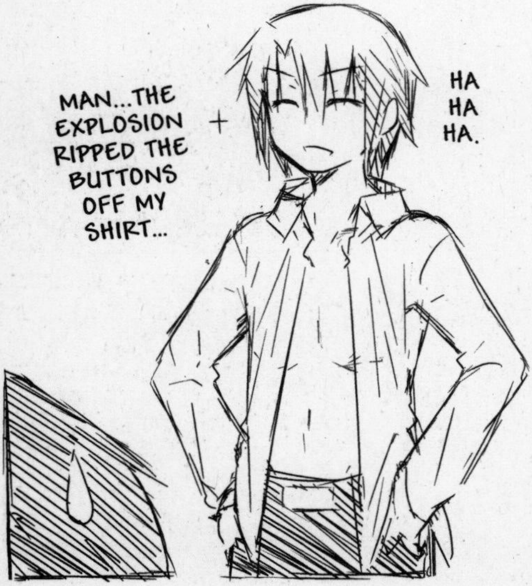
HA
HA
HA.
MAN...THE EXPLOSION RIPPED THE BUTTONS OFF MY SHIRT...

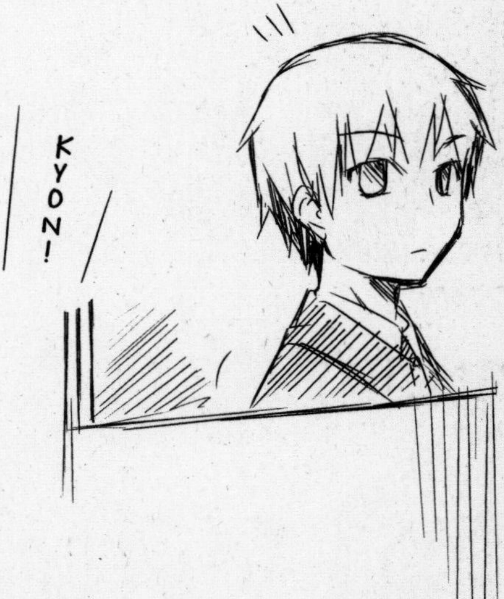
KYON!

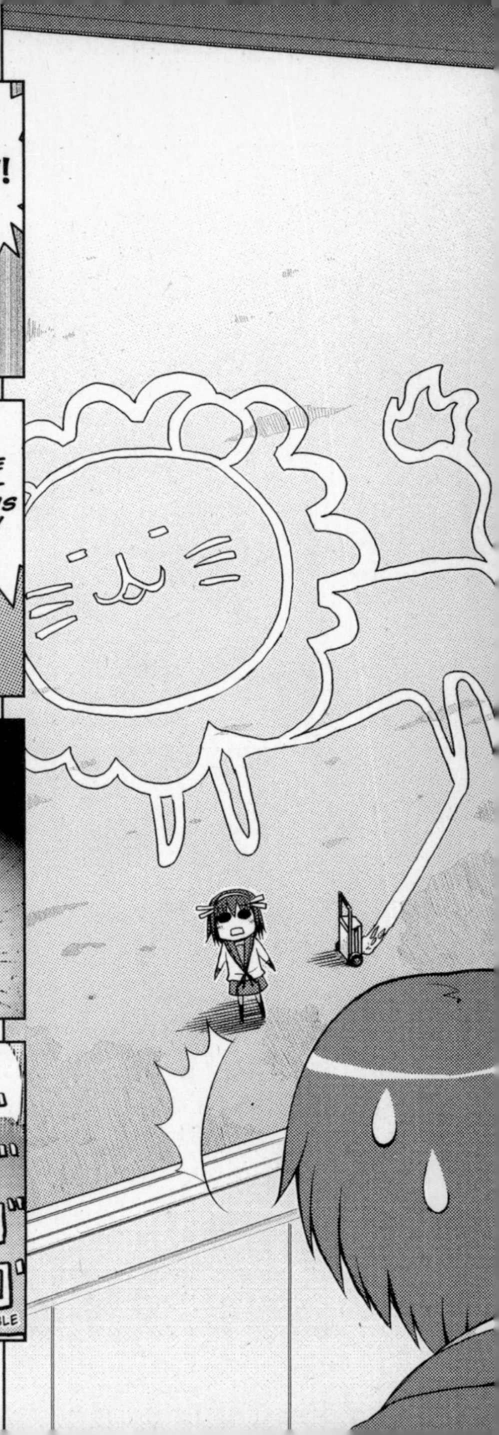

INFINITY LION

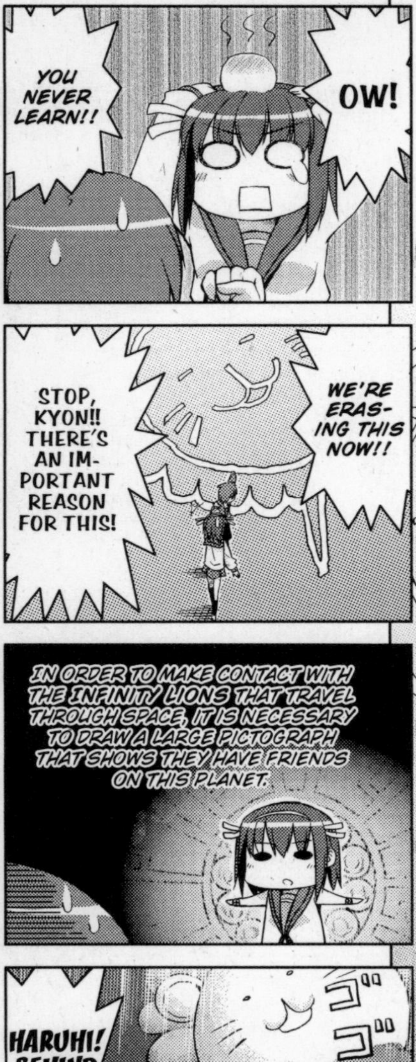
OW!
YOU NEVER LEARN!!
WE'RE ERAS-ING THIS NOW!!
STOP, KYON!! THERE'S AN IM-PORTANT REASON FOR THIS!
IN ORDER TO MAKE CONTACT WITH THE INFINITY LIONS THAT TRAVEL THROUGH SPACE, IT IS NECESSARY TO DRAW A LARGE PICTOGRAPH THAT SHOWS THEY HAVE FRIENDS ON THIS PLANET.
ゴゴゴゴゴ
RUMBLE
THEY MOVE THROUGH SPACE LIKE GIANT COMETS...
HARUHI! BEHIND YOU!!

INFOMERCIALS

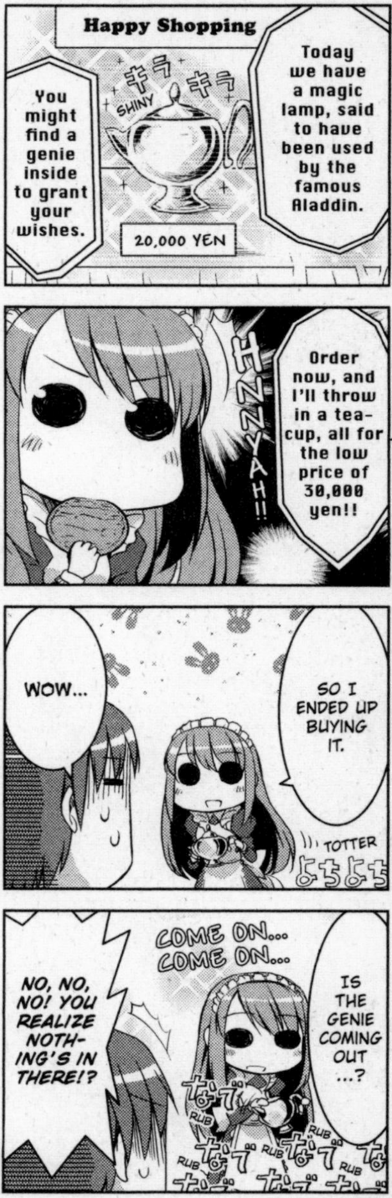
Happy Shopping
Today we have a magic lamp, said to have been used by the famous Aladdin.
キラキラ
SHINY
You might find a genie inside to grant your wishes.
20,000 YEN
Order now, and I'll throw in a tea-cup, all for the low price of 30,000 yen!!
HNNYAH!!
SO I ENDED UP BUYING IT.
WOW...
TOTTER
よちよち
IS THE GENIE COMING OUT ...?
COME ON... COME ON...
NO, NO, NO! YOU REALIZE NOTHING'S IN THERE!?
RUB
RUB
RUB
RUB

ALIEN POWER

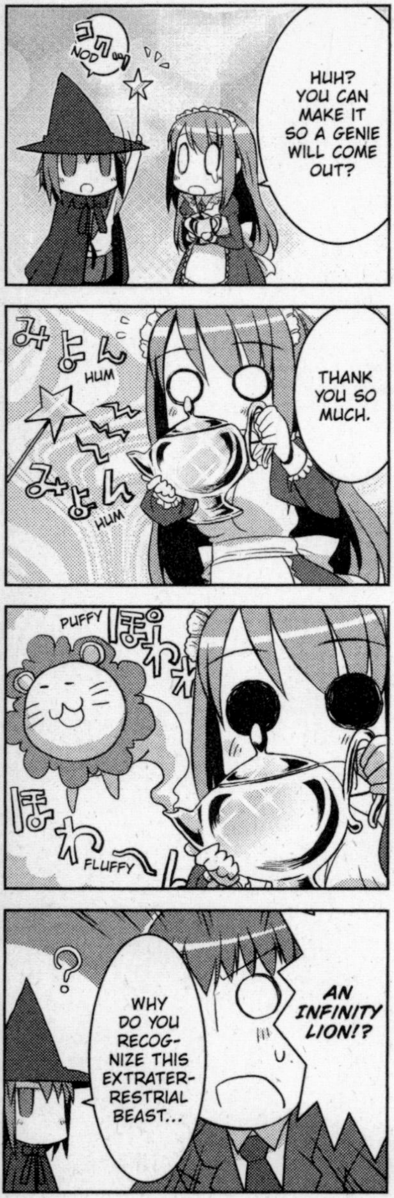
HUH? YOU CAN MAKE IT SO A GENIE WILL COME OUT?
コクッ
NOD
THANK YOU SO MUCH.
みょん
HUM
みょん
HUM
PUFFY
FLUFFY
AN INFINITY LION!?
?
WHY DO YOU RECOGNIZE THIS EXTRATERRESTRIAL BEAST...

•Haruhi-chan •SOS Brigade brigade chief. A troublemaker who's always on the go.

•Nagato •A reticent alien who's always reading. Capable of doing many things with her alien powers.

•Mikuru-chan •Actually from the future. Seems to be the type that's easily fooled.

STRAIGHT MAN KYON

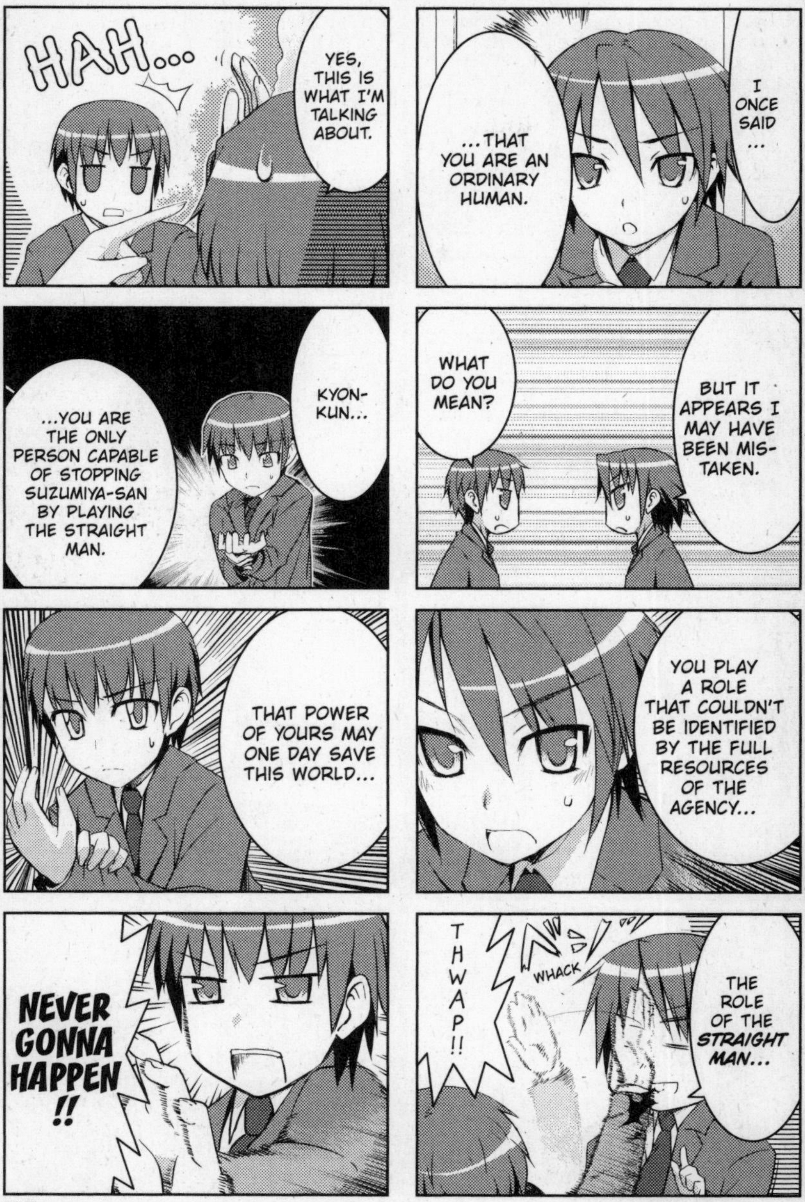
I ONCE SAID ...
...THAT YOU ARE AN ORDINARY HUMAN.
BUT IT APPEARS I MAY HAVE BEEN MIS-TAKEN.
WHAT DO YOU MEAN?
YOU PLAY A ROLE THAT COULDN'T BE IDENTIFIED BY THE FULL RESOURCES OF THE AGENCY...
THE ROLE OF THE STRAIGHT MAN...
THWAP!!
WHACK
YES, THIS IS WHAT I'M TALKING ABOUT.
HAH...
KYON-KUN...
...YOU ARE THE ONLY PERSON CAPABLE OF STOPPING SUZUMIYA-SAN BY PLAYING THE STRAIGHT MAN.
THAT POWER OF YOURS MAY ONE DAY SAVE THIS WORLD...
NEVER GONNA HAPPEN!!

•Kyon •Supposed to be the main character in this story. Possesses a certain special power...or does he?

•Koizumi •An enigmatic transfer student who happens to be an esper. He and Kyon complement each other well.

PULLING THE STRINGS

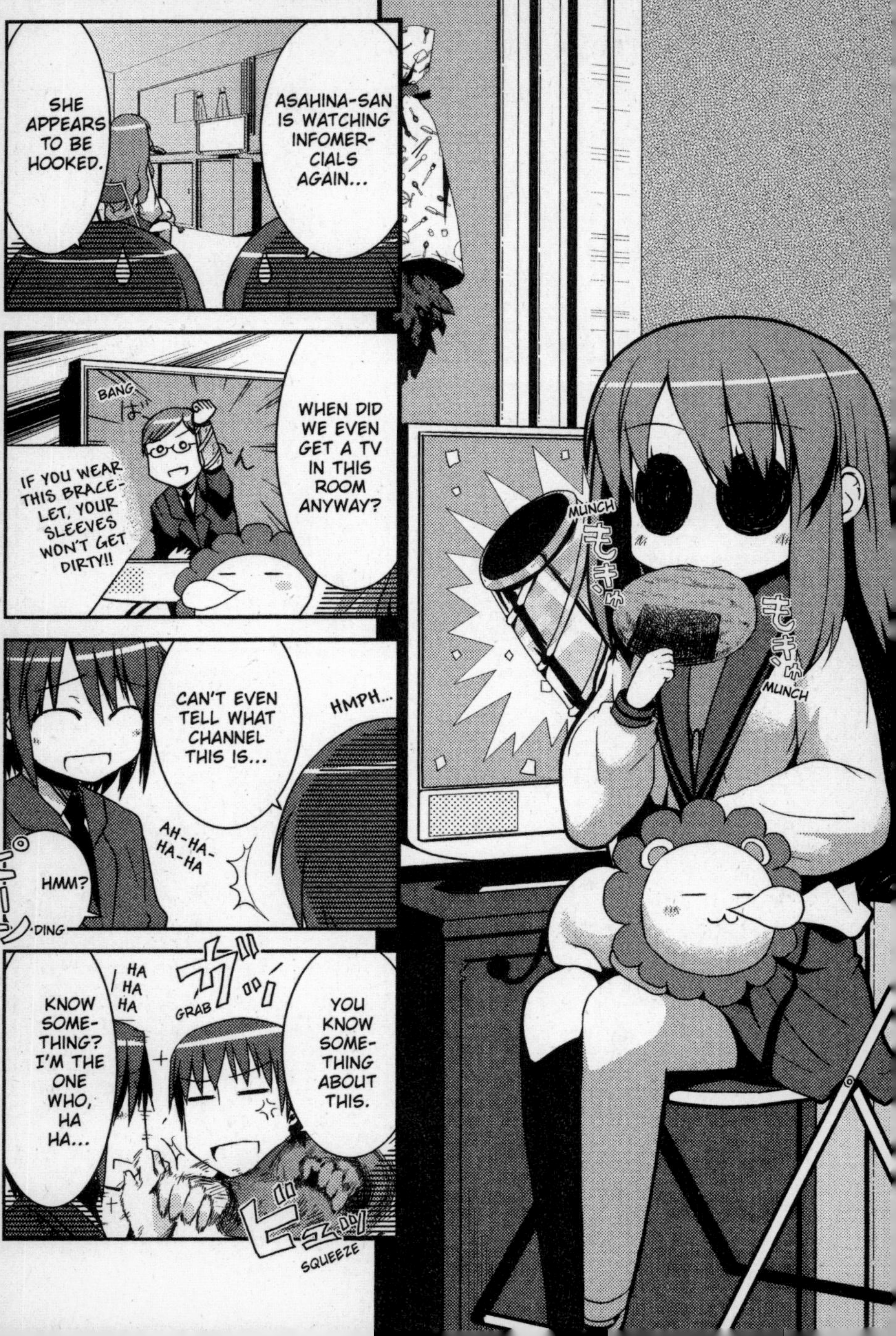
MUNCH
もきゅ
もきゅ
MUNCH
ASAHINA-SAN IS WATCHING INFOMER-CIALS AGAIN...
SHE APPEARS TO BE HOOKED.
WHEN DID WE EVEN GET A TV IN THIS ROOM ANYWAY?
BANG
IF YOU WEAR THIS BRACE-LET, YOUR SLEEVES WON'T GET DIRTY!!
HMPH...
CAN'T EVEN TELL WHAT CHANNEL THIS IS...
AH-HA-HA-HA
HMM?
DING
YOU KNOW SOME-THING ABOUT THIS.
GRAB
HA HA HA
KNOW SOME-THING? I'M THE ONE WHO, HA HA...
SQUEEZE

LARGE PROJECT

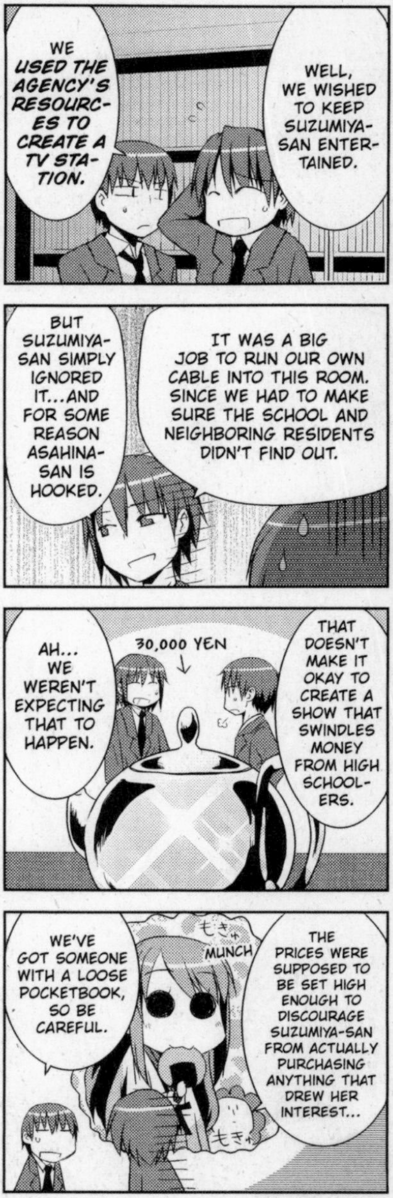
WELL, WE WISHED TO KEEP SUZUMIYA-SAN ENTERTAINED.
WE USED THE AGENCY'S RESOURCES TO CREATE A TV STATION.
IT WAS A BIG JOB TO RUN OUR OWN CABLE INTO THIS ROOM. SINCE WE HAD TO MAKE SURE THE SCHOOL AND NEIGHBORING RESIDENTS DIDN'T FIND OUT.
BUT SUZUMIYA-SAN SIMPLY IGNORED IT...AND FOR SOME REASON ASAHINA-SAN IS HOOKED.
THAT DOESN'T MAKE IT OKAY TO CREATE A SHOW THAT SWINDLES MONEY FROM HIGH SCHOOLERS.
30,000 YEN
AH... WE WEREN'T EXPECTING THAT TO HAPPEN.
THE PRICES WERE SUPPOSED TO BE SET HIGH ENOUGH TO DISCOURAGE SUZUMIYA-SAN FROM ACTUALLY PURCHASING ANYTHING THAT DREW HER INTEREST...
MUNCH
WE'VE GOT SOMEONE WITH A LOOSE POCKETBOOK, SO BE CAREFUL.

BENEFITS

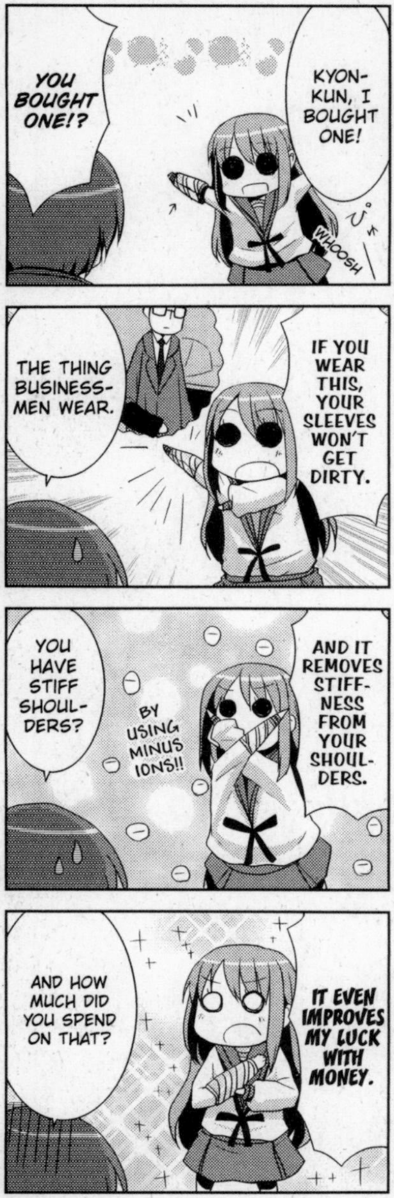
KYON-KUN, I BOUGHT ONE!
WHOOSH
YOU BOUGHT ONE!?
IF YOU WEAR THIS, YOUR SLEEVES WON'T GET DIRTY.
THE THING BUSINESSMEN WEAR.
AND IT REMOVES STIFFNESS FROM YOUR SHOULDERS.
BY USING MINUS IONS!!
YOU HAVE STIFF SHOULDERS?
IT EVEN IMPROVES MY LUCK WITH MONEY.
AND HOW MUCH DID YOU SPEND ON THAT?

•Haruhi-chan •SOS Brigade brigade chief. Always seems to be combative toward Kyon?

•Kyon •Supposed to be the main character in this story. His life is spent playing the straight man.

•Mikuru-chan •Actually from the future. Tricked into buying multiple items from infomercials.

NEW WAY

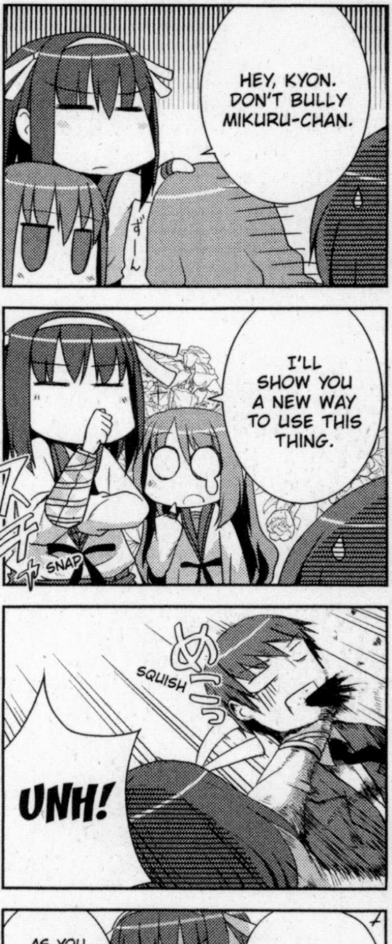
HEY, KYON. DON'T BULLY MIKURU-CHAN.
I'LL SHOW YOU A NEW WAY TO USE THIS THING.
SNAP
SQUISH
UNH!
WHAT THE HELL...?
AS YOU CAN SEE, THE VICTIM'S BLOOD DOESN'T GET ON YOUR UNIFORM.

ANOTHER WAY

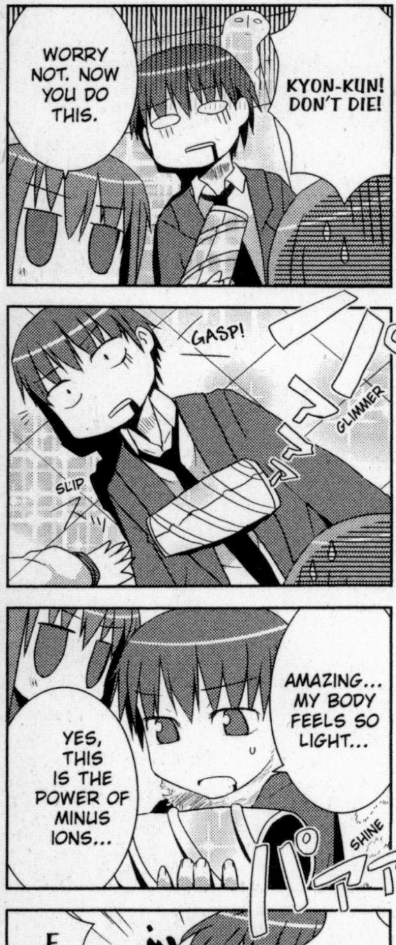
KYON-KUN! DON'T DIE!
WORRY NOT. NOW YOU DO THIS.
GLIMMER
GASP!
SLIP
AMAZING... MY BODY FEELS SO LIGHT...
SHINE
YES, THIS IS THE POWER OF MINUS IONS...
IN YOUR DREAMS!
EEEEEEEK!!
KYON-KUN!

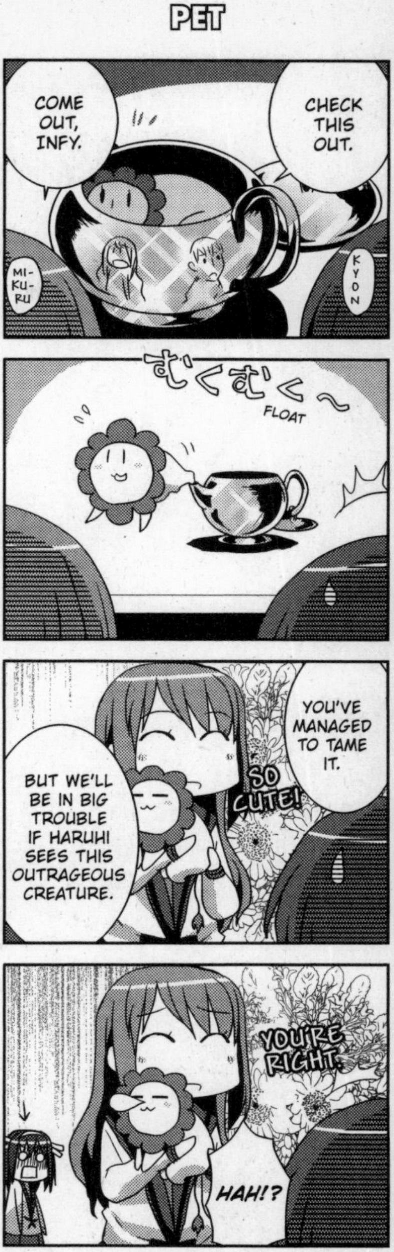
PET
CHECK THIS OUT.
COME OUT, INFY.
KYON
MI-KU-RU
むくむく～
FLOAT
YOU'VE MANAGED TO TAME IT.
SO CUTE!
BUT WE'LL BE IN BIG TROUBLE IF HARUHI SEES THIS OUTRAGEOUS CREATURE.
YOU'RE RIGHT.
HAH!?

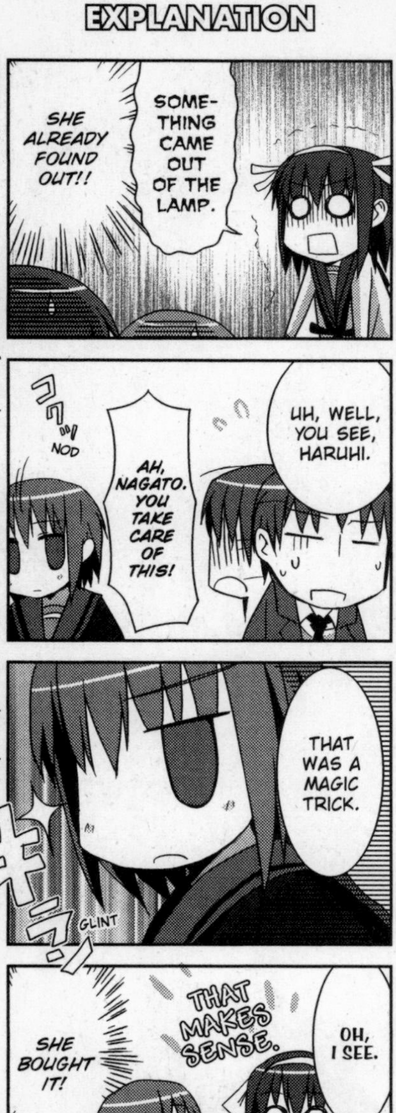
EXPLANATION
SOME-THING CAME OUT OF THE LAMP.
SHE ALREADY FOUND OUT!!
UH, WELL, YOU SEE, HARUHI.
AH, NAGATO. YOU TAKE CARE OF THIS!
NOD
THAT WAS A MAGIC TRICK.
GLINT
OH, I SEE.
THAT MAKES SENSE.
SHE BOUGHT IT!

•Koizumi •An enigmatic transfer student who happens to be an esper. Does various cruel things with a smile on his face.

•Nagato •A reticent alien who's always reading. Capable of doing many things with her alien powers, but she rarely does.

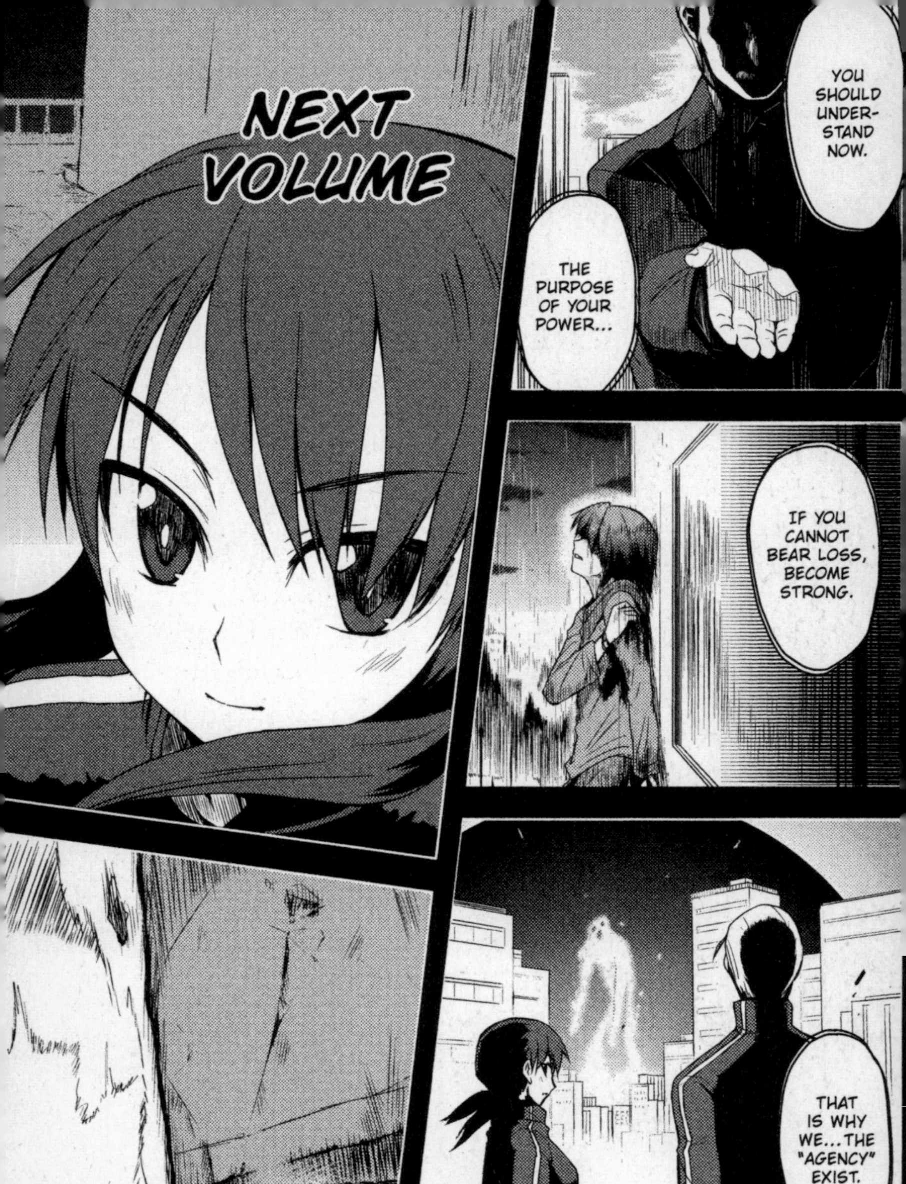
YOU SHOULD UNDER-STAND NOW.
THE PURPOSE OF YOUR POWER...
IF YOU CANNOT BEAR LOSS, BECOME STRONG.
THAT IS WHY WE...THE "AGENCY" EXIST.
NEXT VOLUME

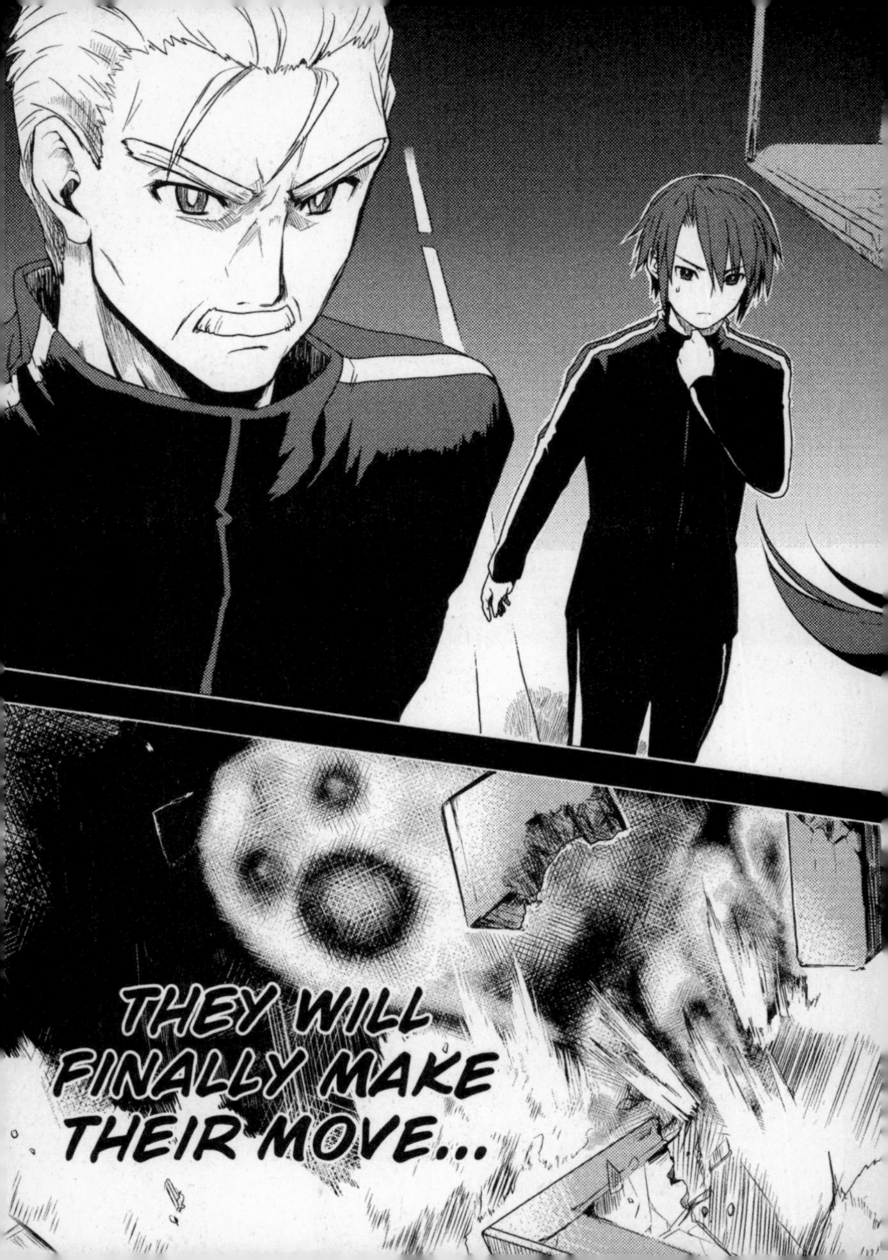
THEY WILL FINALLY MAKE THEIR MOVE...

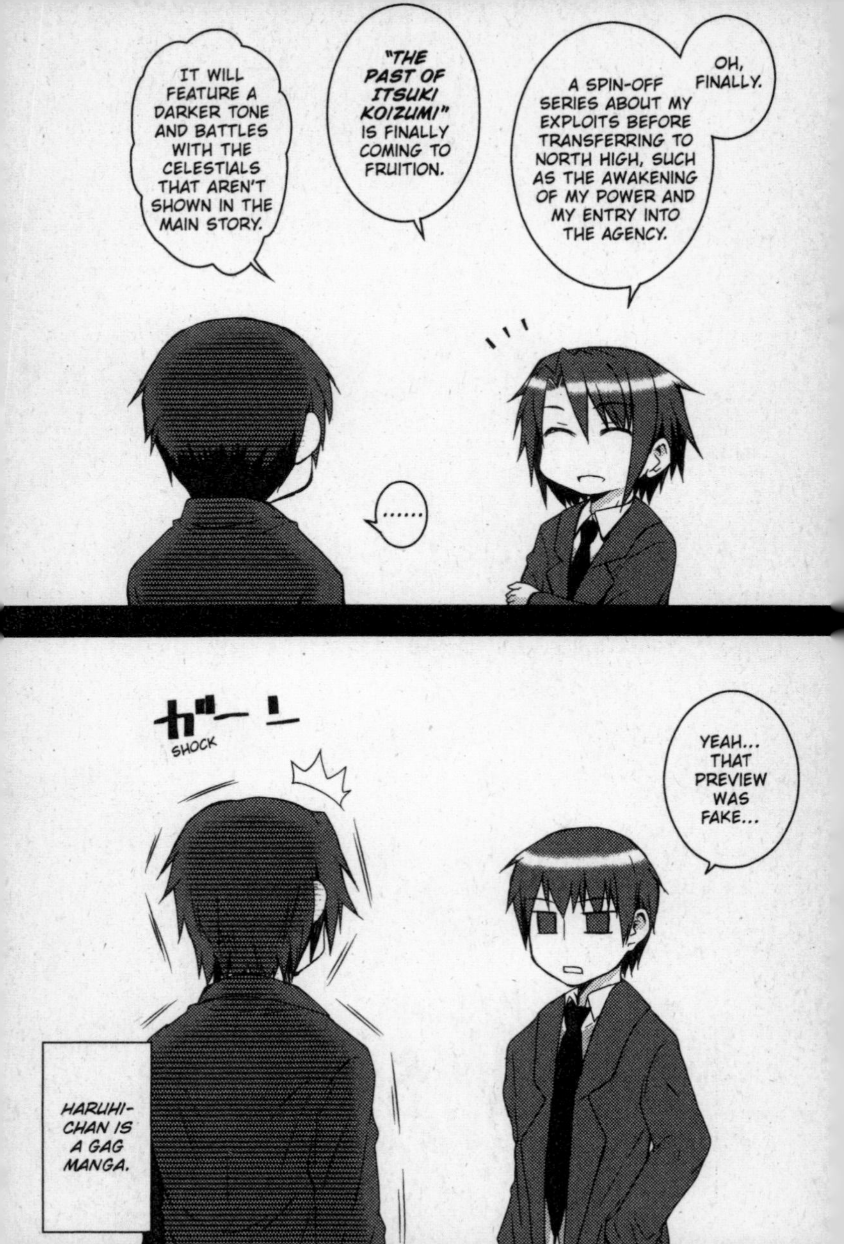
OH, FINALLY.
A SPIN-OFF SERIES ABOUT MY EXPLOITS BEFORE TRANSFERRING TO NORTH HIGH, SUCH AS THE AWAKENING OF MY POWER AND MY ENTRY INTO THE AGENCY.
"THE PAST OF ITSUKI KOIZUMI" IS FINALLY COMING TO FRUITION.
IT WILL FEATURE A DARKER TONE AND BATTLES WITH THE CELESTIALS THAT AREN'T SHOWN IN THE MAIN STORY.
......
YEAH... THAT PREVIEW WAS FAKE...
ガーン
SHOCK
HARUHI-CHAN IS A GAG MANGA.

I LOVE HOW THE HARUHI IN HARUHI-CHAN
IS MORE HARUHI THAN THE REAL HARUHI.
I SHOULD HAVE DONE THIS FOR THE NOVELS
(HALF-SERIOUS).

NAGARU TANIGAWA

THE MELANCHOLY OF SUZUMIYA
HARUHI-CHAN

①

Original Story: Nagaru Tanigawa
Manga: PUYO
Character Design: Noizi Ito

Translation: Chris Pai for MX Media LLC
Lettering: Hope Donovan

The Melancholy of Suzumiya Haruhi-chan Volume 1
© Nagaru TANIGAWA • Noizi ITO 2008 © PUYO 2008. First published in Japan in
2008 by KADOKAWA SHOTEN Publishing Co., Ltd., Tokyo. English translation rights
arranged with KADOKAWA SHOTEN Publishing Co., Ltd., Tokyo through TUTTLE-
MORI AGENCY, INC., Tokyo.

English translation © 2010 by Hachette Book Group, Inc.

Yen Press
Hachette Book Group
237 Park Avenue, New York, NY 10017

www.HachetteBookGroup.com
www.YenPress.com

Yen Press is an imprint of Hachette Book Group, Inc.
The Yen Press name and logo are trademarks of Hachette Book Group, Inc.

First Yen Press Edition: October 2010

ISBN: 978-0-316-08957-9

10 9 8 7 6 5 4 3 2 1

BVG

Printed in the United States of America